WHO'S CLAPPING AT OUR GATE?

A Family's Adventures
Entertaining Strangers in a Foreign Land

Shirley Alberta Roberts Combs

Shirley A. Combs
Prov. 3:5,6

Copyright © 2013
by
Shirley Alberta Roberts Combs
ISBN: 978-1-940609-02-7
Soft-cover

This book was printed in the United States of America.

To order additional copies of this book, contact:

Shirley Combs
733 N.E. 18
Moore, Oklahoma 73160

Published by Jim and Shirley Combs
Editor, Layout and Cover Design
By
FWB Publications

FWB

Table of Contents

Who's Clapping At Our Gate?

Who's Clapping At Our Gate?

Dedication

To our grandchildren with
Brazil/USA dual citizenship:
Jonathan Kemper Combs de Aquino
Julia Marita Combs de Aquino
David William Combs de Aquino
Daniel Queiroz Ferreira
Bianca Marita Combs Ferreira
Isabela Marita Combs Ferreira
And
Our foster grandchildren in Brazil:
Vitória Pena
Jessé Pena
Susana Pena
Ana Carolina Pena

My children,
By telling these stories, I want to hand our faith on to your generation. As the psalmist wrote, things *"which we have heard and known, and our fathers have told us. We will not hide them from their children, telling to the generation to come the praises of the LORD, His strength, and His wonderful works that He has done."* (78:3-4, NIV)

Acknowledgements

When my fifth grade teacher assigned research essays and wrote the subjects on the black board, I immediately chose the subject 'Brazil.' It was only a few hand written pages long with an elaborate, childish hand-painted cover of a pineapple. (I found it in a box of packed things at my parents' house on my wedding day. My mother had saved it. She was my biggest fan and she knew I was going to Brazil as a missionary.)

During the next years I enjoyed writing poetry for special days of family and friends. In the seventh grade my Oklahoma History teacher *volunteered me* to enter a state sponsored essay contest. A few months later I was surprised when my school announced I had won first place in the state. My teacher said he wasn't surprised and encouraged me to continue writing.

In Junior High I was *volunteered* by my choir teacher to write an essay on a trip our choir had just taken to a concert of the Tulsa Philharmonic Orchestra. With the announcement that I had won first place in the state came an invitation to go on stage with the orchestra to receive my certificate. My teachers encouraged me to use my 'gift'.

When we left for Brazil in 1964 my niece, Sharon, gave me a five year diary. I now have a box full of diaries, journals and pocket agendas. Each furlough I had opportunities to remember and share our stories. People encouraged me to put them in a book and I did just that.

To all of the above, I express my deepest appreciation and gratitude.

The Bible tells us to 'remember.' In part one of this book I have included family stories we have shared at private reunions. One of our daughters read a page recently and said, "I remember Daddy telling this in a sermon on deputation."

Our lives have been rich with remembrances and I hope this book will be a way they can be shared with our children and grandchildren after we are gone Home. The short term mission members have opportunities to share right after a trip, but by placing their testimonies in this book, their memories can be preserved for years to come. I appreciate their contributions to this book in part three.

Heartfelt thanks to the many who showed *hospitality* to us as we traveled in the US during deputation in 1964 and during state-side assignments every fifth year.

Many thanks to the foreigners who accepted our *hospitality* in Brazil and brought color, laughs, enrichment, and friendships that impacted our lives for forty-four years.

At an Oklahoma State Senior Retreat in Wagoner, evangelist Bob Thomas, Jr., challenged us that one of our tasks during retirement years is that of preserving our stories. To pass on to the next generation our faith, to recollect our stories to help others understand God's care and providence at work in them. Thanks to you, Bro. Bob.

Who's Clapping At Our Gate?

As I gathered photos for this book, there were so many I wanted to include but did not have them in digital format. A young man who works with our son Kemper converted them to digital photos for me. My thanks to Jerry Johnson, Senior Customer Service Consultant at Farmers Insurance Company, for his photographic expertise.

Once again, I want to thank my sister-in-law Judy Puckett for her help editing the text of these stories. She and my granddaughter Julia Combs de Aquino introduced me to the adventure of photo inserts!

Thanks to my husband, Jim, for living the stories with me and proof reading them after I got them down on paper.

Telling our faith stories can be a spiritual act, and our stories will not be finished until our last breath. So that they won't fade from memory, we are sharing them with you now.

Foreword

One could easily make a statement that a missionary is just like every other Christian. They share the same faith, they have a common goal, and they even make mistakes from time to time. However, saying that a missionary is like every other Christian is like saying that a person who puts a dinghy into a lake once a month is just like every other sailor.

As a 22-year veteran of the United States Navy, I can tell you that the two may be similar, but they are not the same. There is a difference in the level of commitment. Part of the difference is that one is an amateur sailor, and the other is a professional. One of the two can readily decline to set sail if the weather isn't cooperating, the other has weathered typhoons.

While missionaries share many things with every other Christian, it seems to me that missionaries more often than not have weathered storms that most Christians never face. If I'm not making myself clear, let me simplify it for you; missionaries are my heroes.

While I have traveled extensively in my military career, and even gone on several short-term mission trips, I do not put myself into the same category as a career missionary. Further, when a missionary speaks on the subject of evangelism, I pay attention to what they have to say. To me, when a missionary speaks, I am hearing an expert speak; I am hearing a hero speak.

I first met Shirley Combs in January of 2005. I went to Brazil on a short-term mission trip organized by the Greater Kansas City District Association of Free Will

Baptists. In the days to come I was to witness something incredibly powerful.

The first thing I experienced was the welcome by Shirley and her husband, Jim. First they had to pick us up at the airport. They had to try and indoctrinate us into the culture so that we didn't offend people with our thoughtless actions. They had to arrange for our lodging, meals, and transportation.

While we were there to work, it was going to place a tremendous workload on them. Ultimately, while our purpose was to be a blessing to them and the ministry at *Lar Nova Vida,* I felt we were also a burden. Yet in those days spent with the Combs, I felt like I was a part of the family. There was never a hint of being a burden; there was simply warmth and even a sense of relief that we were there to help. Jim and Shirley Combs provided a level of hospitality that was simply incredible.

I also experienced how much Shirley cared for the people of Brazil. A few nights after we arrived in Araras, we were helping to serve a meal in one of the poorest neighborhoods I had ever seen. Many of the children at *Lar Nova Vida* had families in that neighborhood.

One of my companions from North America, a man who also had previous military experience, mentioned that he was more than a little nervous. I agreed with him, this was exactly the type of neighborhood we were taught to avoid when in a foreign nation. Shirley, on the other hand, was walking around the neighborhood looking for the families of some of the children at *Lar Nova Vida.* She was walking down darkened alleys, stepping into the shanties, seemingly unafraid. When I asked her what was keeping us safe, as this looked like a dangerous place, her response was simple.

"The crime bosses in this neighborhood know that I am here to help their children. I'm not trying to bring the police with me; I am simply bringing Jesus with me."

Once again, I experienced what hospitality meant. You see, it isn't just a warm welcome at our home. It is extending that outside the home, as well. It is "bringing Jesus with me." Shirley Combs knows how to do that.

Finally, of course, I observed Shirley dealing with the ministry of *Lar Nova Vida*. Nearly every waking moment was devoted to something dealing with the children directly. There were doctor's appointments, school events, shopping for necessities, meeting dignitaries, and dealing with the paperwork of running a home for children whose parents were unable or unwilling to care for them.

There were the times of prayer with the house parents, as well as the children. There were classes to be arranged, and even taught. There were tears to be wiped away, or a stern scolding to be given when one of her lambs hadn't obeyed the rules.

When I saw the ministry in 2005, it was a far cry from how it started. You see, it started in Jim and Shirley Combs' own home. It was no longer in their home only because the need was too great, and the resources too small in their own home.

Once again, I saw hospitality at work. A willingness to use their own home, and later their own resources, in order to provide a safe, loving, Christian home to children that had no hope.

Yes, hospitality is bringing a warm welcome to a weary traveler. It is carrying that welcome to those outside your home by "bringing Jesus with you". It is a willingness to use what God has given you to His glory.

That is what I observed in that first trip to Araras, Sao Paulo, Brazil in 2005. It drew me back in 2006, 2007, and 2008. It was a desire to learn from someone who exemplified the words of Jesus in Matthew 25:40 (ESV)…"And the King will answer them, 'Truly, I say to you, as you did it to one of the least of these my brothers, you did it to me.'"

May God richly bless *Dona* Shirley, and all those who may choose to read this book.

Alan Kinder,
Pastor
Central Free Will
Baptist Church
Grand View,
Missouri

Preface

Hospitality. Jim and I both grew up as preacher kids and our parents were very hospitable. We grew up with quotes like, "Be not forgetful to entertain strangers: for thereby some have entertained angels unawares." Also, "Use hospitality one to another without grudging." On the list of requisitions for a blameless leader is to "be a lover of hospitality."

As children we gladly slept on pallets and gave up our chairs at the table to receive guests in our parents' home. Our family carried on that tradition on the mission field.

Foreign visitors who arrived at our gate in Brazil brought into our home experiences that helped to enlarge not only ours but the horizons of our three Brazilian born, curious, and hospitable children, Kemper, Cindy and Tânia. Today they are adults with college degrees, families and a world view as Christians.

We also had contacts with missionaries from other groups who worked far away from our mission field but lived in the Amazon jungles or neighboring countries.

They were Peace Corps workers. They were pilots, linguists and nurses to uncivilized, naked people who were transformed through the power of the Word. Theirs was another Brazil, unknown to us, which was brought right into our home as they shared experiences with our family. Years later we had the privilege of flying into the deepest jungle with our children for a lifetime experience.

Who's Clapping At Our Gate?

When relatives came (only four visits in forty-four years), our children were able to show "their" Brazil to relatives on those rare visits. We missed our family and wanted to share our beloved Brazilian people and culture with them. During the years we learned to appreciate a mixture of several cultures in the art of carrying out the Biblical command of hospitality.

I am very pleased with section three where members of mission groups who clapped at our gate included their personal impressions of the days they spent in *Araras*. They wrote about what they saw, felt, did, and what God spoke to them, and I included them in this book. They all had different styles of writing. Some just sent portions of their journals and others shared personal insights.

After we moved back to the US, I had the great blessing of being able to return to our home in Brazil from time to time. In the second section I shared the unusual experiences God gave me on those trips.

Recently I grabbed a flash light, water, radio, crackers, documents, a *pelego* (sheepskin rug), our laptop with this almost finished book, and went into our bathroom closet with Jim. Outside our home was passing the EF5 tornado that destroyed much of our city of Moore, Oklahoma.

Many over the world checked on us, and we and our children were fine. Our home was not hit (until later), so we offered our two extra beds, showers, and washing machine to those who were dislocated because of the disaster. The disaster was so horrific that you hardly knew where to start. The level of destruction was beyond description and everywhere you looked homes, businesses, and schools were reduced to little more than rubble. Where to start? Hospitality. It just felt right.

Then, eleven days later our home *was* hit. When we returned home from our daughter Tânia's safe room in her garage, we drove through darkened, flooded streets. Tânia's and Cindy's homes had no electricity. Ours did have lights but part of the roof came off and it was raining in the house! Oh, well, we had dry beds in the other end of the house which served fine for the next month until we got the roof repaired and back to normal, thanks to Master's Men brethren from Arkansas. A few days later Master's Men from Tennessee came to our house and repaired damages on the inside of our house.

We wanted to help with the search and rescue, but the first days were assigned to professionals. Our Hillsdale Free Will Baptist College, Dr. Tim Eaton, president, opened its dorms and cafeteria and served as the hub for other FWB organizations such as Arms of Compassion, Bridge Builders for the Cross, and Step Into the Waters. So, we helped them. They had combined efforts to help the City Impact Disaster Coalition joined by World Vision and offered hospitality for all those great people.

Hillsdale had volunteers who arrived from Washington State, New York, California, Florida, Michigan, Illinois, Indiana, Idaho, Missouri, Arkansas, and Texas. We had a fellow from London, England and six young people from Israel! Oklahoma is thankful.

Jim and I volunteered at Hillsdale along with volunteers who were nurses, coaches, teachers, policemen, construction workers, mechanics, retirees, young students, pastors, and others. The stories we heard were not all death and disaster, but we heard of miracles and humanity at its best.

Our lives have been blessed in a particular way because God gave us a particular calling. We obeyed. We went. We opened our hearts and home to offer hospitality to many who clapped at our gate. We still want to do that.

I hope you will enjoy the stories we have shared.

Part One

CHAPTER 1
"Who's Clapping at the Gate?"

In Brazil, our missionary family had the unique experience of offering hospitality to many people of different cultures and languages who arrived clapping at our gate. The custom in Brazil is to clap at the gate of the walled dwelling houses until you are acknowledged

Tania, Shirley, Kemper, Jim, and Cindy

and invited to talk or have access to the house.

These contacts from people at our gate in Brazil affected not only our family, but also the Brazilians whose lives were influenced by each visitor.

Who's Clapping At Our Gate?

Non-Christians from India, Paris, Germany, and Japan dined with us. They were Jews, Buddhists and atheists. Christian brethren sat at our table from Africa, Japan, Uruguay, Chile, Colombia, and Panama. Each one left picturesque memories as they shared stories colored by their unique languages, professions and cultures.

The Bible speaks much of hospitality, and we can certainly agree to its benefits. Most of these visitors were not part of a planned guest list. They just showed up at our gate.

Now we joyfully share some of our experiences with those who appeared at our gates during our forty-four years in our beloved adopted country.

The Peddler

In 1965, while we were living in our little rent house during our studies at the *Escola de Portuguese e Orientacao,* language and orientation school in Campinas, São Paulo, the language school scheduled the men to study in the morning and the women in the afternoon for the convenience of missionary families with children.

One morning while Jim was in class, I was home alone and heard a clap at our gate. I was curious to see who was there, but knew I couldn't communicate very well. However, I was always glad to add experience and vocabulary to my short list.

Before I opened the door, I grabbed a small English-Portuguese dictionary and slipped it into my apron pocket. Standing by the gate was a short, smiling man holding the handles of a wheel barrow. Now, we often had vendors pass by our little rent house peddling raw milk (which we had to boil), and fruits and vegetables. All these things we recognized. But the man's wheel barrow was covered with an old tarp.

He started talking in Portuguese to me and I was pretty sure he was giving a sales pitch, but I didn't understand a word and I wanted to take a peek under the tarp. We weren't getting anywhere.

I took out the dictionary and looked up the word *comer.*

"Senhor, comer?"

I wiggled my fingers in front of my lips for the sign *to eat.*

I repeated my question, *"Comer?"*

He looked shocked.

He repeated the word, *"Comer? Nao, nao, nao. Senhora."*

He threw up his hands and started rattling more Portuguese as he pushed his wheel barrow on down the street. Wow. I didn't know if I had offended him and just stood there watching him as he continued on shaking his head.

When Jim returned home, I told him about our visitor at the gate. I couldn't understand Portuguese enough to search for a Portuguese word in the dictionary and Jim didn't have an idea about what had happened.

At language school that afternoon, I shared my story with other missionaries. The Ellisons, Coscias, Robirds from our mission were also studying there, and there were many other denominations represented, also. The Ellisons lived on the same street as we, and the man had also passed by their house. When they heard my tale, they looked at each other and burst out laughing.

Who's Clapping At Our Gate?

"Shirley, the man had *esterco* under the tarp."

The other missionaries who were in more advanced classed had understood and started laughing.

"Okay. *Esterco,* so it must not be something to eat?"

" No, *esterco* means fertilizer – animal manure."

Oh, dear. Well, that was one more new word for my growing vocabulary list.

Students at the gate

While we were still living in our little rent house during *language* and orientation school in *Campinas,* two young women were clapping at our gate. We had been told that clapping at the gate was the substitute for ringing the doorbell or knocking on the door. Who could that be? We hardly knew anyone except our Brazilian teachers and other missionaries in the school. It wasn't the Robirds, or Coscias, or Ellisons. And we couldn't communicate very well in Portuguese.

We invited them into our sparsely furnished living room – a sofa, two chairs, and overturned cardboard packing boxes covered with towels from the mission Provision Closet. Well, they sort of looked like end tables.

The young ladies weren't looking at the furniture; they were looking at us with young shiny eyes. They were speaking broken English, but we understood they were asking for English classes. They were in college and English was a required subject for them.

I explained that I studied Portuguese in the language school each afternoon, and if they wanted

Who's Clapping At Our Gate?

English classes studying the Bible with flannel graph figures, I would try to find time for classes for them. (I still had the flannel graph figures packed somewhere!)

The girls worked Monday through Friday and studied at the university at night. After several attempts and lots of laughs, we finally understood each other enough to schedule classes each Saturday morning.

We were renting a tiny two bedroom house, so we hurriedly made a desk out of some planks of boards over packing barrels and placed three of our four Formica kitchen chairs in the empty front bedroom for the classes. I found the box of flannel graph Bible figures and wrapped a flannel gown around plywood to use as my board. I was ready for my first experience in teaching English as a second language. They were ready for their first experience of studying God's Word in a second language. The illustrated figures helped!

About thirty years later I offered free adult conversational English classes called "The Gospel of Love." I got out the flannel graph figures again and taught the Gospel of John to professional people, business people, and government workers. It gave the same satisfaction of dividing the Word with people who, for the most part, had never heard it before.

Eventually we became fluent in Portuguese and would teach the precious Word for over forty-four years in Brazil in both languages. However, teaching the Bible in English as a second language to two young women who clapped at our gate each Saturday morning is one of the most precious memories I have of that time.

Language Study and Brazil Nuts

During our year of language study in Campinas, São Paulo, a young man appeared at our gate, Luis. He had read a gospel tract in his city of *São Sebastião do Paraiso* in the state of *Minas Gerais* with the address of the Free Will Baptist church in Campinas stamped on the back.

He had worked for missionary Ken Eagelton at the *Evangelandia* camp ground in Jaboticabal, São Paulo. Ken gave him the gospel tract. He had written to the mission and discovered that the missionary pastor there was Earnie Deeds. Earnie started corresponding with him and sent more literature to Luis. He did the correspondence course, **Grande Salvacao** *(Great Salvation)*, and he wanted to know more.

Earnie invited Jim and Don Robirds, who were in language school, to go with him for a trip of three or four hours to visit the young man. The three missionaries spent the night at a hotel with a bath down at the end of the hall. The pillows were long and round like logs and about as hard.

The next day the men easily found the young man's middle class home. He was a fine, talented cabinet maker and found a job in Campinas. He found a church near where he was living.

He had heard the gospel and embraced salvation. And now he was clapping at our gate to visit us in our home. He had some questions.

He asked, *"Pastor, precisa casar-se para ser um bom cristao?"* (Does a man have to marry to be a good Christian?)

We were still in language school studying

Portuguese, but Jim was a good student and understood the young man's words. We soon found out that understanding words does not always guarantee you understand their meaning.

Jim explained that the Bible speaks well of marriage, but it also says that if a person chooses to dedicate himself to God's work, he doesn't have to marry.

"Ah, que bom! Eu nao queria casar com ela." (Ah, that's great! I didn't want to marry her anyway.)

We found out that he was living with a young woman and thought Jim was saying he could as a Christian continue to live with her without the sanctity of marriage. We had much to learn.

A similar thing happened while we were still learning the language. A young man talked with Jim after he had preached, "Ye must be born again."

He said in Portuguese, "I really liked the sermon, because it proves the Bible teaches reincarnation. You must be born again, and again, and again."

Ouch. Once again Jim was learning to be sensitive to both words and meanings in the culture.

Few people have seen the shell that holds our Brazil nuts. Jim gives an illustration of the challenge of breaking through barriers in order to speak to the soul seeking the truth. The Brazil nut has a thick rough shell, tougher than a coconut shell that cannot be easily broken. I have tried a hammer – no way. It is usually opened with a saw. Not an easy job. The nuts inside are in the shape of orange slices, remember? They fit closely in the shell like orange slices, too. When you get the Brazil nuts out of the thick shell, you still have to crack another hard shell around the nut.

The first barriers that sometimes need to be broken when you evangelize in a foreign country are language, culture and past experiences. Sometimes it is a tough, time consuming job of love and persistence. Then when you break through these, there is another spiritual shell that must be broken by the Word and the Spirit. But it is worth it. It is like eating Brazil nuts, once you start it is hard to be satisfied with just one.

Contact with the "Uncivilized"

While in language school in Campinas, São Paulo, we met missionaries from the Unevangelized Field Missions (UFM) who were taking a refresher course in Portuguese. They worked in the jungles of the *Territorio de Roraima*. I remember thinking, "Now, they are real missionaries!"

When we first talked with our International Missions board about Brazil, we asked about jungle work. At that time Free Will Baptists (FWB) had no work with the Indians, and Brazil would soon pass a law that only Brazilian missionaries would be allowed to work with the Indians. Our Brazilian Free Will Baptist churches would later send Brazilian workers into the jungles: Lelis, Junior, José Pedro, Eliseu and Cecilia. Today there are several from our church in training to go as Brazilian missionaries to the unevangelized Indians.

One of the UFM missionaries we met in language school, Sandra Cue from Chicago, became a very close friend. She was working as a linguist with a tribe that had no written language. We were fascinated by the process she and her colleagues used to put the natives' language in written form, next teach the native people to read and write it, and then translate

Nurse, Linguist and Teacher who worked in Roraima in the Amazon

parts of the Bible into that newly-written language.

They opened our minds to the beauty and power of the Scripture and shared the challenge of explaining passages that were difficult for the native Indians to visualize.

For example, Jesus spoke of how he would like to gather His people "under His wing like a mother **hen**".....Those Indians from the Amazon had never seen a HEN! The Missionary Aviation Fellowship (MAF) had to fly in eggs for missionary families. MAF pilots also flew in powdered milk since there were no cows in the jungle.

John referred to Jesus as the "...**lamb** who took away the sin of the world. They had never seen a lamb. Missionaries had a lamb and chicken flown in one day as an object lesson for their Bible translations. The next morning the natives proudly offered the animals to the missionaries – shot with arrows. They couldn't understand how anyone would keep an animal around that wasn't meant for food.

The missionary linguists were trying to find the natives' vocabulary for the story about Paul's **shipwreck.** There was no river or ocean near their jungle compound, and those Indians did not use canoes or boats, much less ships. The Bible mentions dogs and horses, but these also were unknown to the uncivilized native people.

The linguists had to depend on gestures and signs by listening to the Indians' vocabulary for certain objects. They told how their first primers were full of errors, and some of their stories were hilarious. One example: They would point to an object and when the Indian made a sound, they would phonetically write it down. They would point to a wooden table and the Indian would say something like: "xxx." They wrote it down. They pointed to a wooden chair. The Indian said: "xxx." Well, maybe since the Indians don't have tables and chairs, the missionary linguist pointed to a tree. The Indian would say: "xxx." Perhaps "xxx" meant "wood"? Whenever they came to a puzzling situation, they moved on to something else. Later on after they had many lists of new vocabulary, they discovered something. The

Who's Clapping At Our Gate?

Indians don't use their fingers to point at an object. They used their noses, not their finger (xxx}. So, each time the missionary pointed to an object using his/her finger, the native would say the word for finger (xxx).Sometimes pages would have to be cancelled out because of such errors, but they kept on working.

After years of tedious labor and dedication, portions of the Bible were translated and taught to open hearts. The missionaries returned after language study to their compound in the jungles of *Territorio de Roraima*, and they invited us to visit them, which we did at the end of our first five-year term.

By the time we finished our year of language study in Campinas, I was five months pregnant with our first child. We moved to *Araras* at the end of 1965, settled in our rent house and changed doctors.

We had no family – mothers, sisters, or other Americans – to help us, but new sympathetic Christian friends tried to communicate through gestures and broken sentences. My year of language study only gave me a basic vocabulary and phrases, and my doctor spoke quickly and used vocabulary I had never heard of. The Brazilians referred to us as "*Marinheiro na primeira viagem.*" A sailor on his first voyage. They meant we were inexperienced

Missionary Sandra Cue

in having babies. But, one day someone clapped at our front gate.

"Who's clapping at the gate?"

It was Sandra! Our linguist missionary friend Sandra Cue from the jungle mission work. I was due that week, but little Kemper passed the date by several days. She was a single girl, but had been present at the birthing of many Indian babies that would fall on banana leaves out in the open jungle. And she could speak both languages!

There came another clap outside our gate on another day.

"Who's at the gate, this time?"

It was Eula Mae Martin, our Free Will Baptist missionary nurse. Both could speak the language perfectly and both could help put my dear husband at ease. God knew I needed some special *house guests* to help us through the next days.

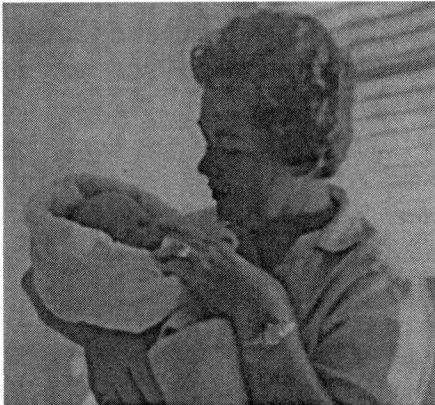
Missionary nurse Eula Mae

I checked into the hospital on Monday with contractions five minutes apart. On Wednesday I was still having contractions, my water had broken and my doctor had left town. The nurses were Catholic nuns and at that time they did not practice caesarian operations. We were fortunate to have those friends with us.

On that same Wednesday my doctor returned to the hospital and saw the condition I was in. In five minutes I was in the operating room for a caesarian and our first-born son, Kemper, was born.

Of course we wanted to let our families know the great news of the birth of our first born. They seemed so far away at that moment. First, we sent a telegram to the US but it took two weeks to arrive!

Next, we tried the telephone. At that time we had one of the few phones in the neighborhood. We called the long distance operator and gave her the contact number and information. She informed us that she would call us back when the call went through. It would probably take two hours.

In about two and a half hours the operator called back with the connection. We had to yell to be heard, but we could hear them well. By the time our second child Cindy was born we could speak the Portuguese language better.

Who would think that communication would change so much by the time we called from Brazil announcing the births of our Brazilian born grand children? What a difference *Skype* makes.

While Sandra was in *Araras,* she spoke at our little Free Will Baptist congregation in a small rented room near our house. She challenged the Brazilians about the work with the unevangelized Indians of their country. She showed slides of the jungle missions and one slide was of an airplane which she introduced as a *missionary.* A young boy, Lelis Fachini, was present with his family and accepted the challenge to help reach the unevangelized. He had airplanes hanging around in his room and had told me he wanted to be a pilot one day. He did became a pilot- with *Asas de Socorro (*Missionary Aviation Fellowship) and was their first Brazilian instructor.

It is Easter the day I am writing this portion, and I received a letter from a father of another young man who was from our work, Jefferson Gaino, and who is a missionary pilot in the Amazon area. His father, William, said (I translate), "Tomorrow Jefferson will join with Lelis to work together for three days in the region of *Ribeirinho* flying in supplies of medicines and food. I am imagining today how a Christian brother I grew up with, now is working with my son, Jefferson. This is truly a *God thing."* Sandra's visit to our city is still bearing fruits in the jungle where she dedicated her life.

After a five year term, our furlough time arrived and we remembered a special invitation we had received during our first year there.

No Gates in the Jungle

On our way to our first furlough/stateside assignment, we flew to a simple airport in northern Brazil. There a Missionary Aviation Fellowship *(Asas de Socorro)* pilot, Eldon Larson, flew us and our two children, Kemper and Cindy, for ten unforgettable days into the Amazon jungle. Unforgettable also was the ride through those mountains and Amazon jungles that left me green with air sickness. But I held on because I knew we were facing the opportunity of a life time. Our tiny plane was met by primitive Indians who wore no clothes, but wore flowers and sticks through pierced ears and noses. They gave us a curious, hands-on welcome.

We later learned that they not only had no clothes but they also had no spoons, salt, furniture (except for handmade hammocks), no matches nor tools and very little variety in foods or fruits. They ate the monkeys and other meats they killed with their poisoned-tipped arrows. They had cassava breads they processed by squeezing out the poison from each manioc root, beating them into round disks, and cooking them over open fires made with sticks and stones. We were about to learn many more things in the ten days we lived among them.

Several naked Indians met us at the landing of the plane. They would beat one hand on their chest repeating a phrase. Theirs was a language unknown to the civilized world and was still being recorded.

We each held our small children tightly in our arms and just smiled as they repeated something to us and crowded around us. When the missionaries later interpreted what they said, a thrill raced through me.

They were saying what sounded like, *"Djedjus wabutu?"*

I asked, "What are they saying? Asking?"

The missionaries answered, "They are asking if God lives in your chest."

Wow! Their language was recorded, the Word was translated and taught, and now God lived in their chests. A naked Indian just witnessed to me. Glory!

On the compound the missionaries had cleared out, there were the log cabins for the married couples with their children, Bob and Gaye Cable, and the

Fritz Harter family. There was another cabin for the single ladies. Sandra was the linguist and Maria the nurse. Soon a teacher Edith joined their team and became our friend. All the houses had an *Indian porch* on the front where the Indians would come and sit and look into their homes. Not much for privacy, but before they had designed the Indian porches, the Indians felt free to just walk in their homes unannounced.

Scattered around were several more buildings. There was an infirmary, a storage/dispensary, and a little school room. The Indians helped them clear a runway for the plane that visited every two weeks. They traded their time for things like machetes or matches from the storage room, since they had no concept of money.

There was one interesting rule the missionaries imposed. When the male Indians showed up to work on the runway, they had to wear loin cloths. Any other time they and the women walked around naked. The missionaries said that their next step would be to teach them to wash the cloths. Stink. Stink.

One day the children and I were in the single missionaries' cabin by ourselves. Jim had gone with missionary Bob and some Indians on an overnight hunting trip with the Indians. Maria was at the infirmary and Sandra in the school house. The cabin floors were made of small round logs which were not comfortable on the feet without shoes. It wasn't difficult to sweep since the dirt fell through the cracks. But what about the creatures that could come up through the cracks? I didn't ask.

The girls had made their furniture themselves out of wood. There were front steps to the Indian porch and back steps from the kitchen. Water had to be carried in from quite a distance. The entire cabin was about 15' x 20'.

The children were taking a nap when I heard a noise at the back steps. Someone calling? I certainly couldn't speak their language if it was a native. Yes, sure enough. There was an Indian woman sitting on the back step. With an arrow sticking into her naked shoulder!

I knew I needed to run for Maria or Sandra, but I hesitated, thinking about our sleeping children alone with a wounded young Indian woman. I finally ran out the front and down to the infirmary. Maria left with me immediately and Sandra joined us in the run back to the cabin. The children were still sleeping, and the Indian young woman was still sitting on the back steps.

Sandra and Maria treated the wounded woman as she told them her story in her native tongue. Her husband had shot her with the arrow out of jealousy. He thought that a man from another tribe was trying to get his woman (which she denied).

I was glad she was taken and treated before the children awoke. I would later hear stories from our *civilized* world that sounded similar to theirs in the jungle.

One day we were invited to visit a *maloca* with Sandra. She said it was a huge, round Indian house shaped like a donut. The hole in the thatched roof was to let the smoke escape from the fire in the center to fend off the cold nights. About one hundred Indians lived in a common house with only hammocks hanging all around inside the thatched dwelling. The hammocks were made from homemade spun cotton threads. We watched the women spin from a cotton ball into a crude instrument made of twigs they held in their hands.

"Are you folks ready for a hike?"

"Sure," we said accepting the invitation. "Let's go since we came to learn all we can."

"It will be an hour's hike straight up."

"Okay. Let's do it anyway," we agreed,

We left the children with a missionary family that had children. We hiked up the mountain following Sandra and the Indians trying not to lag behind like city folk. We pulled at plants to help us up and sometimes I wished for someone to push me from behind. The canopy over and around us shaded us from the sun, but the humidity made our clothes stick to us. The twigs and thorns scratched me through my skirt and the sweat bees were biting my legs.

Finally, we made it. It was beautiful up there, I'm sure, but all I could see were swarms of naked Indians coming out of the *maloca* to meet us. They would squeeze Jim's arms and, once they saw his gold filled teeth, they pulled at his chin for him to open his mouth. They picked up his arm and placed his ticking watch close to their ears. Poor Jim. He just laughed and let them do it.

I hated to say anything, but I whispered to Sandy that I was thirsty after that hike. She turned to one of the Indians and spoke something. She told me that they would go get me some water. I asked if it were very far. She said it would be an hour's trip down the mountain and back up again. Forget it. From her smile I think that was exactly the answer she expected.

Now it was the time for her to whisper to me.

The Indians were about to offer us a snack of something that they only harvested once a year.

"What is it?" We whispered.

She said, "Just eat it and smile like a good missionary, remembering that you are the honored guests."

They picked up big banana leaves from the smoky ashes in the coals on the ground and unrolled them carefully. In the center I saw what resembled pecans or peanuts. I had a hunch they were not.

Sandy accepted one and smiled at Jim and me when it came our turn. I prayed silently, Lord, help it go down and stay down. It tasted smoky on my tongue, but I certainly didn't intend to chew it. It went down. I looked at her for an explanation, but she was talking to the Indians in their language so I waited. Guess what? Sure enough, once a year they harvested this delicacy and had just shared them with us. Larva. Larva? Larva! I really did want a drink of water then.

On the way back down the mountain we followed Sandy and the Indians again. This time I held onto vegetation to keep from sliding down. I noticed the native men and women hiking along with us. The custom is for the Indian women to carry the heavy loads and the men to carry only their bows and arrows.

We followed one young woman with a heavy load of bananas on her head. Probably a stalk of over sixty bananas. Sandra said that the woman had been mute for a few years. Demon possession. After we left the jungle to go to stateside assignment in the USA, I prayed off and on for that young woman. One day Sandra wrote that the young Indian woman accepted Christ, had been delivered of the demon and was talking once again.

Soon we would be leaving the mystery, the enchantment, and challenges of the jungle. The nights were dark, dark with no artificial lights anywhere in the entire jungle and for that reason flashlight batteries were basic equipment. However, it made the stars shine even brighter to our eyes, and the canopy of the sky seemed so much closer. God seemed closer. The laborers seemed so few.

Sandra was always teasing me in language school about not being "namby-pamby." The word took on a different meaning as I watched the courageous, dedicated missionaries and their families living the Gospel in the heart of the Amazon. Our dear Sandra died there among her beloved Indians where she had given her life to record, translate, and teach the Word to the uncivilized tribes. Her body was buried among them, but she is in Glory fellowshipping with the True and Living Word. How fortunate to have had this godly woman and friend at our gate in Brazil.

During the ten days we were in the jungle we never saw a gate. But we left with such an incredible treasure of memories and met Indians who had Jesus *in their chest* because of missionaries who had dedicated their lives to recording and teaching the Word. We will meet Indians and missionaries inside the Pearly Gates together with the LIVIING WORD!

Woops. Hospitality Lessons

When practicing hospitality, you naturally use the customs you have learned and practiced to try to make your guests comfortable. However, we started observing small gestures different from our own customs.

We learned to serve coffee or treats on a tray and never to hand a cup, glass or plate directly into the hands of the guests. I learned another custom the hard way. With my Okie background, it was natural to offer someone a drink of water or some refreshments as soon as their wraps were taken and everyone was settled.

One Brazilian friend discreetly told me that you offer refreshments to your guests when it is time to leave. It seemed I was 'hinting' to them to leave shortly after they had just arrived. Oh, well, they were patient with us.

Brazilians rarely touch food with their fingers, using paper napkins to get hold of any bread or little treats. A toothpick? In public it is considered bad manners to use a toothpick, unless you cover the mouth with your other hand.

Well, don't expect strict punctuality from your invited guests. Most will arrive at least 15 minutes after the time arranged. Don't plan to serve right away, because they will probably go through their arrival rituals of hugs and hellos and then visit a while.

As foreigners we observe. We learn. We integrate. Being a foreigner actually made first contacts easier at times for me. Brazilians are naturally curious and like to hear new points of views and especially like to hear people who appreciate their culture.

English as a second language is required of children in school and of adults in college. Business people need English in commerce. Higher income society likes to travel overseas and wants to learn languages. That is what I speak, so it naturally brought new friends to my gate.

But as the Bible says, "to be all things to all men" so that through some of the many things you do you can win a few. The Bible also says to be hospitable. To love. To give. To share. To give your time. To lift up the Person who has given you hope and to pass it on.

Three Times is Charm

In language and orientation school we learned that you may have to give an invitation at least *three* times before a person feels free to accept. A few weeks out of language school we learned firsthand how it works.

A family with many children, I believe 12, had been evangelized in meetings on a sugar cane plantation outside our city of *Araras*. The workers lived in a colony and their father, José, was in charge of the community garden. The families and plantation owners got their fresh produce from him.

Their older children worked in the cane fields. Three of his sons, Oripes, Joaquim and Joao, wanted more than their weekly Bible studies there and liked to catch a ride into town to attend services in our little rented corner building.

Our rented house was only a block and a half from the rented church building so we walked to and from church. One Sunday we invited the young men to walk with us to our house after church, since that would save them from going the long distance back to their home right at lunch time.

The three of them sat timidly on the sofa in the

living room while Jim and I tried to visit with them with our limited Portuguese vocabulary. I had prepared part of the meal before going to church so it was soon almost ready. We had no canned foods, no convenient frozen items, no prepared sauces, no instant drinks – everything was prepared from scratch. It was hot summer time and we were soon expecting our first child, Kemper.

The dining room and living room section was one open area so the brothers could see that the table was set for five. I was thankful that I had prepared the regular beans and rice, a big bowl of salad, as well as a generous portion of spaghetti and meat sauce. A menu they would recognize and be comfortable with.

I announced that the meal was on the table and I asked them to choose water, tea or fruit juice to drink. All of it cold since it was hot, summer time.

The brothers looked at each other and said, *"Obrigada, Irma, mas nao queremos nada para tomar ou comer."*

We knew enough Portuguese to know they said they didn't want anything to drink or eat.

We reasoned with them that they had left early that morning to get to church and it would be late before they would return back home to the plantation. I showed them the table was already set for them and that it was our joy to share the table with them. We could visit and get news from their family. We talked on and on. Didn't they want to eat before they went back home in the afternoon?

They said again, *"Nao viemos preparados para comer. Nao estamos com fome. Pode comer sem a gente."*

They were refusing again to eat with us. They said they didn't come prepared to eat. They weren't hungry and we could feel free to eat without them. Well, we didn't feel free.

Jim and I looked at each other. The food was getting cold and we had run out of vocabulary to beg anymore.

We slowly sat down at the table and just looked at the three empty places that had been set for our guest. We were about to ask the blessing when one of the young men asked,

"Pastor, o que foi a pergunta que o senhor fez para nos?"

I asked Jim what question he had just asked them. He said that's what they asked, but he didn't remember a question he asked them.

"Pastor, aquela ultima coisa que falou. A pergunta que fez para nos."

They were asking him to repeat the last question he had asked them. Yes, now he remembered.

"Ah, voces estao convidados a comer conosco. Porfavor, nao querem almocar conosco?" You are invited to eat with us. Please, don't you want to have lunch with us?

That did it. Third time is charm. That was the third invitation that was missing.

They all three stood up. We stood up. Everyone shook hands and hugged and the five of us sat together around the table. As we held hands during prayer before the meal, my heart smiled. One more lesson in hospitality learned.

Who's Clapping At Our Gate?

We had many more lessons to learn over the next forty-four years. (We observed that this particular custom has changed some over the years and now most are quite eager to accept our invitation after the first or second time.)

Communicating Brazilian Style

Most of our American guests in our mission teams soon find out that Brazilians are very welcoming and hospitable. Since they are easy to befriend, leaving them can be unsettling.

Most Brazilians don't need much personal space and you may soon notice that. However, it can be considered rude if you back away. They are a 'touchy', tactile people. They put their hand on someone when talking and it is simply an indication that they are interested in the conversation. They seem to maintain more eye contact when listening or talking to you.

In general, conversations are lively and noisy. Sometimes when we are on a bus, in a restaurant, after church, or on a plane, we stop and listen to the noise level and just smile. We love it. Everyone seems to be talking at the same time and jumping from topic to topic.

Recently I was at a baby shower in Oklahoma City with our daughter, Tânia, and granddaughters, Julia, Bianca and Isabela. A Brazilian friend was giving the shower in her large beautiful home for another Brazilian friend. There were 42 Brazilians present. I mentioned to Tânia to just listen. The noise level was high and many were talking at the same time. As I said, I love it.

Don't be offended if someone just jumps in on your conversation. They don't consider it an interruption and they don't have to use ritualistic expressions of permission to interject something. It is accepted and you just get used to it.

I still haven't quite figured out how to interpret their laughter when someone falls, trips, or spills something. Somehow they don't seem to be making fun of the victim and surprisingly the victim may smile, too. Maybe it is a face saving gesture for the person. I still want to sympathize with the person while everyone else is laughing.

Introductions at first seemed ritualistic or formal to me. Men will shake hands and they may place the other hand on a shoulder. Women will touch cheeks and smack into the air, as will men to women. In São Paulo it will be one kiss. But in other areas of Brazil where we have lived, it is twice if you are married and three times if you are single. (The third is for good luck in finding a mate.)

This same ritual is repeated when you leave. However, you add long statements about how it was good to see you, how they enjoyed the meeting, as well as pass on best wishes to family members who were not able to be there.

If someone restarts a conversation by remembering something else to say, after the conversation ends, the good-bye ritual begins all over again. You may be kissed good-bye more than once before they walk toward the door.

If you are the host, you accompany the guest to the door. If you are the guest, you don't announce you are leaving and just walk to the door and open it. It could be considered rude. The host or hostess will follow you and open the door for you.

Even if it is a close friend or family, you walk them out the door and watch them leave out the gate and wave. I notice our family continues to do that here in the United States.

CHAPTER 2
Who's Clapping at our Santa Catarina Gate?

Our Brazilian Field Council of missionaries decided to open new areas to evangelize and establish churches. After researching different needy areas, Missionary Information Bureau (MIB) informed us that the neediest area of Brazil was the state of *Santa Catarina*. Of the cities with which we corresponded only one responded. *Tubarao*, (Shark City) *Santa Catarina*.

After much prayer, we moved to *Tubarão* with our three children – Kemper, Cindy and Tânia, who was 21 days old. Sam Wilkinson and John Craft soon arrived with their families. It was June and winter time, and no houses or buildings had heat so our adjustments began.

Our three families were busy with evangelism, home Bible studies with Moody Science films, Christian Reading Room, English classes, outreach services in neighboring villages and grist mill. After the first term, the other missionaries moved on to other areas.

Since we were the only Americans left in town, we had a unique opportunity to entertain foreigners.

The last coal fed steam locomotive in the country of Brazil was in our city of *Tubarao, Santa Catarina*. *Tubarão* is a coal mining area, and so is Jim's home state of West Virginia. The steam locomotive was a tourist attraction for foreigners. Sometimes an official would call from the Train Agency informing us that they had a foreigner in town and asked if we would we like to meet them. We were the only resident Americans, and they always ended up having a meal with our family. They usually didn't speak Portuguese, and sometimes their English wasn't easy to understand. But we were always able to communicate and gain a wealth of experiences. We homeschooled our children, and it was a great plus to have people from other cultures and background into our home on a one-on-one basis.

What Do Chickens Do Around Here?

In *Santa Catarina* our college student intern missionaries were young men. (During our first five-year-term in the state of São Paulo we had all young ladies.) Since we were usually the only North Americans in town, it was good for us and our children to be able to visit with someone in English.

We try to give these students many experiences while they are with us and expose them to many activities – weddings, funerals, holidays, camps, VBS, and field trips.

One thing they all seem to enjoy are the special and different foods they are served.

Danny Cooper, from Jim's home state of West Virginia, was a blessing and a help with the new work we were in. He easily made friends with our contacts. He still continues in ministry.

Dennis Owens, from Florida, was a joy and great observer while he was with us. One day he said, "Jim, what do the chickens do around here?"

Well, you never knew what to expect from Dennis, but Jim asked him why he asked.

He said, "Well, I've been here almost a month

and I haven't seen a fried egg yet."

Humm. He was right. The Brazilian breakfast is similar to a Continental Breakfast. Bread, butter, cheese, fruits, hot milk with coffee and lots of sugar. So, that is what we serve, also.

After that we tried to be more careful with our hospitality as to our guests' preference so we soon prepared fried eggs for Dennis. He later went with his family to Spain and then to Uruguay as missionaries.

Choo-Choo Tourists

One visitor arrived in town to see the locomotive and ended up clapping at our front gate. He was a Frenchman who spoke English. Around our table I thanked him for the Statue of Liberty. An Englishman tourist wanted to know about the locomotive and arrived at our gate. I thanked him for our motherland while sharing a meal of Brazilian dishes. A Jewish man had visited the locomotive and was sitting at our table. I thanked him and his people for Jesus, our Jewish Messiah. He only nodded his head.

Part of evangelism is fulfilling the needs of others so that they are open to listen to Good News. Some people need to learn English as a second language, and others need a compassionate ear to help them through broken relationships. These foreign tourists just needed someone to offer good, old fashioned hospitality in a strange land. Just like it says in the Bible.

Bikers, World Travelers

A man from Germany and his wife from Japan were traveling around the world by bike. We found out that they met on his travels through Japan and later on she flew and met him in British Columbia where they were married. (I love romantic stories.)

I saw their bikes outside the *Angeloni* Supermarket in *Tubarao*, with a sign written in English, "Around the World – by Bicycle." I waited for them to come out of the store. I had no idea who to look for, but soon a couple left the supermarket and walked toward the bikes. I got out of the car and introduced myself. They were glad to hear someone speak English so we talked awhile. They didn't speak Portuguese and I certainly didn't speak German or Japanese. After a while, I invited them to our house for a meal and for the family to meet them.

They told of their adventures during their world travels. The countries, continents, mountains, deserts, beaches, and forests. They explained how they packed for overnight stops in a tent, with their cooking equipment, food and first aid, and hygiene products strapped to their bikes. They recorded their journeys, and the National Geographic Magazine was interested in their adventures and photos.

The people they met along the way had all

Around the world by bicycle

sorts of reactions to them when seeing the sign on their bikes, and a few invited them to their homes as we did. Even the stories about the different weather they faced around the world added adventure to the family meal as they talked and we listened. Since we homeschooled our children, probably every subject was enriched by the visit of these fascinating, determined people.

The children were impressed by the delicious candy bars the travelers had to eat every few hours to give energy for hours and hours of riding their bikes. They were full of questions, and the couple was patient to answer them in their accented English.

They stayed with us a couple of days and enjoyed hot baths and getting caught up on equipment repair and food supply. They went through a lot of bicycle tires. We wanted to give them something for their trip, but they only suggested the Brazilian equivalent of packages of Kool-Aid. It was a small gift in exchange for the rich and fascinating experience given to our family by two bikers traveling around the world.

They accepted a prayer before they biked away from our gate. Hospitality is good!

Business Man Far From home at Our Gate

The company of Souza Cruz was in our city of *Tubarao*. Usually we are the only Americans in town, but one year we met a fellow American who parked his car in front of our house. We found out he was also a Protestant Christian. He had come from North Carolina to install a machine at one of the largest tobacco companies in Brazil, Souza Cruz. And he didn't even smoke!

Who's Clapping At Our Gate?

We had good fellowship around our table, and he was glad to have somewhere to spend his spare time. It is a lonely feeling to be alone in a strange land around a strange language. He soon moved on, but his friendship was important to our family, and he said he was glad to be able to visit with fellow Christian Americans in a strange land.

Professional Foreigners at our Gate

An American couple was living in the state north of us where he taught in an American high school for businessmen and military families. From beautiful Curitiba, Parana, somehow they found us in *Tubarão* (translated Shark City). What a great surprise when they showed up at our gate. Not only were they compatriots, but they were also from Oklahoma and were Free Will Baptist.

Robert and Deanna Grider and sons, Clifton and Craig, became part of our family for a short time. We had good fellowship in our home even though they were far away in another state. Once on New Year's Eve it was good to be with other Americans as we celebrated together in their apartment in Curitiba.

When they left the school and Brazil, they sold us some of their things. We bought a Great Dane from them for $50.00 – a sacrifice for us in those days. His name was Adonis, but the children called him Scoobie-Doo. He would jump up, put his head and paws over the top of our high back fence that faced the street, and bark. His size and bark would scare people walking by and they would jump and yell. But our small children loved him and Cindy and Tânia rode him like a small pony.

Who's Clapping At Our Gate?

When they took him for a walk, Kemper said he would take *them* for a walk. It cost too much to keep him in food (like buckets full), but he was a good watchdog, and the children enjoyed him so much.

One passerby, however, saw the dog over the back fence and wasn't afraid. He stopped to ask about buying the dog and asked the price. Jim gave him a ridiculous price of US$350 that popped into his head since he felt the kids would miss their dog. The man accepted the offer on the spot. Jim was surprised and said he would have to consult the children first. He went into the house and timidly offered the children $25.00 each if they wanted to sell Adonis. They accepted. When Jim returned to the

The Grider family

man and dog in the backyard he mentioned that it was expensive just to keep Adonis in food and that the children accepted the sale of their Scoobie-doo. The man said he owned a big restaurant in town, and feeding the dog would not be a problem.

Later we heard that our huge, loving Adonis on arriving at the new owner's home, fought with his Doberman and won. The kids said, "Yeah, Scoobie-Doo"!

After our family moved on to another area of Brazil and the Griders moved back to Oklahoma, we connected again after many, many years. Our children and their children are adults now but they can still recall that brief time when compatriots met in a strange land.

Beach Evangelism Team at the Gate

One vacation time we had a group of young adults arrive at our gate in *Tubarao*. They were from the state of *São Paulo* and were members of our Free Will Baptist churches there. They had made the 2,000 kilometer (1,200 mile) bus trip to *Santa Catarina* to help us with beach evangelism. Some were students, musicians, lay preachers, and soccer players. Most of them had never been to that beautiful state settled by Italians and Germans. They discovered that the culture and vocabulary were quite different from their huge modern cities in São Paulo. People who lived on that street would never be the same again.

Tubarão is about 20 minutes from the beach. We had never lived near beaches (There are none in our area of São Paulo, nor in Oklahoma and West Virginia). Our first December there with our home group of neighbors, we practiced a Christmas drama and a cantata. Every one enjoyed the preparation and was enthusiastic. But the week before Christmas our neighbors were packing up to go to the beach. Several even packed up their kitchen stove (which ran on little tanks of propane). They said everyone always leaves before Christmas to go to the beach to get away from the heat and mosquitoes. We were south of the equator and it was summer time in Brazil. When we checked on those attending our church, they had left town, also. You can believe we were better prepared for the Christmas season during the next years.

At times we were the only family left on our street with just the mosquitoes and sultry heat to keep us company. After talking with others and meditating on the best use of our time, we started planning beach evangelism. We took Moody Science Films that presented the Gospel, Child Evangelism material and *portable* musical instruments. At first we visited friends' beach cabins. Later we found a little wooden, rustic beach house with two bedrooms, a tiny living room, kitchen, and a detached one-car garage. It had no inside toilet facilities until Jim added one later.

Jim built benches for meetings in the garage that could be lifted on hinges and fastened to the wooden walls. There we had afternoon children classes. However, it was too small for evening meetings so we put up a white sheet on the outside wall of the garage and showed films on a 16 mm movie projector as the crowd stood.

We sang songs we had taught the children in the afternoon. During those years, TV reception was difficult at the beach, and hardly anyone had one at that time. Once the sun went down, entertainment took place on the front porches where the temperature dropped each night. Table games, music with guitars and accordions, and conversations were the nightly routine. Our evening activities were a novelty for the beach community, and each night the attendance increased.

Jim built six bunk bed shelves on the back wall of the little garage to help house volunteer workers. We kept pressure cookers going each day in our little kitchen to feed the young, hungry group of volunteers who really worked hard, played hard, and made lifelong friends.

By the time the wonderful group left our front gate to make the long trip home, some of those local friends had accepted Christ as Savior. Others carried the evangelism seeds with them and later made decisions.

Oops! Toninho's At the Gate Again!

If anyone has been to Brazil, there is a great chance that he or she has been approached by beggars. They may be seated on the sidewalks near the post office or near busy market places holding out their hands for help. They may be on the steps of a church picking at scabs on their limbs or near the entrance of a restaurant with infants. You can see them at bus stops or airports.

We had our own regular customer frequently come to our gate.

Anthony was the town mascot. He was mentally challenged and had no family. He was probably in his twenties. He made friends with the downtown merchants who were patient with him and usually fed him little snacks. Unfortunately, they also gave him white lightning made from sugar cane since it was the cheapest drink. So the town mascot became the town drunk. The town gave him the nickname "Toninho Louco." (Crazy Little Tony)

At times he would stop Jim on the streets and start a string of disconnected terms in English he had picked up from different places. His pronunciation was not too bad.

"Hey, what time is it? United States of

Who's Clapping At Our Gate?

America, my friend. President Richard Nixon, Hello, my friend, how are you? What time is it? United State of America..."

Brazilians passing by would stop and listen. They knew Toninho and his mental limitations, so they asked Jim if Toninho really was speaking English. Jim would say yes. They would just shake their heads and walk on down the sidewalk. English was a required language studied in high schools and college, and most found it difficult to learn. Jim always got a chuckle out of it because Toninho really was speaking English, but they didn't ask if it made any sense.

When he clapped at our gate, however, he was usually speaking in Portuguese. He would talk a while and end up asking for help. We chose to give him food and clothing instead of money.

By his smell and appearance, Toninho needed more than food and clothing. Sometimes Jim would have him take a bath in a shower in our little laundry area. Jim would pour medicine on the open sores on his legs after the bath. At that he yelled and complained. He said if his wounds healed, people on the street would not have pity on him or give him money. One sore was so fierce looking that Jim wanted to take him to the hospital, but he really became upset and refused to go.

Sometimes Toninho would come to our gate asking for a place to sleep. At first we would put him on a pallet on the floor in a little back room. Oh, no! That didn't last long. He would urinate and the smell was terrible. What could we do the next time he came? He didn't come that often, but no one wanted to face the clean up again.

Who's Clapping At Our Gate?

Jim found a hammock made of nylon mesh which he hung on the screened in front porch for the children. The next time Toninho came asking to sleep, Jim let him sleep in the hammock on the front porch. Early the next morning Toninho was gone and there was a puddle on the tile floor under the hammock. We could open up the water hose to wash the floor of the porch and the hammock quickly dried after being washed in hot soapy water. We thought we had it worked out, but he took us by surprise on his next visit.

One night Jim left our Volks Variante station wagon open. A rare thing for him at that time. There was no sign of Toninho that night, but as soon as Jim opened the car door, he knew without a doubt that he had been there. The smell was overwhelming, and after all the cleaning and disinfectant it lingered for days. The children really didn't want to get in the care, and who could blame them?

Once Jim cleaned up Toninho and doctored him. He had scratches on his face and arms. He said he had fallen because of a seizure, but we thought perhaps it had been an excess of white lightning, too. Jim gave him one of his nice shirts, pants, socks, and shoes. He really looked proud and waved from the gate as he went to the corner and turned.

Later Jim came into the house really upset. One of the neighbors told him that as soon as Toninho got out of sight, he sold the clothes and shoes for a few pennies. . The neighbors already didn't like Toninho hanging around their neighborhood. Maybe Toninho knew that because our house seemed to be the only house he visited. Jim said he was going to be ready for Toninho when he returned.

One day the young man arrived at the gate, and gave his same greetings, and got around to the same request for help.

Jim said, "Toninho, if you ever need something to eat or a place to sleep, we will help you out. But I will never, never give you clothes and shoes again. You deceive me and accept my good clothes and turn around and sell them for pennies."

Toninho was shocked and had an answer to that.

Translated into English he said, "Why you low down, dirty dog, you. After all I have done for you."

Jim asked, "Toninho, what in the world have you ever done for me?'

"Why, I have told all over town what a nice man you are. I have invited lots of people to come here to your house for Bible studies," he replied.

After he left Jim commented, "No wonder our congregation is so slow in growing with that kind of advertising"

Evidently, Toninho got over it because he would return off and on, but never again did Jim waste his good clothes on him.

You know, when you represent the compassionate Lord Jesus and give even a cup of cold water in His name, it feels right and good. Jesus himself said that when we see someone hungry, thirsty, in need of clothing, sick, or a foreigner in our midst and we fulfill their needs, we are doing it unto Him. We can say that it is not easy. Just remember that Jesus paid a high price to help his fellowman and to show compassion while he was on this earth and an even higher price to offer salvation to all of us.

What an honor when He has asked us to do the same thing as His ambassador on this planet. If we try it, it feels right and good.

A Package Arrives at Our Gate

One cloudy day a young lady clapped at our gate with a package in her hands. We had returned to Tubarao, Santa Catarina after the terrible flood that left 60,000 of us without homes and our city devastated. However, the streets were restored, and hospitals, schools, banks, businesses and homes were rebuilt. And we moved back.

We moved back into the same house where water had risen to cover our car and rose up to waist high in some parts of our house. In the same house where we had conducted home Bible services, we were back meeting with our dear group again.

We invited the young lady at the gate into our living room. We were curious about her visit, but waited for her to speak.

"I don't believe we have ever met but I have brought you something I have been holding for about two years," she said.

"Oh, really?" We replied and introduced ourselves.

"Yes, after the flood we found these in our back yard. Our mother washed off the mud and left them in the sun to dry. We live on the other side of town."

We were really curious then.

"One day a school friend visited us and saw

them. She said they belonged to her neighbors and gave us your address."

She unwrapped her package and took out some sheets of paper.

"We were hoping we could find the owners and just now heard that you had returned to Tubarao. That's why we are here today," she explained.

She handed us sheets of large photos. They were bleached out from the sun and water treatment they had used to clean off the mud, but they were of our blue eyed laughing children – Kemper and Cindy. They were taken at the mission apartment in Campinas, São Paulo, when we were waiting for their baby sister Tânia to be born.

The neighbor family who recognized the photos was the Aguiars. Their children attended our meetings and we became close friends.

We had lost so many material things in the flood, but our family and church friends were saved. And now, so were some faded out photos that arrived at our gate.

CHAPTER 3
Back to Our São Paulo Gates

Brazil is the size of the continental United States and we had mission works, Brazilian pastors and leaders in churches in the states of Sao Paulo, Minas Gerais, and Santa Catarina. Missionaries are part of a Field Council of Missionaries who unite in order to work better as a team.

We were working in the state of Santa Catarina when the Field Council asked that we move back to the São Paulo area to work in the local church in Jaboticabal that was without a pastor, supervise the ministry of the *Evangelandia* Camp Ground, and to help in the Bible College and Seminary in Ribeirão Preto, founded by Bobbie and Geneva Poole. The Council thought that different missionaries could make trips to Tubarao, Santa Catarina, to keep in contact with the new Christians there. It was a two day trip, one way.

The decision was pretty easy to make since we worked as a team and followed the vote of the Field Council, but leaving our new Christians and ministry in the city of Tubarao, *Santa Catarina* was not easy. Jim returned once a month by bus to preach and minister to the group on a weekend. Then he would return by bus to continue the ministries in the Jaboticabal and *Ribeirão Preto* areas.

We went to the US for stateside assignment and no one was free to continue contact with our dear Christians there. Some started congregating with other Evangelical churches, and some started a Catholic congregation using Bible studies and Baptist hymnals, without the usual images or idols.

Once again we were the only Americans in the town of *Jaboticabal* and foreigners came clapping at out gate.

A Scientist from India at Our Gate

While the two of us were dining in a restaurant in *Jaboticabal, São Paulo*, I saw a lady beautifully dressed in middle-east Indian attire. She was trying to explain something to the waiter at her table.

I said to Jim, "Look at that lady behind you from India. It seems she is having trouble communicating."

He turned to look at the lady seated at a table across the restaurant. He was smiling when he turned around. "What are you thinking? Do you want to go help her?"

"Well, it's our anniversary dinner and I don't want to mess up the mood," I smiled.

"Do you want to invite her to join us at our table?"

"Oh, I don't know. I can just see if she needs help with ordering. She may not speak English or Portuguese."

Oh, well. On an impulse (which I have never regretted), I got up and walked over to her table and introduced myself. She did speak English!

I quickly found out that she was a visiting professor at the Agricultural College in our city. I suggested she join us at our table and we could continue to get acquainted. I helped her order her food and advised her waiter that she would be moving to our table and to please take her order there when it was ready.

Her name was Pare and she was an oncologist/geneticist. She and her husband Vas had immigrated to Canada from India and had lived there for several years. She was already teaching at the college in town, and her husband would join her later. I shared with her that it was our wedding anniversary, and we had been missionaries in Brazil since 1964. It was a delightful anniversary meal that we still remember.

Since we feel that hospitality is a Biblical means to be a blessing and to serve others, it was natural to invite her to visit us at *Evangelandia,* a Free Will Baptist campground, where we were living with our three children – Kemper, Cindy, and Tânia.

By the time we scheduled a meal together, her husband had joined her in Jaboticabal. For preparing the menu, I consulted the encyclopedia about the religions in India and their preferred diet. The table was full of Brazilian and American foods that I thought would make them comfortable. The meal and atmosphere were so warm and stimulating as we shared cultures and life purposes and visions. I was glad our children could be a part of the conversation and contact with those special and interesting people.

After the meal, and while I was clearing the table, Pare commented that it looked like I had really researched to prepare the menu for the meal. However, she said that really the strict limits of their religion would not allow eggs (I had prepared an American recipe of deviled eggs) since they originally came from an animal. She continued to share that since they had lived in

Canada so long they had even learned to eat meat. And since being in Brazil they appreciated the delicious Brazilian *churrasco*, meat cooked over an open grill. Delicious.

We have lost contact over the years, but good memories remain on our part. Perhaps they have met more people to offer them friendship evangelism.

Six Feet, Eight Inches of Obedience at the Gate

One afternoon in *Araras* the phone rang, and I heard Jim talking in English. He seemed to be talking to someone in Brazil, though, so I was curious. I heard him invite the person to our city and our home, and I was shaking my head yes. When Jim hung up the phone he told me what he had learned.

Notice the difference in height?
Hoop is 7'6" and Tony is 6'8"

The man's name was Anthony White, and he was a professional basketball player with the Blue Life Team in Rio Claro. That was only about twenty minutes away and he was coming soon to meet us.

He arrived at our gate in a small, two-door Santana Volks. Since we were the only Americans in town, we were all smiles as we awaited the special treat of having another American into our home. Our smiles were even broader when we saw that young Texan unfold his tall six feet, eight inch athletic frame out of that tiny car. Most cars in Brazil are small and economical since gasoline stays about $7.00 a gallon. We had never noticed the height of our wrap around front porch or the height of our door frames, but he carefully noticed them all. We had also never noticed the height of our table but we enjoyed many wonderful conversations around our table with him and his wife, Shonda, and two children, Eden and Joshua. Joshua was born when they were in Brazil. However, when he sat down his knees were higher than our table top so he had to adjust to reach the food. Once he brought a friend to our home that was over seven feet six inches tall. Hoop had an even bigger challenge to eat at our table. What delightful times we had.

We found out that Anthony's family was Baptists from Texas. He, his wife, Shonda, and their two children. They were touched by the news of the assassinations of street children and the great need for a ministry to address this problem. Someone in Rio Claro had told them about our *Lar Nova Vida* Children's Home in our city of Araras.

Once he came with a box of canned goods for the children collected by the *Atletas de Cristo* (Athletes for Christ). The highlight was his visit to the children at the home. As they all sat on the floor around him, he talked with them using the Portuguese phrases he had learned. However, when he gave his testimony he wanted to be sure his message got across to the children, and asked me to interpret for him.

One little boy, Alex, asked in Portuguese,

"Why is he so tall?

"God created Anthony that way – all six feet and eight inches," I replied in Portuguese.

"What did the little boy ask you?" Tony questioned.

"Why are you so tall?" I smiled at him seated on the floor.

"Help me talk to him," Tony said. "I want to answer that for him."

Anthony stood up and looked down on the little children seated on the floor. He began, "God created me extra tall so that I could play professional basketball and be invited to play on teams that travel all over the world. In every country, wherever I go, I look for boys and girls so I can tell them that Jesus loves them. I grew tall physically, but I must also grow spiritually, just like you. It is important for you to have healthy bodies and to love God by knowing Jesus as your Savior."

What a role model for those children seated there! Most of the men in their families were addicts, criminals, or unemployed and illiterate. They beat and abused their neighbors, wives and children, and the only religion they practiced was black magic and voodoo to put curses on their enemies.

We found out later that Anthony knew about growing up without a father in the home. He met his father for the first time at 38.

Anthony went beyond just visits with children. He took a personal interest in the Children's Home and offered to arrange a benefit basketball game. He talked with the Brazilian Athletes for Christ and the Christian members of the Blue Life Team, and invited them to play against All-Star Players from various teams in Brazil.

You can imagine what a novelty this was for our city. If a sporting event were volleyball or the national sport of soccer, it would almost be guaranteed to be a success. At that time, basketball was not a popular sport, so advertisement would prove to be important.

Encouraging, good things started happening as we prepared for the event. The city sports arena was offered at no cost. Tickets were printed at no charge, and many volunteers began selling pre-game tickets. Local newspapers printed articles, the radio called us for live interviews, and a little television coverage was given. Friends from other churches offered to help us with the snack shop and prepared hundreds of *pasteis* (fried meat pies), *brigadeiros* (chocolate candy) and soft drinks. Local businesses donated nice sports gifts for door prizes. The competing teams did not charge for their services, and they showed up! We were ready to open the gates for game time.

And in they came. There was a better turn-out than anyone expected, and the teams put on a great night of entertainment.

Our own children from *Lar Nova Vida* ate their fill of snacks, clapped, and laughed at the tallest men that had ever seen in their lives. Best of all, they and others saw male role models giving their testimonies in a sports arena of salvation in Jesus Christ and they gave away Bibles right along with other cherished prizes.

Without the athletes knowing it, the home faced that month a large financial responsibility. The funds from our regular cake sales and special drives were all used to meet the monthly expenses. In our staff meetings we searched for an idea to come up with extra funds for this great need. Well, God used a tall young Texan, far from home, to supply a need in a little ministry in Brazil. The financial need was a tall order, and God sent a tall ambassador to our gate for Christ to bless our lives.

Anthony White now has a ministry and website, ANTHONY WHITE MINISTRIES, which majors in men's ministry. Shonda speaks at conferences on the subject of Health and Nutrition. Through playing professional basketball, Anthony traveled the world ministering the Gospel of Christ in Austria, Switzerland, Germany, Italy, Yugoslavia, Hungary, Chile, Argentina, Peru and Brazil. Yes, we were honored and blessed by having this young family clap at our gate in Brazil.

Will "Snow" Ever Arrive at our Gate?

During all the years we were in Brazil, we never saw snow at our house, but we had invited Chuck and Fleda *Snow* for forty-four years to visit us in Brazil. By the time it happened, Jim and I were gone!

Jim and Chuck were roommates in Bible College in Nashville, Tennessee, when they heard missionary Tom "Pop" Willey speak in a missions conference. He invited students to go to Cuba to help in their ministry. His wife Mable, his son Tom Jr., and his family were there, but there was so much that college students could do to help.

During the summer between Jim's freshman and sophomore years, the two of them decided to go to Cuba together. Jim had been in the Navy and worked a while after his enlistment near Washington, DC, before going to college. He had felt God was calling him to the ministry and spending a summer helping missionaries in Cuba appealed to him.

Chuck had written a letter to missionaries Tom and Mable Willey telling of their arrival in Havana, but the missionaries never received the letter.

Jim and Chuck arrived in the beginning of July, 1960, a few weeks before the first anniversary of the Castro takeover of the Batista regime. While the two were there they saw anti-American signs like, "Yankees go home," and "Eisenhower, the stupidest golfer in the world," and "Americans, don't get in front of this bus."

The guys decided they would keep a low profile and bought Panama hats to wear. But when they opened their mouths, they gave themselves away. The simple people thought Castro would be their savior, but the land-owners who lost their properties did not like him. However, the Cubans in general treated the two student missionaries well.

Back to the airport. They didn't speak Spanish, but when no one met them, they finally caught a bus from the airport to take them *to Pinar Del Rio*, a trip of about four hours. They went to the church in town, but found no one there. Finally, they found someone who knew Bro. Wiley and knew where the Cedars of Lebanon Bible Institute was located. A taxi driver offered to take them there for a certain price.

When they arrived that night, the Cubans were having a youth camp there and were just finishing the evening service. Jim and Chuck introduced themselves and explained their adventures of reaching their place. They put Jim and Chuck in a dormitory with a group of guys who only spoke Spanish. Pop Willey and Sister Mable, Tom, Jr., and Ruth, their children, Pastor Benito Rodriquez, Sister Carmen Rodriguez and their boys, and Pastor Raphael Josue were all at the campground with the young people.

During their visit Jim and Chuck helped build the parsonage on the Bible Institute property. They helped set up tents for revivals in several areas all around Cuba. A missionary and family from Ft. Lauderdale preached and sang for the revivals.

Since there were folks all around them who spoke both Spanish and English, the language barrier was not much of a problem. During the revival services out in the country they ate with the Cuban families who offered them delicious meals out of their very poor subsistence.

After one meal, a young man of one family rode a horse up to the front porch area and asked if Jim or Chuck wanted to ride him. It was smaller than a regular American- sized horse and had no saddle or bridle. It only had a rope wrapped around his nose, through his mouth on the right side, and out on the other side as a makeshift bridle. He was guided with a single rein from one side.

Jim volunteered to ride the horse. As soon as Jim mounted it, the horse took off across a field like a wild horse. He jumped bushes, gullies, and rocks within a barbed wire fence several hundred yards out. The horse was making all the decisions and carrying Jim all around the edge of the fence for about a half mile. Finally the horse turned toward the house. Jim thought he was finally going to stop, and was he happy. The men folk ran to the fence waving their arms and yelling. They were having a good time (at the gringo rider's expense).

Oops. Jim saw that the horse did not intend to stop. He started yelling "Whoa" and pulling on the rope, but to no avail. How do you say "Whoa" in Spanish? This was no bi-lingual horse. The horse just kept wildly galloping back over the field again. But this time he was going straight for the fence- a barbed -wire fence. When Jim saw it and it seemed like the horse would not stop for the fence, he ducked his head and grabbed the mane. Whoa! Stop!

A few feet from the fence, the horse stiffened his two front legs and stopped right there- right at the edge of the fence. The horse's head was right down on the ground and so were Jim's feet. If he hadn't been holding on to the mane, he would have been thrown into the barbed wire fence.

Jim picked up the rope and led the horse back toward the house. Jim noticed that blisters had already formed on his "lower back" parts, and by the time he checked them, they had already burst. The men were still laughing at the gringo limping back to the house.

During one of the revival services Pop Wiley got sick and was rushed to the hospital in Havana. He couldn't drive so Jim was assigned the job. He didn't have a Cuban driver's license but made the 100-kilometer trip in a standard shift car over very simple two-lane roads.

They were stopped by policemen standing on the side of the roads. Since Jim didn't understand nor speak their language, Bro. Wiley (even in his sick condition,) had to speak to the policemen. Jim waited at the hospital until some of the family arrived the next day and took Jim back.

Before they left Cuba, they heard stories from Tom, Jr. and others about how they were allowed to counsel and pray with citizens who shortly afterwards were shot by Castro's firing squad. It was a summer trip they still talk about.

At the time of this writing, Cuba was celebrating the Seventieth anniversary of Free Will Baptist work in Cuba. There were over 800 in attendance. They reported that the convention has 51 organized churches, 70 mission points, 152 small groups meeting in homes, 28 young people studying at Cedar of Lebanon Seminary, and 456 conversions. Jim and Chuck were there over 50 years ago right along with Pop and Mable Wiley and family, and God is still building His church.

By the time Jim graduated from Free Will Baptist Bible College (FWBBC) in Nashville, he and I were engaged. According to the rules he was required to get permission from Dr. Thigpen, the dean of students where we both studied, if the engagement occurred during the school year. Permission granted. Jim had arranged for Chuck to sing at our wedding and for Fleda to play the piano. They showed up in Shawnee Mission, Kansas, and in spite of getting over laryngitis, Chuck still sang and Fleda played.

A year later we were off to Brazil and invited them to visit us one day. We only saw them a few times during the next forty-four years at the Free Will Baptists national conventions while we were on our stateside assignments. He and Fleda visited mission fields in Russia, and Cuba, and had children as missionaries in Japan and Africa. It took them a long time to plan a trip to Brazil.

Finally, after all these years, Chuck and Fleda Snow showed up at our gate in *Araras*, São Paulo. However, Jim and I were in the US! They had gone to Brazil for a wedding in another city, and their missionary hosts took them to our house. We weren't there to open the gate for them, but we were still happy that our empty house could receive them in our absence. That was the only time in forty-four years that we had "Snow" at our gate.

(The next gate at which we will meet will be heaven's gates. Bro. Chuck passed away at home right before Christmas of 2012.)

Who's Clapping At Our Gate?

Who's Clapping At Our Gate?

Part Two

CHAPTER 4
Clapping at My Own Gate

Our children were born in Brazil and married Brazilians, but all moved to Moore, Oklahoma, with our six grandchildren. We arrived in Brazil in 1964. In 2008 we were faced with a difficult decision.

Four years earlier, we had officially retired from International Missions of Free Will Baptists and chose to continue to live in our home in Araras. The home was paid for, our personal car paid for, and Jim went on his fishing trips. I felt satisfied in my ministries and in hosting mission groups from the US in our hospitality house we had built on our property.

The dollar value continued to fall and our personal budget was tight, but whose wasn't? We had been able to return to the US to visit family each year since we had retired. When we were working under the International Mission Board, we could only return every fifth year. For retirement, I was satisfied and fulfilled, except for family.

Family is very important, and every parent and grandparent wants to live close to their children and be a part of their lives. My five sisters were still living, and eleven of Jim's siblings were living. They were scattered across the US, and we couldn't live close to them all, but telephone calls would not be international. Visits would not require that passports and visas be current. And, we could live close to our children and grandchildren since they all lived in the same city.

Would God approve our staying or approve

our leaving? When we were commissioned by our denomination in 1964 by laying on of the hands as we knelt to be career missionaries to Brazil, it went practically unnoticed by the world. But God took note. As I was on my knees before God asking His direction whether to stay or return to the US, the result would not make headline news. But God would take note.

After much prayer we made our decision to move and put our house in Brazil up for sale. Since we had not planned on leaving Brazil "until Jesus returned," mission trips to *Araras* had already been planned by several mission groups. (Our house didn't sell until four years later so we were able to use it for visiting mission groups). In April 2009 we moved into a smaller home in Moore, Oklahoma and for four years we had homes in both places that my heart holds dear.

So I found myself joyfully arriving **at my own gate** in Brazil with mission groups and **clapping** until the caretaker's family opens it. It seems God allowed our leaving, living near family in the US, and also our returning. But there was a purpose for each return, and I would like to share with you some of those stories I've written in my trip journals.

Jairo's Moccasin

It was our last day as residents in Brazil after forty-four years. We hadn't sold our car before leaving *Araras*, so we packed our four suitcases into our Honda and drove ourselves downtown to the bus station. It was not a holiday in Brazil, but it was Thanksgiving Day 2008 in the USA and it was 90 degrees at the *Araras* bus station.

Who's Clapping At Our Gate?

Friends from our church were already waiting for us there and one, Eduardo, was going to drive our car home to turn it over to Afonso, a church member, who worked at a car dealership. He was going to continue to try to sell it.

As we approached the group with our rolling baggage, some took over suitcases while others greeted us in that emotionally-charged moment.

A man approached Jim asking for help. He said someone had stolen his bag of tools. After more than forty-four years of listening to these stories, we had worked out a system. First, we usually don't give money. Second, we do want to help truly needy people, when possible. If they beg for medicine, we take them to a pharmacy. If it is for food, we take them directly to a snack shop. Sometimes they want money for a bus ticket (usually nearby), and we offer to buy them a ticket to their destination. Does it work? It can be time consuming, and many people still insist on money because their stories are lies. Who is to judge? Nothing is really easy.

However, on that day since we were in a hurry, Jim reached into his pocket, gave the man money and joined the other men watching the scene.

The man stayed close by, looking at the money. We had a few minutes so I asked the man a question.

"What kind of tools did you lose? It must be tough." I wondered if he were an electrician or a mechanic or maybe an imposter.

"*Senhora*, they were my craft tools. I sell wooden and leather items and I'm at a loss to how I can make a living without my tools," he said.

He wasn't dressed like a transient. He looked to be in his thirties. I was safely surrounded by people, so I continued to ask questions.

"What is your name, *senhor*? My name is Shirley, and this is Sonia and her sister, Ruth. They are from our church."

"My name is Jairo," he offered looking at the cement floor.

"Oh, that's a Biblical name. I didn't know your name, but I know someone who does know your name and is interested in your problem right now. He is Jesus Christ. I don't know if your folks were Spiritists or Catholics or Evangelicals. But it is not about titles or religions. It is about the person Jesus Christ."

He was looking at us now. "My folks are Seventh Day Adventists. But my father and I haven't talked in many years."

"I don't know about them, but I feel badly about your situation; I know God does, too, and would like to see you in another situation," I said.

"You know, Sr. Jairo, many buses are leaving from this very spot. At the other end of the journey in other cities are people preparing to receive these passengers. Businesses are preparing for new workers to arrive. Families are preparing to receive their relatives. Professors are preparing for students who will attend their classes. My husband and I have families preparing to receive us."

It would soon be time for our bus to leave, but I knew Sonia and Ruth knew where the conversation was going and were probably already praying. So I continued.

"And Christ has gone to heaven to prepare a place for us. For you. But, it is a perfect place and sin can't get in. Now that puts all of us in a bad place. We have all sinned. The Bible says so. But it also says that Jesus has paid the price of sin. We just have to believe. He will forgive everything. We have to personally pick up our *spiritual tickets and passports* that we didn't even have to buy. We can't work for it. No one can do it for us."

"Sr. Jairo, God knows your name. He loves you and wants to help you. I want you to believe that."

At that moment the son of the lady who was to rent our house, joined the circle of men and motioned for me.

I shook Sr. Jairo's hand and left. He continued to stand near the women, and I heard Sonia talking to him as I turned away.

"That lady talking to you is leaving today with her husband after forty-four years in Brazil....." I couldn't hear the rest of the conversation.

Our bus was soon arriving and we started gathering up our things. I knew saying good-bye to my friends and co-laborers in ministry was not going to be easy. They were family.

When I joined the women, Sr. Jairo held out something to me. "I want to give you this. They told me you are leaving Brazil."

He handed me a tiny leather moccasin on a key chain.

"Oh, is this the kind of thing you make? I would like to buy some from you to take as souvenirs to the US."

He shook his head and said, "No, when they took my tools, they took all my things."

Of course, all this conversation was in the Portuguese language, and he surprised me when he started speaking the following to me in broken English.

"My name is Jairo. They say you are American missionary. You make my heart and my eyes feel warm with your words. Thank you. I will visit my father now. Please have good journey."

"Thank, you, sir," I answered in English and shook his hands. We walked up the steps into the bus and waved to the group from the windows.

While seated in the bus on our way to the airport, I breathed a prayer for Sr. Jairo. I thought about all the other Jairos in Brazil who need to know that there is a God who knows their name. A Savior who died for them to make possible the writing of their names in the Book of Life. Faith comes by hearing. Who will tell them now?

Joaquim's Last Good-bye At His Gate

About seven months after setting up a house in Moore, I returned to our home in *Araras* with the Go-Team Mission Group from Rejoice Free Will Baptist Church in Owasso, Oklahoma. They put in a full week of hard work.

The lively group of Americans was to leave Brazil the next day and planned an afternoon of sightseeing. Kimberly Johnson, our missionary helping with Lar Nova Vida and our churches in town, and Brazilian pastor Hélio had rented a van to accommodate our visiting group.

Who's Clapping At Our Gate?

As we were making plans, I felt an uneasiness about my going on the trip. I sifted through my feelings and thought *Joaquim. Joaquim?* Yes, for some reason I needed to visit him and Dona Julia that very afternoon. I couldn't visit the couple that night because we were to go downtown to the city square for an open-air meeting. In the morning we should be packing to leave on our trip back to Oklahoma. Yes, I needed to go and see them right then.

Missionary Kimberly Johnson didn't question my explanation and we were both sure she could handle the translations needed for the afternoon. Right before they left I went to *Joaquim*'s house.

Joaquim and Julia

When I clapped at his front gate he immediately came shuffling down the sidewalk past his caged birds, his fruit trees, and through his flower garden. His first words as he put his key in the gate's padlock confirmed my feelings, "I have been expecting you, Dona Shirley."

The afternoon was spent recalling the meetings on his small open front porch where the first services for the Candida FWB Church were held. The couple talked about their younger days when he could evangelize his neighborhoods in different towns. He talked about his many children (19 total, of which 14 are still living) and grandchildren as a typical proud father would. About how he couldn't read but learned by reading his Bible. He quoted scriptures to support each recalled incident and personal opinion.

Dona Julia made quiet little comments as her husband told his stories. I turned to her and teased, "You know that today is Valentine's Day. You two need to celebrate, you know."(Brazil's Valentine's Day is in June.)

She smiled and cut her eyes up to her husband. "Did you know that we have been married three times? First we were married at the Justice of the Peace. The Catholic Church doesn't accept that without a church wedding, so, we got married there. Then we became evangelical Christians, and we had a nice wedding in our church. Three times we were married, you see."

"And here we are 70 years later. Married and together," *Joaquim* said.

After our visit, I said, "It is getting late and the group should be back soon for our open-air service downtown. I really need to go."

As we all stood up they offered me more refreshments and told me it was early yet, but he then looked at me and said, "Tell Brad (one of the American mission team members) if he can't come by to see us, I'll understand. And tell Pastor Jaime that next Saturday I will be 90 years old. The children are giving me a party and I wish he could be here. I miss him. He is like a son to me."

Who's Clapping At Our Gate?

By that time I had tears in my eyes and sobbed during our last moments of holding each other.

Back at the *chacara* (our country home), I waited in the main house for the group to arrive. They were certainly late. The tenant had moved out of our home and there was no land-line phone. I didn't have a Brazilian cell phone, so I just waited. The hospitality house was locked, and so was all our food.

I opened my journal and recorded the last delightful hours I had spent with *Senhor Joaquim* and Dona Julia. It was a gift.

It was more than an hour past the time we were to leave to go to the meeting down town when I saw a headlight arriving at the gate. It was deacon Vicente on his motorcycle. He came in the house before he said, "Have you heard the news?"

"No, what is it? I don't have a phone. I have been waiting for the mission group to get here," I said.

"They are down at the church. I'm sorry, Dona Shirley, but it is Brother *Joaquim*. After you left him this afternoon, he died. The American missionaries are down at the church moving the furniture around so they can put the casket there. That's what Brother *Joaquim* wanted. To have his wake at the church."

"How did they know to go to the church?" I was numb with the news.

"The family called Pastor Hélio on the cell phone about Bro. Joaquim's death. They returned immediately with the group and went to the church. They asked me to come tell you."

"I'll follow you to the church," I said as I gathered my keys and purse.

Who's Clapping At Our Gate?

It was to be the first funeral at our new church. Very few Brazilian funeral wakes are held at a church. The body must be buried within 24 hours by Brazilian law, and the wake is usually in the home or at a small room near the cemetery.

At the church some were still moving around the furniture and women were in the kitchen preparing the usual snacks, hot tea and coffee for the all-night wake. The Americans silently helped. The church people whispered to me about how touched they were to the see the *Americanos* helping so late at night. They couldn't talk to the shocked, grieving people, but they hugged them and sat with the family until about 2:30 in the morning.

During that time I sat on the bench with *Dona* Julia and some of her children. She told me that when they were at the gate to see me off in the afternoon, *Joaquim* told her he was going to take a bath. As they went back into the house she told him to not lock the bathroom door. She was in the kitchen and heard the water turn on in the shower and then a thud. She ran into the bathroom and found that *Joaquim* had fallen in the shower. She turned off the water and felt for a pulse. Finding none, she ran out into the street and screamed for help. When the ambulance arrived, he was already gone. She said she would cherish the happy afternoon we spent together. Oh, and so would I!

When we finally got back to the Hospitality House there were lots of questions and sharing of answers. I shared with them that one of the sons said the family asked that I speak at the funeral the next morning since I was the last one to talk with him that day. It was a short night of sleep.

The next morning we all tried to pack for our plane trip before going to the church at 9:30 am for the *"celebracao da vida"*, the celebration of the life of *Joaquim Araujo*. His children were scattered over the state, and some traveled all night to get there in time. There were 14 sons and daughters present. (Julia, Vashti, and Aldenilda attended the church there). Various ones gave testimonies to honor their father. Children, grandchildren, great grandchildren and in-laws gathered around the casket and sang Daddy's favorite songs. What a choir. What a scene. What a celebration.

During our six days in *Araras* I kept a journal, so I was able to open my little book and read to the crowd about that wonderful afternoon with the couple. I could share the clever, funny things they had said that afternoon and quote some of the scriptures that their father and our friend had mentioned. I could share the sight of tears in their eyes as they talked about their children and the church they helped to start. I shared my recorded statements of how I listened to the voice of the Father and followed the plans He had for me that afternoon. It was a precious surprise gift the Lord had for me.

Others asked for an opportunity to speak. Several mentioned that they were already preparing for his ninetieth birthday celebration on the next Saturday, but God had called him and he started celebrating early. Several pastors were there and the church was full of people whose lives had had touched. There were people standing outside the front doors, feeling blessed to be present to see their dear friend honored.

The cemetery was in the same neighborhood as the Candida church so there was a caravan of cars following the hearse with the simple pine casket with a satin lining. It would soon decompose as would the body that had not been embalmed. There is no police escort in Brazil. No special car for the family. No headlights turned on, and no cars pulling over to the side of the road. Not much ceremony after a short 24-hour wait. Just mostly the reality of death.

But we had experienced the celebration and hope of a family who could know that this man's faith and life works made a difference in that Brazilian town. Yes, the reality of death, but that death brought the reality of eternal life for *Joaquim a*nd other children of God.

We had said our earthly goodbyes at his wrought iron gate one afternoon, but one day we will greet again inside those beautiful heavenly pearly gates. Glory!

Grandma Quilú
Four months later I was back at my home at the *chacara* in *Araras,* and once again I found out why.

Soon after I arrived, I was approached by a friend. "Did you hear that Grandma *Quilú* was in the hospital? They opened her up and just sent her home this time. She doesn't know about it, but they told the family she only had a few days. *Soraia wants* you to go pray with her. " *Soraia* was her granddaughter and used to be one of our children in *Lar Nova Vida.*

As I drove to her house in a very poor

neighborhood, I prayed and thought. Even if they had called me earlier, I couldn't do any more than I was about to do. Just to be an instrument in God's hands. God doesn't fit into a box so that we can explain Him. Sometimes chills ran down my arm when I prayed for someone and they were healed. Sometimes they were healed without the chills. Sometime they were not healed.

My personal opinion and experience is that the choice is with God. It wasn't my place to promise anything to the family I visited except that God has the power to do His will. That really took a load off my shoulders at that moment.

After clapping at Great Grandmother Bisa's little make-shift front gate, I was met by her great granddaughter, Soraia. She followed me into their kitchen. Grandma *Quilú* was lying on a tiny makeshift bed in Great Grandmother Bisa's kitchen of her two-room home. A kitchen, a bedroom and a bath. *Bisa* was a diabetic and going blind, but she ended up taking care of her grandkids and great grandkids from time to time, including *Soraia*.

I knelt beside *Quilú's* bed on the cool cement floor and reached for her hand without the tubes. A bladder draining bag hung over the side of the blanket. She slowly opened her eyes.

"Dona Shirley, *Soraia* told me you would come. Thank you," she whispered.

"Oh, I was glad to come. We have been friends for years, and I was troubled to hear that you had been in the hospital. We have talked many times about how God is interested in you and in your family, and right now I have come to pray with you. Would you like for me to pray? Do you believe that God hears our prayers?"

I had prayed with *Quilú* and her family many times over the years and explained God's plan for salvation. We got permission from her for *Soraia* to be baptized while living with us at *Lar Nova Vida*. She had been rearing her grandchild, and we wanted to respect that. She always agreed with everything I said, but just did not understand the difference between what she had been taught and what I was telling her.

"*Sim, senhora*," she whispered again.

"First, exactly what do you want me to ask the Lord Jesus right now?"

She look up at her short, little stooped over mother and said, "I am so tired and would like to be able to sleep."

Bisa told me that she hadn't slept for days and nights.

"And I would like to be able to eat something. Nothing stays down*,*" *Quilú* said.

I turned *to Bisa*. "What do you think she could eat, *Bisa*?" I saw that her cupboards were bare. She didn't have a refrigerator.

She said she thought that her daughter could eat some fruit.

Nothing is too hard for God, but I guess I was relieved that Quilú didn't ask at that moment for complete healing from the cancer that had taken over her body. She didn't ask to get up and walk around. But I was there to be an instrument in the name of Jesus, to ask God for her requests. Sleep and nourishment. So we prayed.

After our simple but emotional prayer, I gave *Soraia* some money to go to a nearby store for some fruit. We exchanged our ceremonial hugs and cheek-to-cheek kisses, and I left with the promise to return the next day.

The next day I parked in front of their house and came face to face with a surprise. *Quilú?* She was walking in the street with a towel wrapped around her waist and carrying her bladder bag. She was all smiles and the neighbors started filing out of their houses.

"Do you see, Dona Shirley? Do you see what happened?" they asked.

I couldn't help but be caught up in their happiness. We went into *Bisa's* kitchen and they told me the good news. After I left the day before, *Quilu* ate some pears and apples and drank some kind of juice. She slept all night long. I had seen God work like that so many times, but each time it is so refreshing and renews the faith of everyone involved.

"Guess what? A couple that lives nearby heard about me today. They are going to come and take me to their church tonight. I want to thank God for what He did for me last night and today," she said.

After that she would always tell about her trips to the church. Finally one day she told me that she gave her heart and health to God. She finally saw the difference! And everyone could see the difference in her.

People would whisper to each other wondering how long it would last. I wondered the same thing. She and I talked about that six months later. She was thankful for the time she had to get to know the Lord better, to be with her ailing mother longer, and to participate in the lives of her grandchildren. Before she met the Lord, one son had been murdered; another was in prison, her daughter, *Soraia's* mother, had an addiction and was suffering from AIDS. Some of the grandchildren were going down the same path. She said it all now seemed to be easier to handle.

In October, twelve months after I first prayed with my friend Quilú, I returned from a trip and mentioned that I needed to check on three friends. One was Quilu and I asked how she was doing.

"Oh, you don't know do you? Last week she passed away. We were so sorry you weren't here."

I was, too.

But I was glad that when I promised her that our God had the power to do His will, she accepted it. She passed from darkness and death into the light for the last year of her life. There is still young Soraia and her new walk in the light and the rest of the family still in darkness. Who will be the instrument that God wants to use there in that little slum village?

Dr. Nelson's Silent Request

Soon after I arrived in *Araras* with two energetic friends from Albany, Georgia, someone sent me a message. My friends, Bobbie Jo Lee and Marie Glover, were about to arrive at the gate of a very prominent doctor in the community. He had served the community and area as state congressman and vice-mayor, but most of all, he was my friend.

"Dr. Nelson is asking about you. Could you pay him a visit? He is in the hospital after a fall. He is really bad."

When I checked at the hospital, Dr. Nelson Salome had already been released to go back home. We were leaving in a few days, so I stopped by his house to talk to him and his wife Carmen. He was gone. He had gone for therapy. Carmen and I talked about family, life, being prepared, and making peace with God. I had met her through English conversation classes and I had met him when I went to deliver our first son, Kemper, at the small local *Araras* hospital.

Before I describe my recent visit with Dr. Nelson and the circumstances that impacted the moment, events of many years ago should be reviewed.

In language school in Campinas in 1965, we discovered that I was expecting, and a local Christian doctor was recommended for my pre-natal visits. We finished language school in December and moved to the nearby city of *Araras*. Kemper was due in April so a lady from our tiny church group recommended her doctor to me. Dr. Enio was highly esteemed in the town.

Oops! On my first visit to his office I realized that I couldn't understand him. I had finished a year of language school, but he spoke Portuguese at a very, very fast pace. He was quite attentive and explained many things, but even with a dictionary in my hand I couldn't keep up. It was our first child, and as the Brazilians say, I was "a sailor on his first voyage." I was continents away from my mother and five sisters and there were no other Americans in town. That vocabulary had not been taught at language school and I was really lost. You can believe that I spent time trying to learn it.

Now comes the part where I met Dr. Nelson. After hearing the phrase many times *"quando a fruta for madura, caira"* (when the fruit is ripe, it will fall), my contractions with the baby began. About five minutes apart. Jim checked me into the hospital that Monday evening and we were so excited. My doctor looked in on us in the room that night and left me in the hands of the Catholic nuns who ran the hospital.

All night the nuns did the *"toque"* but said there was no dilation. That's right, no dilation, but the pains were still five minutes apart. They called a young intern to check on me, Nelson Salome'.

Sisters:
Sonia and Odete who
helped me learn
Portuguese.

The next morning my friend, Odete Cressoni, visited me and saw my situation. She explained, in slow Portuguese, that my doctor had to leave town suddenly and the Catholic nuns at that time did not believe in a Caesarean-section birth.

All day and all night my pains continued with no dilation. My water broke. They prepared me for the birth, and Dr. Nelson continued to check on me. But I was told he did not have the authority to go over the nuns. My doctor needed to return.

I held onto the old-fashioned iron hospital head posts as the pains continued. I heard moans and screams from the other rooms, but I was determined not to join their choir. My poor husband was sympathetic, but at times he had to just leave the room. He was a sailor on his first journey as a father, and he didn't have an iron post to hold on to with each pain.

Odete Cressoni was at my bedside and told me something that I remember to this day. "Honey, this is the type of pain you don't want to go away or to diminish."

You want it to get harder and harder because you are going to have a baby in your arms pretty soon. Then it will be worth it all." The Bible says something similar, and she was right. But there was one more night and one more day of pain.

The next day, April 20, my doctor returned. He entered into my room and said, "Okay, Dona Shirley, what was it? A boy or a girl?"

"I don't know doctor. I haven't had the baby yet, but my water already broke."

He sped out of the room. Immediately there were uniformed nuns in my room rolling me out into the hallway. Soon Jim was walking beside my rolling bed looking down at me. He kissed me on the forehead and said he was praying. They gave me a type of spinal tap and I was aware of those in the room - my own Dr. Enio, young Dr. Nelson and missionary nurse Eula Mae Martin who had driven down to be with me. Yes, soon I had our own little son in my arms. Two years later a little girl, Cindy, at the same hospital. Another Caesarean. And, it was worth it.

During the next years we lived and ministered in other cities in Brazil. In 1990 the *Araras* church invited us to return. Baby number three Tânia had been born in Campinas so we moved back to *Araras* that year with three grown children and a foster son, Marcos.

By that time, Dr. Nelson was married to Carmen and had a family. He was probably the most sought-after gynecologist in town. My yearly exams were with him, and he came to be a great friend and volunteer at the *Lar Nova Vida* Children's Home. He never refused to help the poor, and through the years he became very dear to the people. Because of his popularity he entered local politics and went on to become a state congressman.

Now, he was lying helpless in his own home after a fall.

My missionary friends from Georgia, Bobbie Jo Lee and Marie Glover, had repeatedly returned to Araras on mission trips and knew Dr. Nelson's sister-in-law Rita Merenciana, a very hospitable women who attended our church. She prepared us for our visit with him.

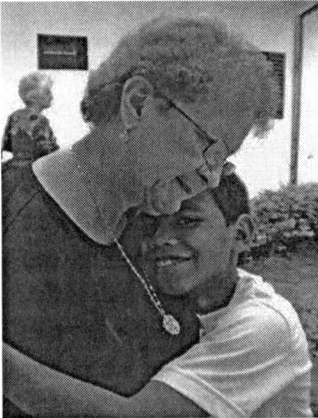

Marie Glover gives one of her famous hugs

"Nelson has had more strokes. He has a nurse 24 hours a day because Carmen can't handle him by herself. He is full of tubes and completely helpless. He can't speak now, but he will know you are there. He really does respect you and was asking for you. When he could, that is."

The three of us prayed hard about our visits the next day. First, we went to the poorest part of town for the missionary ladies to deliver food baskets. After clapping, we were greeted at the lady's broken gate and welcomed into their little shanty. Bobbie and Marie had already given clothes to some children and young mothers there and had bought a table for a blind grandmother who was rearing her great grandchildren. As soon as we were finished, missionary Kimberly Johnson asked us to call her so that she could go with us to see Dr. Nelson.

In contrast to that slum district, we arrived at the very luxurious home of Dr. Nelson and Carmen Salome. Kimberly was already there waiting in her car. Their gate at the sidewalk had a modern doorbell. Carmen met us at the gate and took the four of us into the house. Dr. Nelson was reclining in a chair. His eyes were watery, and he was full of tubes. His nurse was there and greeted us with a smile.

Carmen said to the nurse, "Oh, look. He recognizes Dona Shirley."

I confess that I could tell no reaction from him, but he really looked bad. I knew I didn't know his relationship with the Lord or if he was ready to meet God. I wanted to honor him, but I could not just declare that he had a place guaranteed in heaven if he had not accepted Jesus as his only Savior. I may not have another chance. Oh, how I silently prayed.

I introduced him to our American friends. As they stood around his chair I knelt down by his left arm.

"Dr. Nelson, I am Shirley. Remember me?" His watery eyes turned toward me.

"Today is Children's Day, and I am here in the name of the more than 40,000 babies you have delivered and in the name of their mothers to thank you. That's enough to populate a city! You have been a doctor, a friend, and a counselor to many of us."

My heart was beating in my ears.

"Dr. Nelson, the whole city knows how you love *Araras* and have helped as a doctor and as a politician to make this a better place. You have family and friends who love you."

I touched his arm. He looked over at me.

"I don't know why you have to suffer now in this condition after you have helped so many back to health. But I do know one thing. God has prepared a place for His children where there is no sickness. You won't have to take medicine, or pay your bills, or fill up your gas tank at $7.00 a gallon."

"But none of us deserves to go there and we can't be good enough or do enough good deeds to get there. Why? Because sin can't enter there. It wouldn't be heaven if all of our shortcomings went in with us."

"That's bad news for us. For me and for everyone in this room."

The two Americans didn't understand our conversation in Portuguese, but I knew they were praying.

"But Dr. Nelson I have good news. You don't have to do anything to get into heaven. Jesus has already done it all by dying on the cross for us. That is His gift to us. You know if you buy a gift for your little granddaughter, Jade, and put her name on it and leave it here, she will never be able to open it or hold it. She has to come get it. Jesus bought eternal life for us on the cross but we must receive it, believe that He did it. We need to hold it close to our heart. No one else can repent and do it for us."

"To come here to Brazil these ladies with me today had to pay for a passport and visa to get into this country. Jesus already bought our *visa* to enter into heaven, and we don't have to do a thing. Isn't that wonderful?"

"I didn't want to tire you out, but my heart was full to come here and give you this good news. We need to be reminded that there is hope for a better life one day. God loves you and knows your situation right now."

At that moment I stood up. He was still looking at me, but how I wanted him to talk.

"Carmen, Dr. Nelson, nurse," I turned to them. "Would you accept a prayer for your family and all of you before we go?"

Carmen and the nurse both said together that it would be good.

"Nelson, would you like to have prayer?" Carmen asked her husband. She and the nurse saw some reaction from him and said he agreed. I still couldn't tell.

We made a circle around him while we prayed.

Who's Clapping At Our Gate?

"Doctor, I plan to return to *Araras* in a few weeks and will come back to see you. If not, we can see each other in heaven one day."

As we left I had mixed emotions.

Later I told Rita about my visit with her sister and brother-in-law. She said,

"How wonderful, Dona Shirley. Before Nelson left intensive care at the hospital and went home, he could still talk. He accepted Christ with some evangelical Christians who visited him. He went home with his name written in the book of life. If he didn't understand it all at that time, I am sure he understands it better now. Thank you for visiting him and Carmen. His nurse is an evangelical Christian, so I know she was happy, too."

The angels rejoice over one sinner accepting Christ, and another name is written in the book of life. As I write this, I rejoice again for my dear friend and brother, Dr. Nelson Salome. That was the last time I saw him here on earth. By my next visit he had gone on to glory. Maybe one day *you* can meet him in heaven, inside the Heavenly Gates.

Flood Waters, Soggy Books and Tiny Creatures

Three months later, in January, our 85 year old friend who lives with us asked if I would take him to Brazil so he would not face the cold Oklahoma winter. He would pay for the tickets. You can believe I started packing my bags. We traded winter weather for the summer rainy season of *Araras.*

Who's Clapping At Our Gate?

On a Sunday evening I was sitting on the benches in the Candida church, and everyone's head automatically turned toward the windows and doors as we heard the downpour. Where could the water go now? The ground was already soaked from days and days of rain, and the canal around the town was full.

The evening meeting was over, but the rain storm was not. We waited awhile but decided it wasn't going to stop soon. I got soaked running to my car and rode a few blocks with my hair and clothes dripping. It was January 7 and summer time in Brazil. It had been in the nineties during the day and I was in short sleeves, a skirt, and sandals. The rain storm brought cold, night air. Driving home in the blinding rain and the flooding streets I realized that I couldn't get to my Brazilian home by my usual route. Following the streets to my right to higher ground and crossing the overpass into downtown would keep me on higher ground and possibly give me an idea on how I should proceed. That is where I decided to go.

The visibility was poor because of the downpour and there was a blackout in the downtown area. There were no lights to guide me. So, I went slowly in the darkness. Other cars were stalled as they tried to pass through high waters already flooding the streets, but I felt I needed to risk it and keep on going. My Honda Civic had been through high waters before and I didn't think it could be flooded out easily. But I didn't take more chances than necessary. By keeping on higher ground, I made it to the canal street that would lead to the road toward our home.

With a caravan of cars, I crept cautiously along the canal street. It was a one-way street, but you couldn't see the curbs since it was all leveled with swift moving water. The first bridge would be far enough for me, but before I could reach it I came upon cars stopped. I was right in front of the Samantha Condominiums. Soon others stopped behind me. There were headlights all around me, but the rain was falling so hard that I couldn't tell how many.

A man with a flash light in a yellow rain slicker stopped at each car. When he came close to my car I rolled down the window and the rain blew in. I asked, "What is happening? Why are we all stopped?"

In Portuguese he yelled through the noise of the rain, "The road up front is flooded and perhaps a car has fallen into the river. You can't go forward tonight, and behind you the road is filling up fast with more flooding." The lights behind me started moving and seemed to be turning around to go back the other way. The lights looked all confusing to me.

"*Senhora*, try to back your car around that curve and over the bridge to the *Tupiniquins* gas station. You can see it from here."

Now, I don't like to drive in reverse even on my long tree-lined drive way in bright day light. But somehow I had the courage to do what I had to do. I had no idea where the road ended and the river began, or how far away the curve was, but I kept going in the blinding rain. In reverse. Praying that the other car lights were leading me right.

There were many cars already parked in the gas station, and I was able to drive under the covered area into the last space. It was almost 10:30 p.m. There were food and drinks in the gas station, but I was not hungry. My hair was drying some so I didn't feel so cold. I rolled down my car window to hear the comments all around me. People were sharing their stories and making speculations. They really seemed calm, and we all were just waiting for the rain to stop. Rainy season and flooding came every year and was part of life.

Around 11:20 p.m. two policemen rode up on motorcycles. I got out of the car and asked them for information and direction. When they found out that I lived at *Residencial Morada do Sol*, one said, *"Senhora, don't you have relatives here in town to spend the night? I don't think there is a way to get to your place."*

"I don't have relatives here, and my friends live on the other side of those flooded streets," I replied.

"There is one bridge passable right now," one policeman said. "If you go through Sao Benedito neighborhood, on to May 13 Street, on to Volpe Gas Station, cross the bridge, go to the Anglo School, turn through the Cuba neighborhood, and on to Sao Joao neighborhood, you can get to your road."

Yes, it made sense. I could see how that route would lead me to the highest part of the city. I followed his instructions, went up to the highest point in town, and wound through the dark flooded streets. I had cut through that neighborhood before, but that night it was so dark and the downpour so blinding that I was easily disoriented. I knew the general direction it was taking me, so I kept going.

Finally I found a familiar road that led to my house. I slowly tried to see through the rain and find the street to make a left turn at the entrance of *Residencial Morada do Sol*. The electricity was working on our street, so the control opened the automatic gate to our house. The family living in the front house, Celso, Renata, and girls, had already turned off all lights and they were probably asleep. I drove to the back of the property and down to the hospitality house where I would be spending the night by myself. In my sandals I waded through the gushing water, unlocked the glass sliding doors, and gasped in surprise.

Water rushed out the doors and onto the front porch. I had left the porch light on, so at that time I could see into the living room through the sliding glass doors. Shoes from the bedroom were floating in front of the sofa. I turned on the light and caught my breath. What if the water level had reached the electrical outlets? Would it shock me? I sloshed around in the water to see if I needed to unplug anything but soon gave it up.

I was wet and cold again and needed to change, but my suitcase in the bedroom was on the floor and was full of water. So were my clothes. I waded into the bathroom, pulled a towel off the rack, and returned to the bedroom. I kept thinking about the possibility of getting shocked, so I sat on the bed in my wet clothes and tried to think while drying my hair with the towel. All of a sudden I remembered a box full of 20 Xeroxed copies of my second book. (It cost $27 to make a copy in the US and but only $10.00 in Brazil.) Were they ruined? Where was the box? Oh, no. Oh, yes, it was on the floor also.

I got up, waded through the water, and lifted the heavy box with the soggy bottom. I spread out each book on the long granite counter top with the ceiling fan above turned on high. I hoped by morning to find they could be salvaged.

Who's Clapping At Our Gate?

The alarm clock was wet on the floor beside the bed but it was still ticking. I sat on the bed again and slipped off my sandals. With the towel I dried my feet, wrapped the sandals in it, and put them on the top bunk. It was summer time in January so there wasn't much cover on the bed. The temperature had dropped with the rain. I lay down in my clothes and wrapped up trying to relax. At least I wasn't in the rain anymore as others may be. The poor and homeless. I had felt the Lord's help as I drove blindly through dark and dangerous places. I was lying above water on my bunk bed. I was blessed.

As I lay there, my mind went back to another flood years ago in *Tubarao, Santa Catarina*. I was trapped in the upstairs of a college building with my family and about 80 other people for five days. Sixty thousand in our town were without homes. We found out later that 3,000 from our area lost their lives. There were no roads, electricity, water, communication, and soon no food. Our hospital, banks, stores, schools and homes were all gone. Our car was covered with water, we watched as our furniture washed out through a broken down wall of our house. Bodies were floating in the water, and our lives were never the same.

Of course, this flood was no comparison with that one night. The water would probably drain out of the house sometime before morning if the rain stopped. There was a drain in the kitchen and drains in the four bathrooms. Books and clothes would dry out. I would wash the mud from under the beds and furniture. The house would be disinfected along with many similar places around town. The city would soon be back to normal. Yes, this flood was a lot different.

Who's Clapping At Our Gate?

Uhum. Ooo. What was going on? My neck and shoulder felt strange. If I turned on the light I would have to get my feet wet again. I waded out and turned on the light. On my arms were tiny specks. Moving specks. Crawling down my left arm and around my neck.

I swiped down my arms and wiped my neck. I beat at my pillow and covers in case there were more. I certainly didn't want to get out of bed and into the water. I scooted down to the foot of the bottom bunk and rolled down the covers and swatted and swiped the bottom sheet and pillow case. I rolled layer by layer back up and did the same. Swat. Swipe.

There was no way to know how they got on the bed and whether they were all gone. At least they didn't sting or bite even though they did look like tiny ants. I sat up for a while and decided to lie down. I was blessed with a dry bed and a safe situation. I pulled up the cover and put one hand on my shoulder and one on my neck, just for good measure. I tried to think about tomorrow. Wash and dry and begin again. That's part of life. About three o'clock in the morning I heard a gurgling, swooshing sound coming from the drains. It lasted several minutes. Though I had never heard anything like it, it was a good sound. I was blessed.

Orange Juice or Milkshake in Sao Paulo?
Once again I was on a plane to meet a group in São Paulo and then to minister in *Araras.* This trip I was traveling with Richard Howard, the elderly gentleman who lives with us in Moore. On this trip, I was to learn that ministry was to begin at the airport with a stranger.

It was three thirty Monday morning and the

Who's Clapping At Our Gate?

American Airlines passengers were waking up and lowering our trays for breakfast. Since it was actually seven thirty at our destination in São Paulo, we would soon arrive. Soon after breakfast the captain told us to prepare for landing.

After arriving, we waited for Richard Howard's wheel chair to arrive so we were among the last to leave the plane. At the baggage claim, they unloaded the suitcases and Richard's motorized wheel chair. They dismounted the chair and finally discovered how to get it working. It was a good thing, too.

Since I had my baggage cart and his baggage cart to push and pull, it helped to have him mobile. And the stares at his chair. It was such a novelty in Brazil to see such a thing as a motorized wheel chair.

When they saw Richard in the wheel chair (and me with my white hair!) they took us out of the immigration line and past the x-ray security tables into a more private area. He was very tired from the overnight flight, so the special treatment felt a little like being pampered, and soon we were free to go.

We were to wait for a *Senhor* Ferreira, a driver of a private van, who was to pick us up with the bags and the motorized chair. He was already in São Paulo and would take us to *Araras* on his way to the city of Ribeirão Preto. We didn't know him and he didn't know us, but he set a time for us to be at the assigned place for vans. He would recognize us by the motorized chair, bags, and description. (Remember my hair? Women my age color their hair so I stood out with my white hair.)

We waited and waited. The long distance phone booths were on the third floor and I wanted to phone Jim in the US to ask about the driver arrangements. Should I leave Richard alone in the chair with the bags? He didn't speak the language and he took little naps. I decided to go up the escalator and make the phone call. Jim said he would get the information and I should call him back a little later.

Downstairs everything was fine. I thought with such a long wait, perhaps there was something the Lord wanted done during the delay. People were clustered in groups near bus stops and van stops, but not near us. They waited for short times, but we had been there almost three hours.

A young man was seated on another bench repairing a buckle on his back pack. After about a half-hour, he heard us talking about the driver and van that hadn't arrived. In heavily accented English, he asked if we needed any help. He didn't speak any Portuguese so he was glad to try his English. We talked a while. He had come on a flight at midnight the night before and would leave out that night at 8:00 p.m.

Silently I prayed, "Lord, do you want to say something to this young man through me?"

The thought came: orange juice. Hmmm.

I learned he was from Serbia. He was in college in his country studying hotel business administration and was taking some time out to visit different tourist spots in South America. I really did want to go up to the booths to call the US again. He was a stranger, but had offered to help, so I asked him to stay with Richard while I phoned.

Orange juice. Orange juice? There was that thought again.

We talked a while longer, and I went back upstairs to the international phone stations to call Jim again. He told me the driver had left São Paulo and that we should try to find bus transportation to *Araras*. On the way down the escalator, I decided to order something for us to drink and eat since we hadn't eaten since having that early breakfast on the plane.

At one of the snack bars I asked about milkshakes which I thought would be more nourishing than orange juice. The young waiter told me that his disposable cups to take out of the building were very small, but I ordered them anyway. When I went to prepay, the bill was to be R$47,00 (*reais*). That was over US$20 for tiny cups! Oh, I cancelled my order at once and asked for two cups of orange juice, a cup of coffee with milk, and three cheese bread rolls.

I gave the coffee to Richard and the young man's eyes lit up as I handed him the juice and cheese bread roll. He said he had eaten crackers and water on the plane yesterday and spent R$100,00 more than the agency had told him for his plane ticket to leave that night to Manaus. He had not eaten at all that day.

I sat down beside him on the concrete bench. It was about 35 degrees F. when we left Oklahoma City and about 90 degrees F. in São Paulo. He had told me his name, but it was difficult to pronounce and to remember. (It seemed to have the month of September in it somewhere.)

I said, "Listen, today the Lord seemed to tell me to give you some orange juice. I really wasn't sure. Since He is like my *boss* I obeyed Him and I see that you really appreciated a little refreshment after your long wait. However, I am impressed that He would have given it to you had He been here, but He chose me to serve you. I am honored."

"Now on your trip to other places in Brazil I want you to remember that Jesus Christ knows your name and each of your destinations. I feel He will give you other opportunities on this trip to know He is near you. Open up your heart and mind to Him who is the Way/path and the Truth that He will show you. You see, He has prepared a place in heaven as our final destination if you accept the price he paid so that you can go there. We can't do anything to deserve it. He died on the cross to give us that right, but He is alive today. Maybe someone else on your paths these next days will also be used by Him to show you His love."

"I must run now and try to get us bus tickets to Campinas on the *Capriolli* bus and from there take another bus on to *Araras*. Would you please stay with Mr. Richard one more time?"

He said, "Of course. Of course, I will."

I hurried to the *Capriolli* agency to buy our tickets. They said I must go back and get Richard's passport before I could purchase them. The driver of the bus was there and said he was leaving in the next five minutes and I wouldn't have time to return. He asked the young lady at the ticket counter to forgive that requirement. She did. Hurriedly I explained as we rushed toward the two men waiting that I needed to put a motorized wheel chair in the bus along with the bags. The driver said it wouldn't be a problem, but we must hurry.

It did give a little problem to fit the heavy

chair underneath the bus, but we were soon in line to board the bus. Richard had to go up several steps before reaching the level where we found our seats.

The young man from Serbia waited by the steps.

"God created you and has plans for you. He will shine light on your paths as you travel so keep a watch out for His guidance. Do you understand me?" I asked him as he shook my hands and gave me a hug.

He thanked me and helped me on to the bus as the driver started the motor.

The wait had been a long and tiring one, but I thought as we drove away from that fantastic city of twenty million souls that maybe the Lord wanted to plant a seed in the heart of a young Serbian passing through on a visit. I didn't even have to get a passport or ticket to go to his country. Did I explain it well enough to him? I wasn't sure.

However, I was pretty sure then that my Lord wanted to serve a cup of fresh orange juice to a young man far away from home, and I was honored to be chosen to do just that. The Holy Spirit was very capable to do the rest!

Tears, Trains and Triumph over Trouble

José Carlos appeared at our *chacara* in *Araras* on a motorcycle and honked. What a surprise! What a joy! That morning I woke up wanting to see him and had put his name on my prayer list, but since they lived in another town, I didn't know how to contact him.

I had no address or phone number for him. God knew and sent him as a special gift to me. He was taken to our children's home when he was four years old and went to live with family again when he was in his teens. He always kept in touch and how I love him.

Jose Carlos and Izaura

Someone was getting off the motorcycle, but was using crutches. Izaura? Two years earlier Jim and I had participated in their wedding in *Cordeiropolis*, and we hadn't seen them since. She was a pretty 28-year-old young lady with five children at that time. She was a cook at the Nestle Company, and he worked for a transport company. They were both so happy and attending church together with the children.

As we greeted with hugs and kisses, I noticed the reason for the crutches. Her right foot had been amputated. How? When?

Inside the house after they were both seated on the sofa, he told Izaura that he had been baptized in our swimming pool at the *chacara* and that he learned to play the clarinet and drums in our church. Such good memories. But I was curious about her amputation.

"He calls you his mother," Izaura said. I had helped bury his mother many years ago. His father was addicted to alcohol and drugs and was expected to die soon.

"And she tells everyone that you are her *Sogra Americana"* he said. Her American mother-in-law. I liked to hear that.

Finally I asked, "Probably everyone asks you this, but how did you lose your foot since I last saw you?" She looked down and José Carlos reached over to her.

"I was very depressed. I had lost around 24 pounds. I went to my mother's house and found some of her tranquilizers. I took a lot of them, and they made me crazy."

"But Izaura, what brought on this depression? Finances? Health? Family problems?" I asked.

José Carlos offered, "Truthfully, we had separated, and she was upset."

"I couldn't accept the separation. I took all those pills on Tuesday and woke up on Thursday without a foot. They told me I had thrown myself in front of a train on the railroad track close to my house. The train with 47 cars passed over me."

"Do you remember the pain, the trauma of all that?" I asked.

"No, I don't remember it. My reaction to the medicine was so strong I was out of my head."

Also visiting at that time was Pamela Wilson from Kansas City, who had come to help me at *Lar Nova Vida*. She had visited several times and had met José Carlos. I was interpreting as the story unfolded. She asked, "What about your children? How did they handle the trauma?"

"The children were only a few yards from the train tracks when they saw me and then the train passing. It was hard on them, but even when José and I stopped going to church, they continued to go with my mother. Maybe that helped them. But we are all going together again and helping each other."

I interpreted for Pamela as she said, "The closer you get to God, and the closer your relationship to each other will be. Remember, the Devil is the enemy. He came to steal, to kill, to destroy. God spared your life and he wants to heal, to renew life, to build it again. Resist the Devil and cling to God. Not just go to church. Pray, read God's Word, accept His love and His path for you."

She asked Izaura, "What can be done for you? Can you get a prosthesis?"

"A congressman promised to help get one, but he hasn't done anything and he doesn't answer our calls. My family and friends say it was to get votes. Prosthetics are very expensive, and there is an enormous waiting list. This happened nine months ago. There seems to be an internal stitch that never healed and something is infected."

Again I interpreted for Pamela when she asked, "Could I go with you to see the congressman? I have a webpage for my organization, Hands of Hope, and I would like to write about your testimony. I want to tell the congressman that you told me about his promise for the prosthesis, and I want to know if I could use his name on my webpage."

José Carlos looked at Izaura and said, "Wow. That could really work. It will remind him about the promise...it might just work."

We had prayer with the young couple and saw them several times during the next two weeks while we were helping at *Lar Nova Vida*. They seemed very encouraged and shared their experience and testimony with others. And guess what? The congressman did set an appointment for his interview with Pamela - after we had left for the US. Since then, Izaura has been scheduled for another surgery to correct the infection and speed up the healing.

Two months later, Jim returned to Brazil with another mission trip group, the Rejoice Go Team, and took Izaura some new aluminum crutches.

Tears, trains, and trouble can bring bad choices with terrible consequences, but God gives triumph for the healing of the soul and spirit for those who learn their lesson and humbly accept His help.

In September of that year, Izaura arrived at our gate behind her husband on their motorcycle. She was wearing tennis shoes – a pair. She had received her new prosthesis!

Plane Delays, Funerals and Surprise Opportunities

It was rainy season in Brazil, but the sky was clear as Pamela Wilson and I unloaded at our Hospitality House the boxes and suitcases she had brought to the children at *Lar Nova Vida*. She came with a group from Kansas City on her first mission trip, but has returned alone many times since. She is a beautiful Christian woman who loves the Word and practices praying about every move. That made a perfect combination for the surprises God had for us that week.

Pamela had been traveling two days without sleep, but seemed her bubbly, contagious self. She ate a light meal I had prepared, and I had her lie down for a while. When she heard a young couple arriving, she got up to greet them. They told us they were on their way to see his father, *Senhor José*, in the hospital. José Jr. said the hospital had advised that his father was seriously ill.

All this conversation was being interpreted for Pamela, who turned to me and said, "God is telling me to go to the hospital and see this man."

I explained this to José Jr. He said, "Oh, no. She is very tired and needs to rest. Maybe she can go another day. We don't want to interrupt her sleep."

When I interpreted this to Pamela, she insisted that God was telling her to go right then. She and I had experienced situations like this together, and I knew that God had something special for us and that man's interruptions can be God's intervention.

It was an hour before visiting hours closed.

While Pam quickly changed her clothes, the couple had a snack. They hadn't eaten since morning, and they had come directly from work from their town about twenty minutes away. We all got into our Honda Civic and arrived at the hospital just as it started to sprinkle rain.

Only one person could visit in the room at a time, but José Jr. needed to give his wife assistance so they let them go in together. They told us later about their visit.

José Jr. said to his father, "*Pai*, I know that you didn't raise me or never really wanted much to do with me, but I am here to say that I forgive you, *Pai*, and if I have done anything against you, I want you to forgive me."

"There is nothing to forgive, *Filho.*" His father whispered.

"But I am here now, *Pai,* and from this day on whatever you need, you can count on me," José Jr. said, patting his father's hand.

"And, *Pai,* you are going to leave this hospital room number 27, either to meet God or to go back home. You need to make peace with God. You need to pray *em voz alta (*aloud) to God and ask his forgiveness. Believe on Him. Please, I want you to go to heaven."

When they returned and the next person could go in, I explained to the receptionist, "This lady doesn't speak Portuguese, but she wants to visit Sr. José and pray with him. I would like permission to go in with her." We got our passes and went in together.

Pamela and I entered room 27 not knowing about the conversation José Jr. had with his father. The patient was lying in bed with a blanket pulled up to his chin. Even through the blanket you could see his huge, bloated stomach. One foot was outside the blanket and was bandaged. He had walked on crutches for the almost 20 years I had known him.

Pamela asked him his name, and I interpreted for them and introduced them to each other. "She didn't know your name but she knows someone who does, and she wants to tell you about Him. He is the one who told her to come to visit you."

"Yes, *Senhor José,* this person is Jesus. He loves you and knows all about you. Have you ever asked Jesus into your heart?" Pamela asked. I interpreted.

He replied, "*Acho que nao. Nao vou na igreja.*" (I don't think so. I don't go to church.)

She said through interpretation, "That doesn't matter now. It is never too late to ask God into your life. It isn't because you are good or go to church or because someone did something for you when you were a baby. It's because Jesus died on the cross and has already paid the price for you to go to heaven. Just ask forgiveness, and He will clean up all the past and make you His child."

After I interpreted her words, I touched *Senhor José's* shoulder and asked, "Do you believe that He died on the cross and shed His blood to give salvation to all who believe?"

"*Sim, acredito.*"

"Do you believe that Jesus rose from the dead and is alive now waiting for your prayer?"

"*Sim, acredito.*"

"Do you believe that God's Word, the Bible, is true and that God will save you if you ask?"

He turned his head slowly toward us and shook his head, yes.

Pam said, "I am going to pray, and then you can repeat a prayer with Dona Shirley. Be baptized when you are better."

I interpreted her prayer, and he repeated after me the sinner's prayer that has been prayed around the world in many languages and in many cultures.

His eyes were misty when we finished. Visiting hours were almost over. Pam said, "Halleluiah! The angels are having a celebration, and I am celebrating, too. In 25 years, I am going to knock on your door in heaven, and we can have a good talk and understand each other."

She touched his hands folded across his chest and told him good-bye. "I have to go back to my home in the US, but we can see you again – maybe in heaven." She didn't know it then, but she would be seeing those folded hands again in just three days.

After we all got back in the car, José Jr. and his wife told us about their visit and his witness to his father. We shared that his father prayed to accept Christ. What sharing. What rejoicing.

Pamela said, "You know, if my plane had not been late, you and I would have been already at the *Lar Nova Vida* Home and may not have seen this young couple."

We drove a few more minutes, and she said, "You know, come to think of it. I should have said in 30 years I would knock at his door in heaven. I am too young to be counting on only 25 more years!"

The next days were filled working with children and church families and ducking the sudden rain showers each day. We met with hundreds of Brazilian Christians for a beautiful watch-night service on New Year's Eve.

As we were preparing for church Sunday morning, the phone rang about 8:00 am. It was *José, Jr.*

"Dona Shirley, my father passed away this morning, and the funeral will be at the cemetery at 10:00 a.m."

"Pamela and I will be there, son." Brazilian law requires burial within 24 hours since there is no embalming. They reflect reality. No beautifully decorated church. No escorted funeral procession. No family limousine. Just one of a half dozen little rooms near the gate of the cemetery. A pine box with a net covering the body to keep away the flies. Candles burning to keep down the smell.

Before leaving to go to the cemetery, I called Hélio Torres, a young man who watched José grow up. When we arrived, José had asked Hélio to bring a message and told him about his father's bedside confession to accept Christ as Savior. While Hélio was gone to get his Bible, a priest arrived. José was upset and wanted Hélio to conduct the service. I told him that, since many members of the family were not Protestants, all they knew to do was to call a priest. I was sure that Hélio and the priest could work out something.

When Hélio arrived, he and I went over to the priest who was sitting next to the casket leafing through a small book. We introduced ourselves.

"Oh, are you the lady who called me?" he asked. "I don't know this family."

"No, sir. But I'm sure someone in the family called you. Others are *crentes* (believers) and didn't know that you were coming so they asked this young pastor to speak. How do you think it can be worked out?"

"Oh, no problem. He can just tell me the scripture he is going to use so I won't use the same. Oh, well, just let him go first." Exactly what I hoped he would say.

As Hélio moved closer to the casket with his Bible in his hands, the people who were seated in the chairs lining the walls of the little room stood up. The folks who were gathered in the area outside the door crowded closer to show respect. Hélio brought a great message for the occasion. He told us that after the resurrection, Jesus called his scattered disciples together and gave them a message to give others. He shared that José had witnessed to his father in the hospital with that same message.

"This man has a son here today who loved his father enough that he told him how he could go to heaven. He shared the same good news of salvation that the disciples shared. *Senhor José* is not in heaven because he was perfect or a good man who did good deeds to deserve heaven. He accepted the price Jesus paid on the cross for his salvation, and his son can have the assurance that he can meet him in heaven."

The priest closed his little book, listened, and shook his head in agreement. That's good, I thought. However, when Hélio said there were two destinies after death and mentioned the word *inferno*, (hell), the priest jerked his head up and looked at Hélio. Hélio continued and said that we could be sure that Sr. José was in heaven since he accepted Jesus as the only means of salvation. The priest started agreeing with him again.

Next, the priest stood up and read from his little book, and many chanted after him. He read some more, and they chanted again. He read a part that said that his soul was in heaven because he was baptized by his parents when he was an infant. More chants. I noticed there were no Hail Marys.

He suddenly lifted his head from reading and looked around the room, "He was baptized wasn't he? Did he have infant baptism, does anyone know?"

Everyone looked around then someone said,

"Ask his wife, we don't know."

The widow looked up with glazed eyes and shrugged her shoulders, "Maybe, I don't know. I guess so."

"Very well," continued the priest. "He is in heaven because he was baptized as a baby, and we will now pray for his soul." After more chanting, he turned it back over to Pastor Hélio.

He took longer than Hélio, but the pastor had the last prayer. It was short, but it reminded everyone again the plan of salvation. Not by works, but by faith. Then he opened the little hymnal from our church and led us in a song about heaven. Several joined in with us.

We followed the small walking procession as it made its way through the cemetery and up the sloping streets. Pamela and Hélio walked with José, as his wife, who was on crutches, and I followed slowly behind. It began to rain as we watched the grave diggers slide in the pine box and seal up the hole with bricks and mud.

Pamela was observing but couldn't understand much. She had lots of questions when we got back into the car. "Don't you see, Shirley? That's why God sent us that day to the hospital while he was still lucid. What a great testimony for his son, his family, and for us. God is so good."

Remember the old hymn? "Speak, my Lord. Speak, my Lord. Speak and I will gladly follow you...." How sweet to hear the voice of the Lord. How sweet to obey.

Cell Phone Shocker

Jim handed me the cell phone in the Hospitality House in Araras. It was the second day of our mission trip with Dr. Jim and Bobbie Lee and Marie Glover from Albany, Georgia.

"It's Ivani," he said and handed me the phone.

She grew up in LNV and was now married with a child and lived in São Paulo. I walked to the porch for better reception on the cell phone.

"*Tia,* (Auntie*)* tomorrow I am going to *Araras.*"

"Oh, good. We want to see you. We just got here yesterday," I said.

"*Tia,* Ana Paula died!" She started sobbing.

"What? Ana Paula?" I was shocked. Ana was her sister. "When? How do you know?"

"Someone called saying they had found Ana's cell phone and started dialing trying to find family. They said that September 5 was her birthday and she was found dead the next day. Knife wounds. They told the name of the cemetery where she was buried and that only one person was there at the burial. That person had paid the burial expenses."

All of this was spilling out through her sobs so she handed the phone to her mother-in-law, Laíde.

I had a birthday present for Ana Paula. No more hugs and smiles from her? That meant she would have died the same day we arrived in Brazil. The Brazilian law requires that a body be buried within 24 hours, so was she buried before the family even knew about it?

For the last few months I knew Ana Paula was

living in São Paulo with Laíde and Ivani, so I asked about that. Laíde said that about a month ago they came to *Araras*. Ana had been sick and was better. There was an argument between Ivani and her mother-in-law, and Ana Paula said she didn't want to go back to São Paulo with them. About an hour later a couple from the nearby town of Limeira came to get Ana Paula. They said she used to live and work with them before. She was in the car with the couple when they told her goodbye and that was the last they saw of her. They tried to call her on her birthday, but there was no answer.

Ivani and Ana Paula had been taken to our children's home by the police when they were six and seven years old. They lived there until they were 18 and 19. They were both in their mid-twenties at this time.

"Laíde, it seems unreal. Like a cruel joke someone is playing!" I said.

"The woman who called gave the address of the house where the police went to see the body. She also gave us the name and address of Ana's friend, and the name and address of the cemetery. We are going there to the cemetery this weekend, and we invite you to go with us."

Ana dead? Already buried? Our sweet little song bird. She had loved teaching children and singing. How I would cherish a hug and some time with her.

"Yes, Laíde, I will go with you. Let me know when you arrive in town."

I hung up and walked into the Hospitality House. I couldn't talk. Jim was lying down on the sofa. How do you say something like this?

"Ivani said she is coming to *Araras*

tomorrow," I began. I felt like I was in a daze and just began slowly telling what I had heard. He kept saying "Ana Paula? Ana?"

So many questions. Was she alone on her birthday? Depressed? Why didn't authorities search for families? Did she try to call someone?

At that time, Renata walked in the door with clothes from the clothes line. She and her family live on our chacara as care takers since we are gone so much. Jim asked me quietly if I was going to tell her. I said that I would later when I had gathered myself together. When Marie came out of the bedroom, Jim started telling her and I finished. Then I told Bobbie Lee. They both loved her and brought little gifts for her. How thankful we were to have these sweet co-laborers with us at this awful moment. That heart wrenching moment.

The phone rang. Jim handed it to me. It was missionary Kimberly Johnson who had just heard the news from Ivani's cousins. Kimberly had been their house mother when they were youngsters in LNV years ago. Did we do enough? Soul searching. Just one more chance to hold her and encourage her. Never again? Our hearts ached together over this terrible news.

Ana's husband, Reginaldo, who was recently separated from her, drove up in front of Hospitality House and asked to talk to our visitor Dr. Jim about the Jiu-jitsu project for the boys that he was sponsoring. I wondered if he knew. After the men talked he turned to me and said he had something sad to tell me. He knew! I told him that Ivani had called me. We cried together and prayed together. What a terrible ending to a dear life.

He said, "You know, I can't believe that it is

true. I know Ana wouldn't do anything to herself. She is a strong person. Someone who had stolen things from her threatened her a while back. Should I tell the police about it?"

Who knew? We discussed it a while and wondered if the person involved would just sling mud and lies to cover up. We all had a disturbing afternoon.

Kimberly called before we left for prayer meeting that night. "Shirley, who have you told about your phone call from Ivani?"

"Those of us here at the *chacara*, and Reginaldo came by already knowing. Why?"

"Well, I called that cemetery. They had nothing registered for a burial of a young woman of that description. The police had no records of a woman's body being picked up at that address. I called a social worker from there who said she would go to the address tomorrow. Nothing has been confirmed so I called Ivani and told her not to go there this weekend. You shouldn't go near there until something has been confirmed. It could be a trap for you. It is all very strange." I certainly agreed with her.

"I'll go up and tell Renata not to mention the death to anyone until something is confirmed." I walked from the Hospitality House up to the main house to tell her. The house was closed and their family was gone, so I called her on their cell phone and gave her Kimberly's message.

When I disconnected the cell phone, a phone number appeared, the first on my contacts list. In red. It was: Ana Paula. Call the number, I thought. What? What if it is an old number? What if strangers have her phone now? What would I say? Call the number. Call the number. Okay, so I dialed.

"Alo." A female voice.

"Alo. É o numero de Ana Paula?"

"E', yes."

"Ana? Ana Paula?"

"E'. Sim, it's Ana Paula."

Oh, my heart. It did sound like her voice.

"Ana Paula, are you okay? It's *Tia* Shirley. We are in Araras."

"You are? Oh, I want to see you." She sounded surprised.

"Are you okay, Ana Paula? Are you safe?"

"I am fine, *Tia*. I was sick with pneumonia, but I am fine now. I have even gained a little weight."

"But are you safe?" I asked again.

"Yes, I am. I'll go see you and show you that I am fine. Why are you so worried about me?"

"Honey, have you talked to Ivani? Do you know what she told me?"

"No, I haven't talked to her," she said.

I explained to her the whole nightmare. What someone had told Ivani and Laíde. What Kimberly found out when she called the cemetery and the police. The whole cruel story.

"Have you heard anything about this at all?""

"No, but someone mentioned that a person had been around asking questions about an *Ana Paula* and wanted to know if it was I, and I told her no.

"Really, I am fine. That was a terrible story they told Ivani."

"Yes, you must call her. She is heartbroken.

She is suffering with all this. Reginaldo came here today, and we cried together and prayed together. Are you in trouble, are you safe?" I asked.

"Don't worry anymore. I'm fine."

"But who would do something like this? So crazy! So sick!"

"There is a person who stole things from me and from the family I live with. We made out a police report and she got really mad. Maybe it was that girl."

"Okay, I'll hang up so you can call Ivani. She will be shocked but relieved. What a terrible thing to happen to her. Why would anyone be so cruel?"

"I'll call her right now," she said.

"I'll call Kimberly back. She called the cemetery. The police. No one confirmed the terrible story." I sent hugs and kisses over the phone with great relief.

"This weekend I will see you."

I had to ask just one more time, "But, are you safe? Do you need help? Can you leave work?"

"I can change my hours to go there," she said.

"Where do you live, Ana?"

"I live with a nice family. They have a little boy, and I am safe."

"They told me you lived in a terrible place. A dangerous place."

She said, "No. I'll go there this weekend, and you will see that I'm okay. I love you."

As soon as I hung up I called Kimberly with the wonderful news. Ana Paula is alive!

Ana Paula called right back saying she talked to Ivani, and all was better now.

"You'll see the little birthday present we have for you. We'll look for you this weekend." I finally felt I could breathe freely again, but I felt I had been in a battle.

At prayer meeting that night Kimberly leaned over and whispered to me that Ana had called her. After she went to her pew, we exchanged looks that needed no words. A death message had cruelly been sent on a stolen cell phone, and our hearts wanted to celebrate that it was false. A lie. How do you celebrate a resurrection? A cancelation of a death message? But now it was time to celebrate the truth with thanksgiving. The truth had set us free.

A few days later our Ana Paula clapped at our gate and ran into our waiting arms!

Leaving Nightmares for Little Girl's Dreams

For the Twentieth Anniversary of *Lar Nova Vida* in Araras in 2011 we were calling the alumni/ex-residents for a little celebration together with folks from the Albany, Georgia Mission Team, Dr. Jim and Bobbie Jo Lee and Marie Glover. One phone call was to our little Jaycee, one of the former residents. She is now a secretary in the city government office, and I had to catch her at home at night before she went off to class. We had a similar meeting in January, and she wasn't able to go.

During the phone call, she couldn't promise that she would make it, but declared that *Lar Nova Vida* was important in her life and really gave her a new chance for a future. Before I continue with the anniversary celebration, let me tell you about the young girl on the phone.

I remembered another phone call many years ago. Seven years, in fact. We were on stateside assignment and happened to be in Oklahoma when we received a phone call from a board member of LNV. After we talked a while, she brought up a question.

"The court house has asked us to shelter a girl, and we wanted to talk to you about her". Usually on our year-long stateside assignments, the vice-president and board made those decisions without calling me.

"Okay. What's her story?" It had been 14 years at that time since we opened a Children's Home in *Araras*. We had recently opened another home for our girls and their younger siblings near our church in *Jardim Candida* neighborhood. She would be the two hundred and twenty-fifth child we enrolled to shelter. To give them a safe place to heal their little wounds that life had thrust upon them.

"How old is she?" One of the first questions I always ask.

"Well, she is thirteen," she answered.

"The court knows that our limit to accept a child is twelve years old."

"Actually, she has a birthday tomorrow," she hurriedly offered. "That makes her twelve today."

"Our constitution allows us to make exceptions if they have a smaller sibling needing us or if they have already been in our home in the past."

"Yes, but the case worker was insisting that we are their only hope to help her."

She continued to tell the child's story, and it was shocking. The authorities had found this pre-teen girl living with a man to whom her parents owed drug money. The court felt the parents had traded her for their debts. Neighbors in the *Vila de Barro* said she had been living with the man for a while and had quit school.

LNV workers told the case worker that they would rather she wait for us to arrive back in Brazil in just a few days. But they said the situation was so urgent that they wanted to take her out of it and give her to us immediately.

By this time, I agreed that it was urgent, and we could help this little wounded lamb. I couldn't stand to think of the danger she was living in and what she had been subjected to at her young age. May God guide us to take this child away from this absurd, cruel, nightmarish situation and allow her to be a child to dream youthful dreams.

Soon we arrived in Brazil and met beautiful Jaycee. She had long, black straight hair and a slim body just barely budding into womanhood. The house mother said she was sweet natured and obedient.

Each time I looked at her I felt there was something I was missing. I went to my records and checked enrollments for the year 1997. Yes, it was there. Jaycee and her four siblings lived at LNV for a very short time. We had taken in 23 new children that year counting those five. I wondered how the family and beautiful children made it after they left. Now we had a second chance to help one of them.

She received all the medical exams given to our new children, and we checked her for other things because of her grown–up *exposure.* Thankfully she was reported as healthy.

Now to find a school for her. Brazilian schools

begin the scholastic year in February, so it was midterm when she joined our family. Under ordinary circumstances it would not be easy to find a vacancy. Thankfully God is not hindered by circumstances. Let me give some background before I continue.

Since the children's home had recently rented a house in *Jardim Candida*, all the children were in a different kindergarten, grade school and high school. I wanted to start her in the school with her age group, but we had never had a student there. However, years earlier the superintendent of the junior high and high school in the neighborhood had invited Jim to be a counselor to some of the older students. He had asked me to give motivational lectures to the school's professors. He had also invited the praise team from our church to have a program for an anti-drug assembly.

The young praise team had as members a policeman, José,' a lawyer, Sergio, a school teacher, Rita, and businessmen. They gave talks, and could they sing and play. Later the director said the parents of the students called him, and he was prepared for some negative feedback. No! The parents wanted the praise team to return and have a session for them.

So, I found myself seated before this young superintendent asking him to give our young Jaycee a chance. I asked that she be able to enroll to audit classes at first. They could observe her for a semester and evaluate her participation.

He listened carefully and finally said he would have to take it before his board of teachers. Oh, yes, one more bit of information. A teacher on that board attended one of our churches.

Who's Clapping At Our Gate?

Was God preparing us for this very hour with these contacts from years ago?

Without telling her entire background, I gave him enough information to show how urgent it was to get her back into the normal life of a young teen. He set a day, and I returned with Jaycee. He really gave her a lecture about attendance, obedience to rules, and the hard work it would take to catch up with her peers. She meekly agreed to work hard and be a good student.

She didn't disappoint us. She kept up with her extra work load and became an exemplary student. She was a good example of how important it was for LNV to give a child a chance at a normal life.

She was on her way to recovery. Then one day we were advised by the court that her *boyfriend* was given visitation rights on Saturday mornings. Incredible! The house mother or I had to be present in the sitting room during his visits. You can believe we were.

How would she react? He was a handsome young man, and I could see how she was flattered by his attention. She had taped his photo inside a closet door. But, oh, I wanted her feelings to not return to the old paths. How I wanted her future plans and dreams to include a Christian home and family, and an education to take her as far as she dreamed. We told her that the Lord had plans for her. Plans for her good and happiness. How I wished the *boyfriend* would just lose interest and go away.

Away he did go. He was sent to jail for selling drugs and didn't look her up again after he was released.

Before we moved from that house, our foster son, Marcos, had a prayer session with our older girls.

Unlike Jaycee, some of the other girls seemed depressed and restless, and we were praying for deliverance from evil forces in their young lives.

During the prayer, however, Jaycee was the one who manifested a spirit disturbance. We hadn't expected that. As Marcos prayed, she was standing with her eyes closed and her body started swaying. No strange voice manifested, but the other girls' eyes were wide open. After the prayer, everyone was quiet and serious as Marcos spoke to the girls. The house mother, Julia, and I hid that scene in our hearts as we continued to work with her and prayed for her salvation.

After having children sheltered in seven different rent houses, it was good to have them all in our two permanent houses in *Jardim Celina*. The Brazilian law is for ten children per house mother, but at times we had 20 children in each house. The courts said that reality and community needs annulled that law.

With the move, our Jaycee changed schools and continued to do well. One private computer school offered scholarships for some of our children. She was one of the children chosen to study there, and it proved to be very important to her future. We also provided guitar lessons for her along with others. But, we needed at least one more guitar. She approached me about it, and we put it on our prayer list.

Not long after, I had a call from a man from the US. He said, "My son is part of E-Team Brazil, and this group is to go to *Araras* to work at *Lar Nova Vida*. We were wondering if you could use a guitar. My son could take it to Brazil with him when he goes. Is that something you could use?"

Yes! Oh, yes.

Some weeks later the E-Team Brazil was at our church for Thursday night prayer meeting at the *Jardim* Candida Church. As part of their presentation of drama, music and testimonies, the young man told through an interpreter about his father's phone call and called Jaycee to the front of the church. He placed in her hands a beautiful pearl blue answer to prayer. Once again God showed a child being healed of her *wounds* that she and her prayers were important.

In time she accepted Christ and was baptized. She seemed to have more confidence in herself and in her new faith. However, during that time her mother's young body did not resist the toll that her choice of lifestyle and vices had taken on her. We always taught our children to pray for their parents and family and to forgive them.

When she was a child, she somehow accepted their lifestyle as normal since it was just like most people living around her in their slum village. But with the changes in her life, she became impatient with her mother and father. We encouraged her to visit them, but she sometimes was reluctant.

One day we received news that her mother was critically ill with an enlarged heart along with many other issues. By the time Jaycee and I arrived to visit, her mother had passed away. Jaycee said she hardly recognized her mother. The once slim, blond mother of five was now a bloated body and lying on the table.

After that, we visited with her father who was working and had one child with him. Also, an uncle and aunt made contact with us at *Lar Nova Vida*. They had taken in one of her siblings and wanted to encourage Jaycee after the death of her mother.

They sat across from me several times in the LNV office and I sensed that their interest was taking another dimension. Along with her public school, she was enrolled in a VoTec course that prepared young people for their first job. The couple already had children of their own who were her age, plus her sibling, and many other responsibilities. Eventually they started asking about the process of getting her guardianship.

Finally the sad, sweet day arrived when we handed her and her little bundles to her very own relatives.

Her uncle was good to drive all the way across town on Sunday evenings so that she could continue to go to church with LNV family. However, with gasoline costing about seven dollars a gallon he finally asked her to find a church closer to their house or go with them to their non-protestant church.

She kept in touch and kept us informed about good things developing in her life. One day it was, "*Tia*, I got a job as a secretary in a city government office." What a conquest for our girl.

Then came an e-mail saying, "*Tia*, I was accepted to the college on a partial scholarship. I hope to save money from my job to pay the other part of the tuition."

Other children have gone on after leaving LNV to finish high school and to take specialized courses, but she was our first to enter a regular college. We don't know how far she can go under the financial strain, but she is living her dream.

Who's Clapping At Our Gate?

God is still writing the chapters in her life and in the lives of the other wounded lambs who found healing in the arms of the Good Shepherd.

The Twentieth Anniversary Alumni Meeting was a great blessing with lots of hugs, testimonies, laughter and tears. And Brazilian pizza. There were 37 present (Jaycee was not there) that night in a small living room of *Tia* Sonia's house. Even though the dear missionaries from Albany, Bobbie Joe Lee and Marie Glover, could not understand much of their Portuguese conversations and songs, they could see the joy and love. They could see the results of twenty years of dedication to care for and evangelize more than 300 needy children.

Those ex-street children were now setting examples for the children still at LNV. Some came from other cities by bus and motorcycles. Others in town came by motorcycles, buses, walking, and one drove up in a car with his family. There were mechanics, secretaries, nurses, beauticians, factory workers, drivers, and parents gathered around the guitar for hours. There were deacons, evangelists, musicians, children's leaders, and praise leaders giving thanks for the children's home who introduced them to Jesus. Jim and I were honored to be part of that true celebration!

How thankful I am that God sent these little wounded lambs to our gates so that we could now see them as healthy adults. Now they may arrive at our gate by bikes, motorcycles or cars, but their love for us and God is a precious gift.

Oh, yes, Jaycee was at our Fourth LNV Family Reunion. She was still working, studying, living with her uncle, aunt, and cousins. And she brought a nice-looking boyfriend to the party for us to meet. She was still free to follow her dreams.

Mounting Up With Wings, By Tomorrow?

It was still dark and I was already sitting on the side of the bed at our hospitality house. Thinking. Praying. Jim reached over and rubbed my back, and my eyes filled with tears. He rolled over to go back to sleep, and I got up to start my day.

It was June and cold in *Araras*. The next day I was supposed to return to the U.S., but the authorities had told me I couldn't leave the country before Tuesday, if then. We had experienced four great weeks of hosting mission teams of college students, high school students, church leaders, and grandkids. They helped in the children's home and participated in the ministry of our local churches. Now, a very serious accusation was hanging over my head. Leaving the next day, authorities said, was **impossible.**

"Lord," I prayed, "this is too complicated to even know what to say. I need to talk with the lawyer at 9:30 this morning. Then I may need to go to the travel agency to cancel my flight tomorrow. But I don't have answers right now. I want your answers. I'll pack, Father. I can pray and fast today. I'll just go through every scheduled hour and wait. Waiting. But, I want to wait in peace."

A thought came, "No fasting. They that wait upon the Lord, will renew their strength."

Who's Clapping At Our Gate?

Dr. Jose Martini

José Martini, a lawyer, was waiting for me when I arrived at his office at 9:30 am. When he rose to hug me I was reminded how tall and handsome he was. He and his wife, Graziele, grew up in our church. His partner and lawyer, Rosangela, had filled him in about my meeting with her the day before.

He picked up the phone and dialed the police station. After identifying himself, he asked, "Would it be possible to speak with *Senhor* Luiz Fernando about the case with Dona Shirley and *Lar Nova Vida?*"

He was told that the *escrevente, (scribe) Luiz,* had been on duty all night and wouldn't be in today.

"I would like to go there with Dona Shirley. She is scheduled to travel to the US tomorrow so I would like to register that we tried to be heard today before she travels."

We went to the police station to wait our turn to be seen. There were people standing and sitting all around. Some would ask me as they passed if I had been waited on. I pointed to him and said, "I'm with him. " Dr. José (lawyers in Brazil are given the title of *doutor*, i.e., doctor*)* was in a suit and many called him by name. I was glad to be standing by him.

"Is this what **impossible** feels like?" I asked myself.

The secretary apologized and explained again that *Senhor Luiz* had worked the night shift and would not be in today. I would need to come back Monday morning. That meant that I could not leave the next day. Not before Tuesday.

"I can call him, if it is an emergency," she offered. That didn't seem right to me.

Dr. José answered, "If there is anyone else who could take *Dona* Shirley's statement, you don't need to call him. She has been here before without being able to be heard, and now she needs to leave tomorrow."

Once again the sympathetic secretary explained that my case was with *Senhor Luiz* and he was the only one who could hear me. Just then another young lady approached the counter and whispered something to the secretary. Her eyebrows raised in surprise.

"The third door on the left, *Dr. José*." She raised her hand to point down the hallway.

We went to the third door and a young man seated behind the desk invited us in. He smiled slightly, shook hands with us, and said, "I'm not supposed to be here."

"Well, your receptionist yesterday and today did a good job of trying to protect you from working today. Shouldn't you be sleeping?" I asked.

He shook his head. "Really, I don't know why I came. I hadn't planned on it." Now I was smiling. "I can't believe I am sitting in this chair," he said.

Dr. José and I were perhaps thinking the same thing. Maybe I would be traveling the next day after all. I would "mount up with wings" on that American Airlines flight.

"Since we are all here anyway, what is it you need?" he asked as he motioned for us to be seated. I sat in the only other chair and Dr. José remained standing.

Dr. José explained to him that I had gathered more information since I had been to Senhor Luiz's office a few days ago. I had returned twice, but was not able to talk to him. He presented him with the documents I had and explained the situation.

I gave my statements and explanations as he typed out the report on his computer.

Five years ago I had opened a savings account as the legal guardian for three of our *Lar Nova Vida* children. Their 29-year-old father had died of *chagas,* a heart disease caused by an insect bite. The children were entitled to a pension. The government deposited the pension in one bank, and I took the money and placed it in the savings account in another bank. Someone had reported to authorities that there should be more money in the savings than the present bank balance showed.

I had spent weeks while in *Araras* investigating, gathering five years of records from the banks and the government deposits, and putting together an answer for the difference in the bank balance. I didn't even know what the *"apropriacao em debito"* (misappropriation of funds) notice I had received meant, and I was shocked when my son-in-law, José Augusto, a law school graduate, explained it to me!

They were saying I was responsible for also receiving the pension the first ten months of 2005. I presented proof that I started receiving the money only in the eleventh month of 2005. Their mother had fled from the law to another state. She presented the authorities there with the birth certificates for her three children and said as the *poor widow*, she needed their money to take care of them.

The guardianship of the children had been taken from her and given to me as the president of *Lar Nova Vida*. She had illegally been taking the children's money. She had been in and out of jail on drug charges, and the story was that she finally received a longer sentence for killing a man at a bus station. I had taken her children to that city to visit her. But, in 2005, she was already out, and in hiding.

Dr. José had counseled me on how much to say and how to present the information. After Senhor *Luiz* read back to us the statements I had made and he had registered, Dr. José and I signed it.

"Okay. What happens when you send your report to the court house? I returned to Brazil in October of last year to clear up the savings for the children. Their pension had been discontinued for some reason. I returned again in January of this year and checked with lawyers, banks and the government offices. They said I had done everything I needed to do. Now since I received notice from the current president of LNV that I had this accusation against me, I am here again in June. The children still have not started receiving their pension again. Could it be that I will be called again on this matter?"

Dr. José offered to represent me and take care of anything that would come up in the future while I was in the States. He felt that the report made that day should clear up everything. If not, I could take care of anything on my next visit to *Araras*. *Senhor* Luiz agreed with him.

The two young men began saying comforting words to me that brought tears to my eyes again. They told me how important *Lar Nova Vida* was to our city and how it was unjust for people to make accusations. I had heard similar words from people at the bank, the government office and lawyers' offices, but it was so good to have the "balm of Gilead" applied to my soul again.

When we shook hands to leave, I told him that I hoped he could go home and rest.

He said, "*Dona* Shirley, I have known you from the other police station in the other district. I have known your love and dedication, and I am glad I could help you. Maybe it was destiny for me to be here today."

"When you left work, *Senhor Luiz*, you probably didn't know that God would use you to be the answer to my prayer this morning. I asked for answers to the **impossible** and for peace. God has used you to give me both. He brought you here for that. Thank you. He can do the same for you, someday."

How thankful I was for an advocate like Dr. José. He and I both had an Advocate in Jesus Christ who took my case to the Father in heaven. "They that wait upon the Lord will renew their strength. They will mount up with wings as eagles!" I had bags to pack and a plane to catch!

Clapping at Our Kids Gates

If you have adult children, you may remember the first time they invited you to their home as a guest. I remember. And that moment was like, "This is what it is all about."

When you clap at the gate of a child you picked up from the gutter, nourished him back to life, loved him, educated him, evangelized him, and saw him grow into a young adult, the expectation is almost overwhelming. He meets you at his gate as a healthy young man, a citizen in good standing and with a sweet, lovely wife. They embrace you, invite you in and have a meal prepared for you. Tears come to my eyes just to remember the scenes that repeated themselves over and over.

Jim and Shirley celebrate their Fiftieth Anniversary

Jim and I left Oklahoma to go to our beloved Brazil to start the celebration of our Fiftieth Wedding Anniversary. We celebrated our second anniversary in the city of São Paulo while in language study and a dear friend and devoted sponsor of our children at Lar Nova Vida, Pamela Wilson, took us to the fantastic city of Rio de Janeiro for our Forty-fifth Anniversary.

Who's Clapping At Our Gate?

Now, the Fiftieth Anniversary was going to be very special as we spend it in the city of Araras, Sao Paulo, and Easter in Tubarao, Santa Catarina.

We were the first to clap at the gate of Jose Carlos one Friday night while we were there. He and his wife, Izaura, invited us and 35 more of the LNV family to their home for a praise service, family reunion and 27 pizzas. These were our children who were now using *hospitality evangelism* to reach out to their extended family members. Jose and Izaura are very active in their local church, and I was so pleased to hear the reports of our other grown children.

Kleverton and Jessica

On another day our first child to be taken to our home by the police in 1991, Kleverton, invited us to his home. He was nine years old and had been beaten for not taking home enough money after begging in the street when they first took him to our house. He was now a deacon and married to a fine Christian girl, Jessica. She had made one of Pastor Jaime's (Jim) favorite dishes – *costelas* (ribs), and proudly placed them on the table. We filled the walls of that little house with laughter, praise, and prayer.

One afternoon we clapped at the gate, unannounced, of the very humble home of four young people who had grown up in our church and Lar Nova Vida. Their life was a struggle but they continued to study, to work and to serve God. To break the cycle destined for the poor.

We were treated royally to an afternoon tea and felt so loved and welcomed. They kept bringing out Kool-Aid, canned fruit with cream and crackers.

Jim just looked at me with a sad smile. Later I found out we were thinking the same thing.

Our sweet children were taking from their meager supply to give us their very best. What sweet, unselfish hospitality.

Celso and Renata

Couples who were youngsters in our church, Afonso and Maria, Jose and Leslie, Celso and Renata, now had families, careers and ministries. They ministered to us as they invited us into their homes for meals and fellowship. Sonia, Rita, Adelina and Noemia served us in their homes

Who's Clapping At Our Gate?

Afonso,
Maria, Jose,
Leslie

Iraci gave us a bed and meals in Araras and Lavinio's family and Gabriel's family gave us beds and meals in Tubarao. Our spiritual children.

Hospitality is so personal. The Portuguese Bible mentions it six times in the New Testament as a command. There are many examples in the Bible and those who gave hospitality to Jesus were a diverse group. A leper, a tax collector, the Pharisees, the house of Mary, of Zacchaeus, the house in Emmaus and in Galilee.

Our spiritual children in Brazil could not have chosen a better, more memorable way to show love and thankfulness, and to help us celebrate our Fiftieth Wedding Anniversary, than with their sacrificial hospitality.

When we returned to Oklahoma, our own children and grandchildren gave us an awesome Fiftieth Anniversary celebration that they planned while we were in Brazil. The best part was we had no part in it and were we in for surprises! They had brought old and new friends from near and far. The decorations were beautiful and the program delighted our hearts. Our children and grandchildren sang in Portuguese and English, my comedian sister, Carolyn, and her husband, George, entertained us. Jim's sister, Judy, told on her big brother and her husband, Jim, led us in repeating our vows. My sister, Dolores, sneaked photos to them for a delightful video show of our lives together. We were so blessed.

As I said, when you are hosted by your own children in a foreign land or right at home, it is so special. "That's what it is all about!"

Cousins with me
Carla, Ana Paula, Ivani, and Camila

Part Three

CHAPTER 5
Who Are Those Gringos At Our Gate?

Missiologists and missionaries know that it is not good for the national churches around the world to be dependent on sources outside their countries. So what is the importance of groups helping on distant fields? How can it work together with the challenge of leading mission churches to be strong and indigenous?

While in Brazil, I was moved by a video of the story of a family working together to get ready for harvest time. The husband, wife, and children work long, hard days and look forward to a wonderful harvest. However, the father dies. His widow and children do all they can, but exhaustion and discouragement come and they can't complete the harvest in time.

Suddenly, a rumbling sound is heard and trucks and tractors are seen coming over the horizon. Neighbors from all directions come rolling in and help the family do what they could not finish by themselves. The family rejoices with relief to see help arrive. The neighbors rejoice that together they could help after the family did all they could do. The harvest is saved by a united effort.

That is what I have seen with the mission groups I have participated in. They arrive for a few days and help and encourage hard working nationals and missionaries.

A young church had built their church building after much sacrifice. A group of American Free Will Baptist men arrived for a few days and helped put on the roof that allowed them to use their building sooner.

A children's home had sacrificially built beautiful buildings, giving shelter to almost forty children and caring for them for 24 hours, seven days a week. They struggled to give them the best care in food, clothing, medical attention, school supplies, spiritual training, and transportation. There were just no funds left over for material and labor to paint the buildings.   For an unforgettable week, Free Will Baptist men, women, and teens arrived, painted and left beautifully- painted homes for thankful children and workers. The friendship and love shared during those days, in spite of language barriers, encouraged all those involved.

One American friend, Bob, asked a question in Sunday School recently. It started a discussion on why go with a group to a mission field instead of sending the money the group would spend on transportation and documents, etc. to arrive on that field? Good question. So this is our answer:

1. Sometimes it may be better to give the collective amount that would have been spent, if you can raise it.

2. A group may do something faster than paying local labor when time is of essence.

3. The ministry and spiritual participation can't be easily done by hired locals. (Testimonies, sermons, teaching, singing, drama, instrumentals.)

4. The building of friendships and fellowship impacts the local ministry and missionaries.

5. Mission team members have on-hands experiences that God uses to change their own lives.

6. Local churches are impacted by personal reports from a church member on his or her return to the US.

7. Funds allocated for definite projects may or may not be used as the giver intended. There needs to be a personal link dedicated to their intentions.

Who Are These People?
The people on the teams who came to our gate are people who are willing to serve and to learn. Usually our groups are small and are made up of laymen and laywomen. Sometimes the leader of the group has a ministry in his/her local church, but most of the members don't occupy prominent places in churches as preachers or teachers.

Three young pastors from Rejoice Church

Some are whole families made up of parents and children. Some are high school and college students. Some are professional people and business owners who leave their busy schedules to face language and culture barriers in order to serve others.

Once, a group of all pastors sat around our table. Another unforgettable group was made up of young ministers – music minister, youth pastor, and children's pastor of the same church. They were full of talent and energy and won hearts with long-lasting memories.

Rejoice Go-Team

One year we had three young nine-year-olds who came with their parents, and they did a good job of bonding with children and teens in our church and in *Lar Nova Vida*. In contrast we have had remarkable, serving senior citizens who showed wisdom and strength to all ages through their testimonies. Sometimes they were the first to report to work and the last to finish. God bless the white-hair brigade.

Jesus sees in His children potential leadership for the Kingdom. It may appear to others that their abilities would be limited in a foreign setting, but their hearts are big and they get things done. They have a sincere yearning for God. They want to be pliable and molded in the hands of the Master. If you want to be used, Jesus can use you anywhere.

The following are stories from the *gringos* who went to Brazil to share themselves with their fellow Christians in a far country.

Before the mission teams started arriving each year, Jim's baby sister (one of 13 siblings), visited us several years ago and shares the first story with us.

Judith Combs Puckett, Oklahoma

In the fall of 1996, my niece Tânia was attending Hillsdale College in Moore, Oklahoma, near our home. She was planning her trip to Brazil to visit her parents for Christmas and asked me to consider going with her. I had tried to arrange a trip a year earlier and already had my passport, when plans fell through. Our two baby granddaughters were about to celebrate their first Christmas, so it was difficult for me to leave. Fortunately, my family agreed to have an early Christmas together before I left. I quickly made all the arrangements at work and at home to make the trip.

**Jim's sister
Judy Puckett**

It was a long but enjoyable flight on the jumbo jet with hundreds of passengers, many of them excited Brazilians returning home for Christmas. Jim and Shirley met Tânia and me in São Paulo, about two hours away from their home in Araras. After claiming our baggage and going through customs, we left the airport. My first impression was warmth since I had left the northern hemisphere in the dead of winter and was now emerging into the heat of summer. It was a pleasant change, and my senses heightened with the sight of everything green and the aroma of flowers in bloom.

We drove along a modern interstate highway through the huge metropolis of São Paulo, a city of 19 million. We traveled for what seemed like 30 minutes before the skyscrapers disappeared and the countryside emerged. Ironically, alongside great wealth and modern structures in this very contemporary city, extreme poverty was also evident. Cardboard, plastic sheeting, and discarded wood were the materials used for homes of the poor in the ghetto area of the world's seventh largest city.

We stopped at a cafeteria-type roadside restaurant on the way home to have lunch. The quality and presentation of the food was impressive, especially the beautiful pastries. We also stopped at a small grocery store in Araras, *Supermercado Favetta,* to buy bread before arriving at Jim and Shirley's home on the outskirts of town. I was surprised to see rice and beans, a staple for every meal, stocked in 50-pound bags in the store.

As we approached their home, I saw that the entire complex was surrounded by a large wall. They explained that every yard has either a wall or fence as protection from burglary. The farm or *chácara*, a plot of ground large enough for several buildings, was beautifully landscaped with fruit and nut trees, grapevines, crotons, hibiscus, and other lush tropical plants. The main house had a large veranda on two sides with space for outdoor furniture, and hooks for a hammock, which I enjoyed several afternoons during my stay.

There was a beautiful swimming pool and a large open covered hospitality area with picnic tables beside the pool. Attached to this was a pool guest house with two small bathrooms. Behind the main house was a small three-room house that served as housing for a caretaker and his family. In exchange for rent, the man maintained the grounds and his wife helped as a cook and housekeeper.

The day after I arrived, Shirley took me to visit *Lar Nova Vida* (New Life Home) for children. At that time, it was still in its infancy, just about five years old. They had happily received a parcel of donated land, completed most of their structure, and recently moved in. During my first visit to the Home, the children were gathered in the dining area awaiting visitors. *Papai Noel* (Father Christmas - Santa Claus) was about to arrive and distribute gifts sponsored by a local community group. The Nestle Company had just donated money for a new van, much needed by the home, and a group of Nestle employees arrived to deliver the check and personal gifts for the children. It was a joy to watch their faces light up as they opened their new toys, a first for many children who had been rescued from living in poverty on the streets.

Most of the children were very outgoing, and were intrigued when Shirley introduced me as Pastor Jim's sister. They held my hands and asked me questions, which I could not answer since I didn't speak their language. A few shy, quiet ones kept their distance, but most were noisy like children everywhere, busily playing with their gifts. I also met the cook and house parents. I would see them all again at church on Sunday, and later at Jim and Shirley's home on Christmas afternoon.

During my visit, I attended church at the second Free Will Baptist Candida Church, where Jim pastored at that time. The language barrier was not difficult for me because the service was somewhat familiar, and I understood a little of what was being done even if I didn't understand the conversations. Since it was the Christmas season, the church conducted several special events during my stay. The music was lively and loud, and everyone seemed to enjoy it as much as I did. I even recognized one of the songs, "Celebrate Jesus, Celebrate," and was able to sing along.

Another unique experience was going Christmas caroling with a church group. Caroling was not part of the Brazilian Christmas tradition until recent years. This American tradition was something I had done before, but singing in another language was quite a challenge. I had been able to participate in singing at church because I had a hymn book and could read (if not understand) the words. However, standing in the dark streets and at the doors of the homes we visited, I could not read the words and felt somewhat lost. However, after singing the same songs several times, I was able to take part and thoroughly enjoyed seeing people respond to our singing, seemingly very pleased to have us there. Though some were Spiritists and others Catholics, they welcomed this evangelical church group. Music is the universal language and has a way of opening up hearts to the gospel message.

On New Year's Eve, the church held a watch night service during which we took communion and had a feet washing service. These were very meaningful times to me, thinking about how the body of Christ all over the world is unified through our faith in Him. Some of the singers in the praise team were daughters of *Senhor Joaquim* and *Dona Julia*, an elderly couple in the Candida Church who had 19 children. Following the service, we enjoyed a midnight banquet of typical holiday Brazilian dishes brought by the members.

I was privileged to be part of other special occasions during the holidays. On one occasion, Kemper invited the staff of his language school to their home for a dinner party. It was a very interesting mix of guests from various countries, each bringing a dish from their culture, with Shirley providing the main course.

One teacher brought her husband, a soccer player in Italy who was home for the holidays. One person was Japanese, and another was a Brazilian lady who had worked as a secretary to the former President of Brazil. Everyone was able to speak and understand Portuguese as well as their own native tongue, and some also spoke English. Since I was the only one who didn't speak Portuguese, Kemper and Shirley were constantly translating for us throughout the meal.

Tânia took me to *Riberão Preto*, about two hours away, where Cindy and her family lived. While there, I visited their church where second-generation missionary John Poole was the pastor. After evening services, we went to a *pizzeria* with a large group from the church. The group included Luciana Francoi Campos, a young lady I knew already who had visited the US and attended our Combs Family Reunion. Even the pizza was different, topped with almost any food you could imagine, including corn, green beans and boiled eggs.

Cindy's family came back with us to Araras for Christmas. As we traveled, I loved seeing the beautiful green countryside with huge trees and lush vegetation for mile and miles. The picturesque scene was how I had always pictured Brazil in my mind's eye.

We all went to buy groceries so each of us could make special dishes and desserts. I was surprised to find that the super market in *Ribeirão Preto* was huge, about twice the size of our modern Wal-Mart stores. I couldn't believe the number of check-out lanes – around 30 of them – all busy ringing up customers. I bought the ingredients to make cheesecakes, one of Jim's favorites, but found I had to substitute several items that were not available there, including cream cheese and graham crackers.

We had a large family dinner on Christmas Eve and exchanged our gifts. On Christmas Day afternoon, Jim and Shirley hosted a *churrasco* (Brazilian barbecue) inviting all the children and adults from the *Lar Nova Vida* Children's Home, as well as their parents who lived in the area, and the caretaker's family. For hours Jim and José Augusto continued to load meat onto the grill as about 65-70 of us enjoyed the delicious meal around the picnic tables in the pavilion. The kids frolicked in the pool all afternoon, stopping just long enough to eat a second and third time. A few stayed very close to their parents since this was the only time some had seen their family in months.

One striking contrast to our American culture at that time was the mixture of racial and ethnic groups. There seemed to be every combination of Europeans, Africans, Asians, and Indians who were intermarried, and it seemed to make no difference among them. This was true in every part of the culture, but I especially noticed it in the churches since that isn't always the case in the United States.

Jim and Shirley were busy every day during the two weeks I was there, constantly interacting with neighbors, townspeople, church members, *Lar Nova Vida* staff and children, and their own family. That activity didn't stop at sunset, since their phone often rang in the middle of the night.

Before leaving Brazil, they took me with them on errands allowing me to see glimpses of ordinary day-to-day life. We were also invited to visit in the home of one of their church members, an upper-income family. Their home was adequate and functional, but not nearly as elaborate as I expected for a well-to-do business owner and his family.

Cindy and Tânia also took me to a mall in Rio Claro, giving me a glimpse of the retail clothing market and fashions worn by Brazilian women.

My trip to Brazil was very enjoyable and enlightening. Everywhere I went, I was warmly received, and a few people practiced their English in conversations with me. I hope to return someday and see more of this beautiful country and the friendly, welcoming people who live there.

CHAPTER 6
Go Team Rejoice Made a Big Difference for One Family

Each mission team that goes to Brazil not only completes the suggested projects given by the church administration or LNV board, but asks what they can do for the Brazilian pastors and workers or what they can do for the helpers at the Children's Home. One year the Rejoice Free Will Baptist Church in Owasso, Oklahoma made possible a very special gift. A specially made, manual wheel chair that could not be found in Brazil. It was for the son of a deacon in one of our churches in *Ribeirão Preto, São Paulo*. I asked him to tell his story from his own heart.

Death Message at the Gate
(The following is translated from Portuguese to English)

Mardem Ferreira, Brazilian Deacon
Soon after we married we had our first son, Rodrigo. At that time I worked with fruits and vegetables. After seven years, our son, Demerval, was born. For the second time my wife, Maria, passed through a period of depression which lasted about three to four years. It was a time when I wasn't able to work much since Demerval was still a baby and I had to help her to take care of him. Sometimes I would go to work and have to return home quickly because she was sick.

We were Catholics. Not practicing Catholics,

but more from tradition. We looked for healing for her in all directions except in the true direction. We even went to the lowest level of voodoo Spiritism.

We had a neighbor, Dirce, and she was already an Evangelical Christian. She liked us a lot. She was always inviting us to visit her Church. One day we were so tired of *running after the wind* and my wife said that she wanted to go to the church of that *Lady*. We marked to go with her on Sunday.

When we arrived at the church, I read the sign: *Igreja Batista Livre*. (Free Will Baptist Church) It wasn't easy on those first visits since we didn't understand anything about the Bible. The people there seemed so different from us, but with time we started noticing that those people took a great interest in us, and this was making a difference in our lives.

The Ferreira family

Maria began to improve a little at a time. Soon we began to go to church camp meetings where we saw many people giving testimonies of their lives. People converting to a belief in Christ. At the end of the camps people would leave crying. This showed us we needed to continue there in the midst of those people whom we found different.

We became interested in knowing more about the Word of God. We felt we were in the right place for that, because the church had many people who were students of the Word of God. And many of them wanted to help us also know the Word.

It was at that time that I perceived that God talks to us through His Word. We came from a religion that did not know the Bible. I came across a scripture in Matthew 22:29 when Jesus said: "You don't know the scripture neither the power of God." I discovered there how much we do wrong by not knowing the Word.

Soon I was learning more and more of the Bible and how it was showing us where we came from and where we were going. In John 8:32 it says: "You will know the truth and the truth will set you free." I saw through this verse that we were spiritual prisoners, and we didn't know it.

That was the reason we blindly searched for God. We even searched for Him in Spiritism. God started giving us a clear understanding of His truth. That is when we began feeling true happiness. Our happiness was contagious for other people. Our lives were being transformed and everything we did, someone from the church was with us. We began to see in the church one large family that we didn't know before. We were never alone again because brothers and sisters were always with us.

We never missed a program in the church. Our children liked it very much and made many friends. They could hardly wait for time to go to the camp or family retreats because everyone would be together.

After a while we noticed that the woman (my wife) who was always unhappy, always wanting to stay alone and not talk to anyone, and crying all the time, was not there anymore! Now she was a woman who felt happiness in everything she saw and did. My wife was born again. She is a new creature and born again.

By this time we had been in the church for four years, and we made the correct decision to follow Christ in baptism. We knew by then that this was what we needed to do and that we were on the right path. We never wanted to leave that path. What we wanted to do was to be baptized. So Missionary Pastor Bobby Poole scheduled the service and baptized us in 1984.

In 1988 I was ordained as a deacon of the church. I was very timid before I became a Christian. Some of my customers were doctors and professional people, and I could not look them in the eye when I needed to talk to them. What a transformation! I started sharing Christ with these same people and with anyone I had contact with, without timidity. Just a contagious enthusiasm to share God's Word. Soon after our baptism I started taking part in the spiritual leadership of the church. I started for a while leading the prayer meetings which God used, not only in the life of the church but in my life also. Every week we were in communion with the people of the church. Like Joshua 24:15 says: "I and my house will serve the Lord."

We started to have Bible studies, prayer meetings, and family devotions in our home. Not only in our home, but I also did this in other homes each week where God used us marvelously. Our house became a meeting place for all ages of our brethren from the church, and this made us very happy.

This went on for a long time until our first and greatest tribulation happened. The great valley that was to appear for us to face. I entitle it: The Unexpected.

The Unexpected

Everything started when our youngest son at 14 years old became involved with drugs. We were already evangelical Christians. I had been a deacon in the church for several years and had a ministry of leading the prayer meetings and having Bible studies in homes.

But the Lord says in I Peter 5:8: "Be sober, be vigilant; because your adversary the devil, as a roaring lion, walks about, seeking whom he may devour." When he says "seeking whom he may devour," I believe it means someone who is following the path of Christ. His strategy at times is not to attack that person who is on his knees, but to attack a beloved one who is not vigilant or who is not doing what pleases the Lord. Yes, they would be an easier target and would hit you directly at the same time. That is the reason Jesus said: "The devil came to kill, steal and to destroy."

That is the way the devil tried to destroy us during many years of struggle.

Our son Demerval was not able to free himself from drugs. There were some periods of his being placed in a rehab home and other attempts to help him, but nothing happened. Things got worse instead of better. One day he had his eighteenth birthday, and the next week he was in jail for the first time. He was stealing in order to support his habit.

Who's Clapping At Our Gate?

I was working with fruits and vegetables, and I delivered to the house of a very well-known lawyer in our city, *Senhor Saad.* When I talked to him about Demerval, he was able to get Demerval released after 13 days. I had visited him once during that time.

Praying a lot during these days, the Lord gave me a word in John 10:3: "The sheep hear his voice: and he calls his own sheep by name, and leads them out." He gives them direction and security, and with this promise the Lord strengthened me.

But the Lord was always with us and told us: The battle is not over, and you must persevere. So our whole life was to pray for the life of Demerval. It even looked like the more we prayed the more bad things happened. He just couldn't stop using drugs.

He would leave in the evenings only returning the next day, and we couldn't keep him at home. He would come home, take a bath, eat, and sleep all day. We couldn't get him awake, and we thought maybe he wouldn't go out that night. But we were wrong. When the sun started going down he would wake up, and no one could hold him back at home. He went back to the streets. Many times I went out looking for him, but I never found him. His *friends* were not truthful and said they had not seen him.

Every night my wife and I knelt down in our bedroom to pray and cry for the life of our son. But Proverbs 14:26 says: "In the fear of the Lord is strong confidence: and his children will have a place of refuge." Always the Lord gave me a Word saying: Even though Demerval wants to stay far away, I will save his life.

Demerval finally reached the point where he

used crack cocaine. That was the most difficult time for all of us. How many times the sun rose with me on my knees praying for our son. How many times I went out to look for our son. How many times I went out looking for him during the wee hours of the morning.

Finally, it happened that my son went to jail for the second time. He stayed there for six months. At that time I had a prison ministry. I never thought I would find my son in one.

In the prison ministry we saw many spiritual battles, people used by Satan. Many times I was confronted by people completely surrendered to the will of Satan. But I also observed victories among those who heard the Word of God. The Word transformed the lives of many prisoners, and one is now a leader of an Assembly of God Church.

Time passed and, without our knowing it, Demerval was transferred to an agricultural farm 230 kilometers (150 miles) from our house. It was more difficult for us to visit at that distance, and visits from the family are very important to the person in treatment. We made our visits every two weeks for one year and four months. After this time he was finally released.

At this time my business was restoring furniture and Demerval started working with me. He was doing very well. I had bought a 1984 used Chevette. It was my first family car. The only thing I had before were old Kombi Volks buses (1961 then 1973) that I used in the work I had before. But Demerval started wanting to buy the Chevette from me, making payments a little at a time. He already had his driver's license, and he wanted to drive it at times. But it was my very first car. Each

Sunday when we left church, he was sitting in the car wanting to drive it.

One Sunday the Sunday School lesson really spoke to me. When I left church Demerval was already waiting on me in the car and asked for the keys. He was always reminding me that he wanted to buy the car. But that Sunday before I left the door of the church God had spoken to me. I got in the car with him, and he said once again, "Dad, why don't you sell me this car? I'll pay you just right."

That's when I looked him in the eyes. I took the keys and held them up for him to see. I said, "Demerval, I am not going to sell you this car. Today I am giving you this car."

I could see the shine in his eyes, then tears and great happiness. We hugged each other and cried together. For a long time after that I could feel a peace in my heart so great, followed by happiness. Like I had conquered something greatly waited for.

Demerval continued working with me. Soon he traded the car for one newer. He was always proud of the car. He continued to work and put his money together and soon traded that car for a newer one yet. It was a 1998 model. But he wasn't ready to deal with material gain.

He started going out a lot. He started using drugs again. Not like before, but for someone who has had problems so serious before, it is a great danger that he could fall again. He was still going to church, but he used drugs anyway.

One of his friends bought a large motorcycle. He was desperate to take the bike for a ride. Twice he asked his friend to let him ride, but he refused. On the third time, he left his new car with his friend and wanted to just take a short ride, so his friend gave in. The worst thing happened in our lives.

The Crash

Demerval crashed the motorcycle into a car and suffered a cranial traumatism– a TCE *Grave,* breaking the plexus of his right arm. We found out when a young man came desperately running to our house and called at the gate,

"*Senhor* Mardem, Demerval had an accident and died. He is at the corner dead!"

It was 1:30 p.m. and my wife and I were having lunch. I just looked at my wife and said, "We are not going to despair. We have to believe in the Lord, now."

We got in the car and quickly headed up to the place, praying all the way. When we got close to the place, there were many people and two ambulances. But when I looked at the scene only God could give me strength.

His head on the right side was caved in. His eye was almost popped out. He was lying in a pool of blood. The paramedics were treating him like a dead body. When they found out we were his parents, they backed up some. We knelt by his side. My wife held onto his hand, and I lifted his head a little in the middle of that blood. I closed my eyes and prayed,

"Father, your word of promises over the life of Demerval hasn't come to pass, yet. Please have mercy on us, Senhor."

Right then Demerval opened his eyes. He appealed to God, "Jesus, what have I done? Raise me up from here, Lord." He fell unconscious.

At that same time I remembered God's word. "If you call upon me in your anguish, I will rescue you." God always gives me a word of promise when I need it, so I knew I would wait upon the Lord.

The ambulance people started transferring him into the vehicle and we followed him to the hospital. We arrived there immediately. In the emergency ward they tried to revive him.

30 Days in the Hospital

It was 2:15 p.m. when they took him to the surgery room. I stayed there waiting. Praying. Later I went up to the second floor to a waiting room. I stayed there until someone advised me that he was being brought down to another section. It was 2:25 a.m.

The moment I saw them carrying Demerval on the stretcher/gurney, I didn't recognize him. He was full of tubes and wires from machines. He was swollen and his head was all wrapped in bandages. The doctors were running quickly beside the stretcher. His broken arm was wrapped and his face was all dark with bruises.

The paramedics were saying to go quickly, go quickly. I didn't know what to say anymore. "God have mercy on my son." I continued to stay there. Waiting and praying. After 3:00 a.m. I returned home.

I found my wife, her sister, and Demerval's wife all crying a lot. I tried to calm them and told them that he would be better. All this happened at 1:30 p.m. on a holiday Wednesday afternoon on November 2, 2005. It was *O Dia dos Mortos,* The Day of the Dead. One more great battle was beginning in our family.

Thursday morning at 7:30 we were already at the door of the hospital, but the visit at the ICU only began at 9:00 a.m. When we entered the unit, there were nine beds with patients in all sorts of difficult situations. I confess that I didn't recognize my son because he was much more swollen and his face all black with bruises. His head was wrapped and we saw written: *without bone.* We couldn't understand why that was written that way.

After a while someone from the hospital arrived in the room. It was the hospital psychologist. She began talking to my wife and asked how she was related to the patient. She said, "He is my son."

She asked, "Have you seen something like this before?"

Maria said, "No, but I had expected to never see my son again."

She began trying to comfort Maria, and Maria would say, "He is in God's hands. He knows what He is doing."

On Friday we went to the hospital early and went home for lunch. At about 2:00 pm, the hospital called saying the doctor wanted urgently to talk to the parents of Demerval. We immediately left for the hospital. Doctor Fernando, one of the doctors who operated on Demerval, was waiting for us. He gave us news that was not encouraging.

"The clinical picture for your son is not good. It is getting worse. The blood clots have taken over his entire head and we needed to open it again," he said.

I asked, "Doctor, is there a risk he could die?

He answered, "Look, like I already said, his clinical picture is not good. It is most serious. If he stays like he is, he dies. If we open his head again to take out the clots, he could die in the surgery. I think we should try to save him."

I paused a moment and said we needed to pray. I told the doctors, "Look, do what you think you need to do." We signed the necessary documents for the doctors and returned to our home. Only God knows how heavy our hearts were at that hour.

On the way home God had put on my heart to have a prayer vigil. I called our pastor John Poole and told him that Demerval was worse and we were going to have a prayer vigil for him at 8:00 p.m. At ten till 8:00 p.m. 26 brothers and sisters arrived to unite in prayer with us.

We began to pray and to praise God. It was a marvelous time of worship. At fifteen minutes before midnight the last one to pray was Andrew, the pastor's young teenage son. He was kneeling in the middle of the living room crying before the Lord. He could hardly pray but when he finished his plea to the Lord, we immediately all felt a peace fall on us in that room.

We felt like the time when God had spoken to His people of Israel in Exodus 3:7, 8, "I have surely seen the affliction of my people and have heard their cry for I know their sorrow. And I have come down to deliver them."

This was the word that came into my mind and heart at that moment, and all of us were at peace when they returned to their homes. My wife and I lay down and rested a little. Seven hours later we were back at the hospital to hear a report about the surgery.

When Dr. Fernando saw us entering in the hallway, he looked at us and quickly held up his two hands and said, "Look. A better report now. Since he is young, his body reacted well. The clots all disappeared!"

That's when I told him in a firm voice, "May God be praised and thanked in all our lives!"

The doctor said, "Well, continue with that faith, because only God can correct this situation."

Every morning and afternoon at visitation time Maria and I would be there at his bedside. My prayer was always the same as I stood at the foot of his bed holding his feet. "Father, may these feet rise up from here to testify to Your great work in the life of this my son. For the honor and glory of your name, Amen." This prayer was made for 30 days in the ICU where he was.

Some of the doctors were used like those in the Biblical story of Jairus. They would say, "Look, you need to get used to seeing him like this. Perhaps he could be like this for the rest of his life."

He didn't move at all – not even to blink his eyes – his eyes remained open at all times. He could move nothing, nothing. But always when someone said something contrary to our hope, I would say, "But in the name of Jesus, our Savior, he is going to walk." I wouldn't despair and just couldn't see him paralyzed that way for the rest of his life. Near the end of 30 days in the hospital, the doctors started advising us that they were going to release Demerval to go home.

My wife started worrying a lot. The situation he was in, he could not move anything. Not even a little finger. Not even his tongue. He had an open trachea and every hour the secretion in his throat had to be suctioned so that he would not choke. At the hospital it was hard for her to stay in the room when they were doing the procedure. Now it would be her job to do this when he went home. She began to pray and pray with all her might.

The next weekend the doctors said, "Today Demerval is going home." My wife asked, "But doctor, is he going home still in this shape?"

"Yes, you stay in the room with him, and I will return with the release papers and see how he is."

We waited in the room, but Maria was very stressed out about the open trachea. The doctors soon returned from the infirmary with bandages and medicines. The first thing the doctor did was to take that tube from Demerval's throat. He cleaned everything and put a bandage over the hole. He said, "Now you don't have to worry about cleaning this place. It will close up by itself now."

With a great sigh Maria declared, "Thank you, Lord."

The doctor said, "Now what Demerval needs most is great hygiene and love from you folks." With that we took him home.

Paralyzed But Home

We arranged a hospital bed for him. Our older son, Rodrigo, helped us a lot. He was in the United States but was always participating in our needs. He paid for his physical therapy and always helped us with expenses at home and everything that Demerval needed for his recuperation. Even though he was far away, he never,

never let us lack for anything. He was with us daily as we faced the battles.

I thank his wife Tânia and their children, Daniel, Bianca, and Isabela, because I know that they sacrificed to help us all these years. Like God says in His word "He will recompense and reward." God is pleased with those who give with happiness, because we could see in their faces a semblance of happiness and contentment when they gave.

Also, we thank the many Christian brothers and sisters and churches who were with us in prayer. Even churches in the United States helped us. One church, Rejoice Free Will Baptist in Oklahoma, provided a specially designed wheelchair. May God pay them back many times over.

But we returned to our day to day battles which were not easy We bathed him daily with him on his bed because he couldn't move anything. He was fed through a tube for one year and eight months.

We prepared a room especially for him. We have a two- story home and his room is on the second floor. Demerval's room has a balcony. In the mornings we rolled him in his bed onto the balcony to get some sun which did him a lot of good.

Sometimes we gave him a bath out on the balcony. It had a high fence around it to give privacy, and we could tell by his face that he liked it. Sometimes on hot nights we rolled his bed out there under the stars. I would talk to him showing him the stars.

One night a plane was flying low over our house, and I said, "Look at that big plane passing over us." When I looked at him, I saw he was happy and his eyes followed the plane. It was an important sign with his eyes. They had been fixed before and didn't move. For us it was an incomparable happiness to see this small progress. How faithful is our God to us.

Even at that, Satan didn't stop shooting his flaming arrows at us. Once in a while people would visit us, and on their way out they said things like, "He looks like he won't get any better." And sometimes they would say to Demerval's wife, "You are a young woman and pretty. I have seen cases like this before and I can tell you that it is almost impossible to reverse his condition." For some one that is not spiritually grounded, it can be a problem. And that is what happened. His wife left him.

But we were not discouraged, and continued to take care of him with love and tenderness. We learned how to communicate with him. He blinked once to answer yes and twice to answer no. This is how we communicated with him for a long while.

At this time we had his two small children with us. Gabriel and Guilherme. They had always lived with us, and their mother had another child by another man by this time. I talked to her and told her I wanted to be the guardian of the two boys. Since she knew that my wife and I had always taken care of them in love, she agreed. The guardianship that I have is permanent. It gives us the authority to care for them as parents would.

After 11 months Demerval began to talk. Each day we could recognize his improvement. He always had physical therapy, and we took him twice a week to hydrotherapy. At first it looked like there was no way he could do it, but we wouldn't let ourselves get discouraged. Demerval had a great desire and determination to walk again.

We were always at the doctors looking for some way to improve his treatment. But one day we learned that his hips had calcified from being immobile for so long and because of the medicine he took for his cranial trauma. Being calcified made it impossible to walk. This news was another great setback for him.

But I didn't forget my prayers in that ICU unit in the hospital asking the Lord, "Father, may these feet rise up from here and testify one day to your great power."

We were able to get a consultation with hip specialists. Demerval was so happy and hopeful to have surgery to be able to walk again. This was his dream. We went to the hospital, and after the doctors talked to us they ran many x-rays. Finally they called us in to give us the results of the x rays. Three doctors were on one side of the table and Demerval and I were on the other side. They looked at Demerval and said, "Look, this type of calcification of the hips leaves us nothing to do."

I could tell that Demerval was losing control and he said, "Do you mean that I will never walk again, Doctor?" He answered, "There is nothing more we can do." Demerval began crying broken hearted.

At that moment I placed my hand on his shoulder and said, "Stay calm, son. They are doctors and they are human. Just like you and I are human and limited. But we have a God that goes beyond medicine. They began the healing of your body but it isn't over yet."

That's when I began testifying to the doctors about our faith. I told them that to know Christ as Lord and Savior of our lives was the most important thing that any human being could have. The last word in our lives had to be the Lord.

One of the doctors got up and left the room but the other two stayed. One of them told me to keep believing like that.

We left, and I know that Demerval was very discouraged. But in my heart the Lord was speaking from I Samuel 2:30, "I said indeed that your house, and the house of your father, should WALK before me forever. For them that honor me, I will honor, and they that despise me shall be lightly esteemed."

The next week Demerval was doing hydro massage when his physiotherapist stood him up in the swimming pool, leaning against the side to see his equilibrium. He brought him a little away from the side to see his reaction. He said, "Come to me, Demerval."

Demerval began walking toward him by himself. It even surprised his doctor. He started walking all the way to the other side of the pool to the honor and glory of our God. From that day on he didn't stop. Each day he walked more and more.

This was a great victory for us, which we could testify to our great and marvelous God. Each time that God gave us opportunity to tell of these blessings it gave us great happiness to talk to people. We tell how God has been merciful to our family.

The field of medicine said he probably would never talk. Today he talks.

They thought he would not be able to eat regular food. Today he struggles, but feeds himself with his one good arm.

Who's Clapping At Our Gate?

They said he would probably never walk. Today he can walk short distances.

When we started telling our story, we never dreamed that the Lord would take us so far away, because we testified even in the United States four times. They could see for themselves at the end of the services when Demerval would rise from his wheelchair and walk across the front of the church and back. I said he walks a little like *Robocop* but he is walking, praise God! In His word He says, "He is able to do far more that we could ask or think." To Him we give glory.

This shows us how faithful our Lord is. We are traveling to our true country (heaven) and we will continue on because if God is for us, who can be against us?

If you have something in your life that has been a weight and burden and you haven't obtained the victory yet, dearest friend, remember that it is the Lord that says in Mathew 11:28, "Come to me all you who are weary and heavy laden, and I will give you rest." This word is today for you. This is the promise of God for your life. . Hold on to this promise because God is Faithful. You will be victorious.

May the Lord bless you and keep you!!

Thank you, Lord.

Mardem Feirreira and family, Ribeirão Preto, São Paulo, Brazil,

CHAPTER 7
Rosana and Her Second Chance Team from South Carolina

When we hosted our first large groups of mission teams, we didn't have our hospitality house to receive the guests at that time. The month we had a group of 18 from one church in South Carolina and some from other churches in the state, our Brazilian families opened their homes. Several men stayed at the Candida FWB church with sleeping bags in the balcony and one shower down stairs. Some girls stayed at Sonia Krepsky's house. Roberto Oliveira hosted some at his house. Some women stayed at Lina's house. We hosted nine at our house.

We scheduled team volunteers from the group to be official drivers to collect all these people and take them to either the church work site or the Children's Home. At noon we collected them from the two work sites to serve them lunch together at the Children's Home. Then back to the work sites after lunch and again in the evening to take everyone to their host homes. Maybe you can see where we got the idea for a hospitality house? Hey, we had a great time, and it was all worth it.

How did it start? A message on a marquee at a Free Will Baptist church in South Carolina invited the public for services where missionaries Andy Moore and

David Aycock from Brazil were speaking. *Rosana Guimaraes*, a Brazilian, saw the sign and attended evening services. After the message, she went forward to talk to missionary David, and they prayed together. She told me later how wonderful it was for someone to pray with her in her own language. The Moores gave Rosana a book I had written about our ministry with street children in her country of Brazil. She was touched – her Brazilian "children" in Brazil were being cared for by Americans. She was a Brazilian in the USA and this was her opportunity to help. But how?

She called *Lar Nova Vida* in *Araras* about their needs. The house father answered her call. He told her that the home had an open shelter on their property that could be closed in and put to good use. I was not there at the time, but she shared her testimony and vision with other Free Will Baptist churches and organized her state to help with the projects.

Later she contacted me with her idea and Jim designed the building.

The South Carolina group arrived in São Paulo and were taken to *Araras* by bus where they participated in many ways. They took gifts for the children, a hard-working attitude, and much love for the Brazilian Christians. They met the mayor of *Araras* in his office where he thanked them as volunteers in his city to help with *Lar Nova Vida*. They provided material and money for labor for an Activity Building on our property. They had newspaper coverage in which Rosana gave a stirring, courageous testimony of her faith in Christ. The kids loved being around them.

In churches they gave testimonies, sang, and

preached. Rosana could help us translate for the group, and one of the very competent members of the communications team was Mark Cowart who grew up in Brazil as a missionary kid. He was a great help in all areas. They had a busy, blessed ministry to *Lar Nova Vida* kids and staff, as well as the church and city folks.

The Activity Building serves as a chapel, library, a place for choir and orchestra concerts, music/classrooms, offices, a nice room for benefit dinners, bazaars, and a gym for Jiu-Jitsu classes. At times it has also served as housing for older kids and staff members. On some days during rainy season you may walk through the chapel and see lines and lines of clothes trying to dry during the damp and rainy days.

The highlight for many groups is the soup ministry in a slum area. Their group was there in the beginning years. The Cabrini family owns four *Tiradentes* Supermarkets in *Araras*. They furnished the vegetables from one market which we spent hours cleaning and preparing for the huge pots of soup. Another of their markets furnished 150 bread rolls to hand out with the soup. Once a year these markets give a ton of food to LNV – sugar, flour, rice, beans, pastas, and special boxed liquid milk that does not require refrigeration until opened, and more. They have not only helped our home, but many other charitable organizations in town. And, the Cabrini brothers, Eixe and Junior, also visited our family in the USA.

With the help of this energetic group, we would load up the old Volks Van group along with the huge pots of soup and sacks of bread and drive to the slum area. Some families lived in tents with dirt floors, no water or lights. But on the evening we served the soup, folks would line up with their pans or plastic bowls and wait for the prayer. The volunteer groups couldn't speak Portuguese, but they would smile and serve in Jesus' name. They saw scenes they would not soon forget.

I wasn't present at Rosana's conversion, so I want to give you that story from a missionary who was there that night. The following is copied from an article by Annette Aycock, in *Heartbeat* magazine:

Rosana Guimaraes/Annette Aycock, South Carolina
Seeking a sign from God, Rosana's eye caught sight of a simple church sign which led to her transformation.

Rosana Guimaraes is a beautiful, vibrant Brazilian. She is the wife of Eduardo and mother of Carolina, age 12. She had been searching for hope and meaning for her life for many years. Her search really began after her brother, Rogerio, moved to Canada and met a Christian woman named Joanne who led him to the Lord. Rosana saw the transformation in her brother's life and desired what he had.

Joanne continually prayed and witnessed to Rosana by phone over a four-year period. On one particular night in September of 2000 Joanne prayed with Rosana and told her that God was waiting for her. "God will send someone or something into your life…a person, a SIGN!" she exclaimed.

The next day Rosana was driving her daughter home from school when she spotted a sign in front of a church close to her house. The sign read, "Please come join us for our missions' conference. Tonight: Andy Moore from Brazil." The First Free Will Baptist Church of Florence, S.C., was holding their annual missionary conference. She turned the car around to get a second look at the sign. Did she really see what she thought she saw? She stopped in the parking lot and prayed, "God, is that the *sign* you wanted me to see? Please, God, help me."

Rosana had only lived in Florence for two months, but she knew this was not a coincidence. She went inside the church and learned that Andy Moore would be speaking that evening and David Aycock, who was born in Brazil, would speak the following night. She was urged to attend.

The Brazilian was there to hear Andy preach. She was very impressed that such a young couple as the Moores would leave their country and go to hers in search of lost souls.

The next night Rosana returned to the church and brought her family. 'What happened that night completely changed my life," Rosana declares. "David, his wife and their four children had decided to return to Brazil as missionaries. David talked about my country, my people, my culture, and my life. He was so sure of the work of the gospel that I started to open my heart to God. He showed us a Brazil that I did not know.

"David said, 'God loves you so much that He will bear your hurt and sorrow for you. You just have to open your heart to Him' I stared up at the altar and whispered, 'Please, God, I need you."

At that moment I felt His presence. It was so intense. It was better than anything I had ever tried in my life. This was love sweeter than anything. "There have been many miracles in my life – a loving husband, a perfect daughter, good friends, and living in this blessed country – but this miracle was the greatest. This was the miracle of God's love."

After the service, David asked Rosana if she was ready to give her life to Christ. She told him she was ready for God to come into her heart. "At that moment, David led me to the Lord in my own language," the vibrant Brazilian declared. "This was a true moment of GLORY! Praise the Lord!"

One week after Rosana was saved the Moores gave her a book, *A Second Chance,* by missionary Shirley Combs.

Rosana leads the South Carolina mission team

The book relates the ministry of saving street children in Brazil. Rosana read two pages and knew in her heart that God wanted her to help save the children of her country!

The new Rosana called Shirley Combs in Brazil and said, "Madam, I am a brand new Christian, and just started my relationship with the Lord. I am amazed at the job you are doing with my children in Brazil. What can I do to help you?"

Shirley responded, "Rosana, to me, just knowing that you are a Christian is already a blessing. If you want to come here just to be with us, come and let our children bless you with their love."

Rosana says she was "very excited about it" and started talking with Eddie Hobbs and other people of her church. She learned of a need and was able to gather 18 Christians from her church and some other South Carolina churches to go to Brazil in June 2001. They became the **Second Chance Team.** Their plan was to finish an activity center for *"Lar Nova Vida"* (New Life Home), a children's home which cares for more than 30 destitute street children. Today most of them are Christians.

Rosana and Eddie Hobbs arranged a group training and orientation session with James Evans of Benchmark Ministries in Nashville, Tenn. Then a video team from Foreign Missions accompanied the group to Brazil.

Rosana traveled 1,500 miles and gave her testimony in 23 churches, the South Carolina State Association, five woman's auxiliary meetings, and three pastors' breakfasts. Most gave love offerings. Some people participated in a walk-a-thon, others washed cars and trucks, and some held garage sales. They raised over

$26,000 - $8,000 above their $18,000 goal.

When the team departed for Brazil, their luggage carried more than 700 pounds of clothing, shoes, and toys for the children over and above the cash raised for construction. One South Carolina store donated five boxes of clothing to the cause.

Although the volunteers were unable to complete all of the work needed on the building, they showed love and care for the children in the home. "I really believe the team made an impact," says Rosana. "They came with their work clothes on and the people of Brazil could feel the love they had for the children."

The blessings of this trip moved Rosana to encourage others to do something similar. "It is important for you as a believer to go to other countries and participate in missionaries' work there because it will change your life forever."

A church sign! A simple thing, but God used it to help change a life, which led to mobilizing a group and blessing others. (Written by Annette Aycock, *Heartbeat* Magazine, Vol. 43, No. 2)

CHAPTER 8
Brad Leads Okie Teams

Rejoice Go-Team

"Some are called to go, and some are to send," my preacher father taught. And since 1964 many, many churches have been gracious and obedient in sending our family to Brazil. I was attending a Free Will Baptist church in Owasso, Oklahoma, that my father started when I went off to Nashville to attend Free Will Baptist Bible College (now Welch College) to prepare for a life of missionary service.

Each furlough Jim and I would visit many, many generous and interested churches, and one of my very favorites was the church in Owasso. For most of those years it was pastored by Rev. Leonard Pirtle and his wife Carolyn, an extraordinary couple with a great world vision. It is now called Rejoice Free Will Baptist Church, and (at the time of this writing) it is pastored by Rev. Casey Carriker.

Rejoice Church helped us put out our field prayer letter, by snail mail at that time, and always gave us prayer support. When we began the ministry to Brazil's needy street children, *Lar Nova Vida*, Rejoice Church helped set up a sponsorship program for the children and opened an account especially for the children of *Lar Nova Vida*, called, Rejoice Ministries International – R.M.I.

They have a church mission board and a Go-Team that visits various mission fields. For many years they sent groups to our precious Brazilian children and churches. They are called "*igreja irma*" (sister church) by the Brazilian Christians.

One year their Go-Team helped put the roof on a church. Several times they helped paint a church and LNV. They moved the children's playground equipment from one lot to other. They lovingly prepared gift packages for children and workers. They were invited to speak to students in English classes in *Araras*. Their preaching, singing, teaching, and sharing their talents expressed their love to the children and adults of *Araras*. There are many stories of their groups ministering these over ten years which I will let them share with you in their own words.

M. Brad Bickerstaff, Oklahoma

I have been to Brazil 14 times in 11 years, and all were special and rewarding.

The first trip was Thanksgiving of 2000 when Pastor Leonard Pirtle, pastor of Rejoice Free Will Baptist Church in Owasso, Oklahoma, was looking for someone to make his first trip out of America. I checked some things out and Deborah, my wife, and I were able to travel with Pastor Pirtle on this trip. True, the flights were long and exhausting, but were well worth it to see the children of *Lar Nova Vida*. Wow, what an awesome blessing.

Over the 14 trips I coordinated for Rejoice Church, we had various group sizes. 32 was the largest group and the smallest ended up being me, a group of one, when the other three guys had problems with their visas.

Back to the 2000 trip. I was very touched by children at *Lar Nova Vida* and made plans to go back the following year. Jim and Shirley said that many short term missionaries say they would come back and told the children as well. Jim and Shirley said we, Deborah and I, were the first ones to actually go back to visit the children.

The second trip had lots of tears of joy as the children were so glad to see Deborah and me. They latched onto to us and did not want to let go. When we went to church, they would sit around us and on us, getting as close as they could. It was wonderful.

We had many experiences over the trips and years. Some of them are as follows.

Deborah and I were on a trip by ourselves, and we found out all the children, 30 or so, needed new shoes. Shirley made some contact with the owners of the Sonia Shoe Store, so we took all the children to their store. They closed up one hour early so we had the store to ourselves for one hour. Each child received a pair of shoes and they were so excited. I believe this came to a little over $325 (US dollars).

Brad and Deborah Bickerstaff

On another trip a couple years later, we took them shoe shopping again. This time it was a special occasion for two young ladies, Ana Paula and Ivani.

They were sisters who were graduating from the eighth grade and they received an extra pair of shoes for graduation. In Brazil, students are required to complete through the fourth grade and encouraged to complete the eighth. Students who don't have to drop out to work to help support their family, may continue through the eleventh grade.

Because of a shortage of school buildings, they utilize their buildings with three different sessions throughout the day. They go from 7:00 am to 12:00 noon, then 12:30 pm to 5:30 pm and the older ones who work, can study at night.

After a couple of trips, we got the hang of *churrasco (*a Brazilian meat experience) and would stop at the Appaloosa Restaurant on our way from the airport about an hour from *Araras.* This was no ordinary lunch. It was all the meat one could eat, with a huge salad bar and *guarana'* to drink (a very delightful ginger-ale-like soda pop drink).

Initially, when we started stopping there, it was about six US dollars for the meal. On my last trip in March 2011, it was around fifteen US dollars. Very well worth it and if you are ever in the area, I highly recommend it.

We would fly from Tulsa-Dallas-Brazil most of the time, leaving Tulsa around 4:00 pm and arriving in Brazil around 7:30 am the next morning. A chartered Van would pick us up if we were with a group or sometimes, after I could manage the language better to catch the right bus, we would go on a one and a half hour bus ride to Campinas where Jim and Shirley would pick us up. We liked to stop and eat at the *churrascaria,* and then go to their house to rest most of the first days of each trip.

One of Deborah and my trips ended up being 12 hours late with no way to contact Jim and Shirley. Our flight out of Dallas diverted to Cancun, Mexico. They announced over the intercom that it was due to the hurricane in the area which did not make sense to me. We were in an airplane and could fly around it and away from it.

Deborah and I were fortunate to be in business class on that trip, and the pilot came out and advised those of us in business class that the number two engine was using lots of oil and true, he said we could fly on one engine and get there, however, he thought it would be wiser to divert to Cancun.

They would bring in another airplane from Miami, offload all the baggage, reload it on the other plane, load the passengers and continue. While in Cancun, we were stuck in an in-transit lounge and could not go anywhere. We finally arrived in Brazil about 7:30 pm that trip.

As the coordinator for these trips, I made all the arrangements for the travelers, flights, passports, visas and transportation after we arrived in Brazil. Oh, did I mention, I became the designated driver while in Brazil? Jim and Shirley would let me borrow a car or Volks Kombi, all of them standard shift and most with no power steering, to transport our short-term missionaries around the *Araras* area. I drove the groups to and from *Lar Nova Vida*, churches, sometimes fishing, orange grove picking, delivery of soup to the Villa and Tent City. I became pretty familiar with the area and could get around well.

It is awesome driving in Brazil. The have *pare* signs (we call them STOP sign in the US), however in Brazil, if no one is coming, you better not stop. It is considered a yield sign and you just roll through it and keep going. Otherwise you may get run over or honked at and receive some stares. I received many stares as I am a tall, white skinned, fair haired redhead.

One of the most memorable trips was a couple of years ago. Kimberly, Pastor Pingo, and Shirley planned a sightseeing trip for our group of about eight. At the last minute Shirley felt impressed to stay to visit with *Senhor Joaquim* and *Dona Julia* while we made the trip.

As we were touring around, Kimberly received a call. It was a sorrowful call as we were informed Senhor Joaquim had just passed away. I believe he was 89 years old and the *Jardim Candida* Free Will Baptist Church had started on their front porch.

Shirley spoke at the funeral and mentioned that *Senhor Joaquim* asked about me. Moments after she left their house that afternoon, he fell dead in his home and we were all glad that she had that last afternoon with him. Our mission team prepared the church to receive the coffin for the all-night wake. Even though we couldn't speak the language, most of us sat with the family at the church until about 2:30 am.

The law in Brazil insists that the body be buried within 24 hours since there is no embalming, so we all were at the church at 9:30 the next morning. The church was full and people stood at the door and looked through the windows. The man's many children sang his favorite hymns around the casket of polished pine. I believe *Senhor Joaquim* and his wife, Julia, have 19 children. Three of their married daughters were attending the Candida church where the Lar Nova Vida children attended. His daughters are very special ladies and have wonderful singing voices.

We followed the procession to the cemetery and then had to hurry back to the hospitality house to pack our bags to leave for the US that day.

The funeral was quite an experience. Nothing like in the States. My eyes are blurry and I still get chocked up about it.

The Holy Spirit moves so freely when I'm at church in Brazil. I do not speak much of the language, but during a service, I get chills up and down my back and feel very blessed to have been in the presence of our Holy Spirit.

I sometimes sit and ponder and those sensations come back very quickly. I tried to sing along from the words on the overhead projector and tears just rolled from my eyes. Wow, what a cleansing and, oh, so powerful.

Deborah and I have sponsored several children at *Lar Nova Vida,* the last being Ezekiel who is a handsome young man. He has two older brothers, Messias and Elias. He and his brothers learned to play musical instruments in the church.

Unfortunately, the evil one wants to lure them and take them to the streets of *Araras.* There they get involved in drugs, gangs and alcohol. After the boys were returned to their families, they returned to the streets. The children's home found rehab help for them.

Who's Clapping At Our Gate?

The last we heard about Ezekiel, he was going back to church. God will need to put His hand of protection on him and around him. We pray not only for Ezekiel, but for ALL the children of *Lar Nova Vida*. For the spiritual well-being of those of the past, present, and the future.

There is just a great need for these children, for they barely had the clothes on their backs. LNV is a safe haven for them. Those that are awarded by the judge to go there have a much better chance of survival than being on the streets. They have medical needs, personal hygiene, food, clothing, shelter, education, play time, and spiritual nourishment all provided for them by people who love them.

We ALL are missionaries of Jesus Christ to spread His Good News throughout the world. In John 14, we are paid with JOY for the work we do to make known Jesus Christ for those who come across our paths.

There are so many more areas that could be discussed about the fourteen trips in eleven years. One was a song that I jotted down on a piece of paper that was being fed to me. The name of it is "Make a Way Lord". Hopefully, a way will be out there in the future, if I can find the correct folks to take it on.

Please pray for the children and if you can, assist with their many needs.

Janettia Lisenbee Alexander, Oklahoma

My trip to *Lar Nova Vida* taught me so many important lessons and sharpened my understanding of bringing light into darkness. I had been a sponsor of Lucas since he and his older brothers first went to *Lar*

Nova Vida when he was six years old. He had often been in my prayers, but I longed to someday meet him.

The opportunity came several years later in the summer of 2000 when I was asked to go with another couple to learn more about the children and to participate in a musical festival. Upon our arrival in São Paulo and our drive to *Araras,* the lessons began. Stretching for miles along the highway were piles of what I thought was trash. Shirley pointed out that those were actually cardboard and plastic tents where people lived. Unbelievable.

Not long after unloading our luggage at Jim and Shirley's house, we hopped in the van and made our way to the children's home. There I finally met my child, now a teenager, Lucas! He was shy at first, but we seemed to immediately connect. Shirley translated for me, and I gave him a brand new soccer ball, an OU hat, and a shirt. You would have thought that he won the jackpot.

I spent as much time as possible with him for the rest of the trip, but it was so hard not being able to communicate with him. I just wanted him to know I would never forget him and that I considered him to be my Brazilian son.

I soon learned where Lucas' mother lived when the Combs and a few people from their church took us to the *mud villa* for their weekly soup ministry trip. The evil and darkness there were palpable. It was thick and troubling to my spirit. I seemed to sense the danger of some of the men standing near the huts. I could see the emptiness and despair in the eyes of some women holding their babies. Yet, Jim and Shirley loved on them, fed them, visited with them, and cared for them like they were their own. Light in the darkness.

Leaving Brazil was bittersweet. I was ready to be home, but sad to know that would be my only meeting with Lucas. I later learned that the timing was perfect. Only a few months had passed when I received the news that Lucas' mother had been murdered in the villa. Though he lost his mother, I was sure that he knew his *American mother* was praying for him and thought of him every day. My husband and I talked about bringing Lucas to the US to live with us, but felt God telling us that He had plans for Lucas there in Brazil.

Much time has passed now. Lucas married and has a family of his own. What blesses me the most is that Shirley told me that he continued to serve the Lord and his family went to an Evangelical church there. He was one of the children who made the transition from darkness to light and was able to stand firm in the light after leaving *Lar Nova Vida*. Thank you, Lord. Thank you.

Julia Horstman, Oklahoma

Time has flown by since we went to Brazil to meet new friends and help in some way to bring a little something special into the lives of the children of LNV. Since that time my father has asked us to move in with him and Mom to help him care for Mom. She lost her battle to Alzheimer's this last December 8, 2011. Like our time with Mom, God gave us special time and memories of Brazil and the wonderful people we encountered. One thing Papa told me once was "Kids are kids all over the world." He was right. Regardless how much or how little a child has, a special light shines in their eyes when shown love and attention.

After our church's first group returned from Brazil my husband, Chuck, and I were struck with the desire to go ourselves and see what we could do to help. We held a few fundraisers, one being a motorcycle run. My best friend, Alisa Olglesby, and I stayed at the church while our husbands led the ride. They were given various ideas, hand signs, and advice about the bike runs after the ride, which would have been great to know before. Neither had been on a ride before. The Good Lord saw us through it anyhow and we all had a lot of fun.

Wes Holland, who had been to Brazil before, tried to teach us a bit of the Portuguese language. Poor Wes. He has such a God-given talent for languages and we DID NOT.

Finally the day of our trip arrived. After prayers and packing our bags, we headed to the airport. Most of the flight was overnight, and while most everyone on the plane slept, I – Miss Insomnia – paced the aisles of the plane and visited with the Lord and the few of our group who were awake.

Rejoice Church Group from Oklahoma

On arrival in the São Paulo airport, we went through customs. Alisa gave them her x-rays showing the metal she carries in her back from surgery. Most of us went straight through with no hitches, but a couple were selected to go a different route and had to open every item they had with them.

Once on our bus to *Araras,* we were in awe of the enormity of the cities and beauty of the land. One thing that struck me was seeing huge building and houses, busses, trucks, cars and people everywhere. And right in the middle of it all were shanties and lean-tos made of tin, boards, and cardboard or whatever they could build themselves for shelter. These people lived right among all those with affluence.

Those who had little to nothing would build a "home" where ever they could throw up a shelter of any kind. Thank you Lord for the much that I have, and help me not to be stingy or greedy with it.

We stopped at *a Churrasco* Restaurant and were introduced to Brazilian cuisine. What a feast. Then on to *Araras.*

Once we reached Jim and Shirley's place she clapped at the gate to have someone open it. We got settled in and enjoyed stretching our legs, checking out the compound, and taking in all the beautiful vegetation. I love plants and Brazil's are outstanding.

We learned that it is important for homeowners to wall their property to protect themselves from people coming in, and protecting their things from getting stolen.

Who's Clapping At Our Gate?

One of our mission projects was to paint the children's home and play with the kids. Alisa and I were limited on painting skills due to each of us having back problems from separate car accidents. Alisa's resulted in surgery, and mine resulted in back spasm set off by movements in raising my arms overhead.

Alisa noticed there was only one mirror in each house. It was located near the bathrooms and the little kids would have to be lifted up in order to see themselves. It was very important to her that the kids have mirrors in their rooms so they could see themselves and how they looked. I agreed. So we spent more work time with putting up boarders and shopping for mirrors for the kids.

Most of the kids were in school while we were painting. One of the older boys, I think it was José Carlos, helped us paint. I couldn't communicate in Portuguese and he couldn't in English. He would make a "who-who" sound, and I would answer back. I added more of a monkey sound ending to it. He let me know that was a bad thing, and not to make that noise. I never did find out what it was, but I think that they are considered bad luck or something.

When the other kids came home from school, we got to play with them. It was so rewarding to us to see the kids' eyes light up with the changes to their home. Though we didn't speak each other's language, our smiles, hugs, and games said a lot.

Julia and Chuck with
Dalvan and Alex

Many of the kids had
sponsors, but not all.
Chuck and I had been praying about sponsoring a child,
and one young man was laid on our hearts. He was the
oldest of three brothers. Dalvan was a sweet young man
and he seemed surprised that he would be chosen to be
sponsored. Shirley told us that it was good we had
chosen him, because the older kids were often
overlooked for the little kids.

God knows all, and if we keep our hearts and
minds open to Him, He will lead us. I heard the three
brothers had gone to live with their elderly father, but
after his death they returned to *Lar Nova Vida*. I
understand now that Dalvan has left the *Lar Nova Vida*
Children's Home and is trying with his meager resources
to take care of a special-needs brother and a sister. He
continues to be a sweet young man and continues to love
the Lord.

We had taken a couple of soccer balls to the
kids. They were so excited and began playing right
away. Alisa's two sons, Justin and Alexander, played
with the kids. About half an hour into their game, the
kids came back. They seemed almost frightened, but
definitely sad. The soccer ball had just popped.

We just smiled and shrugged to show them it
was alright. Things happen. They laughed, grabbed
another ball we offered them and started over again. We

decided that next time we need to buy a much better-quality ball. They surely played hard.

While the older boys played ball, some of the younger kids showed us how they could run, climb on short walls, and jump. They were so excited to entertain the strange talking *tias* and *tios* (aunts and uncles). What a delight they all were, both boys and girls from babes through teens.

The girls were more laid back and less active than the boys, but they enjoyed the gifts we shared with them. Each of the kids was delightful, sweet and loving. Each had his or her own unique story, trials and tribulations.

One special memory was making soup in the church kitchen with the girls from the home, the church ladies, and the ladies of our group. It was a fun bonding time. After making the soup in huge pots, we sat and shared a meal together, then we were joined by the Go-Team men and Brazilian men who had come from their jobs to take the soup and bread to the slum village where some of the children had relatives. It was called a tent city or something. Sorry, I can't remember the name. They lived in tents, with dirt floors and no electricity. Water was shared at a common faucet.

When we arrived in the old Van bus, the adults and children lined up with their bowls and pans and waited for the prayer. It was so fulfilling to be able to help feed people who are truly in need. Though some may have been drunk or stoned, they were respectful and seemed very appreciative of getting prepared food. We were warned that it could get ugly there and despite how bad the situation was there, I did feel the Lord's presence surrounding us. It made for a sweet event.

The ladies went to a special ladies night at the church, and we gave our testimonies. Speaking in front of people terrifies me, but I made it through. The ladies were all so open and understanding. I was so blessed by them. They made me feel special.

On Sunday we all attended church. Interacting was so sweet. We sang with them and for them, and they sang and shared with us. During Sunday School, we all divided up and paired off to teach and work with the kids. Bryan Oglesby and I were with the young ones, about five, six and seven years old. We sang "Jesus Love Me" in English, and I taught them how to sign it. The kids were so excited to learn and delighted with signing and singing.

Leaving was bittersweet. We were so glad to have the privilege to go there and give a helping hand. There is no place like home, though, and no matter how wonderful a place is, it was time to go home.

But even to this day, a piece of my heart remains in Brazil with those precious children and the wonderful people who gave them such good care. We tried to give a little something to each and every one, but they will never know how richly we were blessed because of them. I pray they will each keep the Lord God, our Savior, in their hearts.

Deborah Bickerstaff, Oklahoma

Thanksgiving weekend in 2000 would be the beginning of a change I could never have imagined. Who knew that Brazil (*Araras*) would hold a key to unlock some of God's love I had been keeping safe

Who's Clapping At Our Gate?

inside?

It all began in 1998 when as a widow with two young teen boys, I met and married a man who had joined Rejoice Free Will Baptist Church. M. Brad Bickerstaff was a very sweet, intelligent, people loving young Christian man who had a passion for Christ as all *baby* Christians do, a refreshing presence to be around.

He also loved traveling - by plane would be his favorite. So, when Brother and Sister Combs came to Rejoice Free Will Baptist Church and Shirley gave her testimony of being a missionary in Brazil, Brad was ready and willing to go to Brazil. When Shirley gave the invitation for any and all to visit, Brad came to me with the idea to go visit the Combs and the children at *Lar Nova Vida.*

I was a little reserved to say the least, not because I didn't love the Combs and the work they were doing. I'm just a little uncomfortable about new adventures. Why, who knew what those Brazilians would think of this middle aged, average American woman?

However, I did agree to go. After all, not only was Brad my husband but he was also my own personal travel agent. So, off we flew, butterflies and all, on a long 10-hour flight. This was just the first leg of the journey that would last years for me. I'll explain that later.

Wow! Look at the enormous city of Sao Paulo, Brazil. The city looked like it would never end. This is Brazil? The third world country I had thought about in my mind just did not match the view out the window of the plane.

When we landed and met the Combs, we had

another two-and-a-half-hour car ride before we arrive in *Araras*. But first, our gracious hosts would stop about midway for us to fill our stomachs at the famous *churrasco* restaurant, Appaloosa.

By the time we arrived at the Combs' house, my stomach and eyes were too full to contain all I had seen in just a few hours. I had been in this beautiful country with such contrasting people groups, of rich and poor, so many, everywhere I looked. Not just a handful of homeless men like I had noticed back home, but hundreds, if not thousands, of poor men, women and children. Brad and I were to stay about a week. How could my mind contain all I was seeing and hearing?

Lar Nova Vida children were like the children I loved and knew back in Oklahoma, only a little darker and speaking a different language. They were still loving, tender children ready for open arms and loving hearts to care for them. Time will not permit all my thoughts to be shared however, when Brad and I left, we both knew we would be back.

Brad and I would return to Brazil every year until 2007 when his mom, Rosa Bickerstaff started having dialysis treatments. Then the next year my grandmother was hospitalized and had part of her leg amputated, and then went to a nursing home. I stayed with her through the hospital stay and two weeks after she was sent to the nursing home. Brad continued to make trips to Brazil, but I stayed in Oklahoma taking care of family.

Meanwhile, we had started sending money to sponsor a child named Ezekiel, and I had met his older brother Messias at *Lar Nova Vida*. Needless to say, my heart melted for our god-son, Ezekiel. His brother would run away from LNV with their older brother, Elias, to visit his mother and ended up in the streets. How sad to go from Light to darkness, something I hated to see when I went back for visits.

Our trip in 2009 would be my last visit for many reasons. Many changes had come about, both in Oklahoma and in Brazil at LNV. Jim and Shirley Combs retired, and my husband lost his job connected with American Airlines. Before I left Brazil, I would see Ezekiel for one last time.

I had spent so much time that week watching him at LNV, playing soccer with the two American boys who came with their parents on this trip. Ezekiel would see me watching him as he "slaughtered" the two American boys in a game of soccer. Just as my own boys looked to me for loving approval, I saw the same look in Ezekiel's eyes. Yes, I showed him my approval by clapping and cheering for him as he made each goal. I loved him more as his soft, sweet heart allowed the American boys to score a goal.

It was the Sunday night service. My husband was ill and had stayed in bed to recover. Ezekiel and I were sitting at church, and I was trying to let him know how much I loved him. He had been having trouble in school because he would miss classes to run home to his family and brothers.

Monday we were due to fly back to North America. My mind was swirling around with thoughts of what would happen to my god-son Ezekiel. How I wished I could take him back with me, but now church service was over and they were calling all the children to load into the Volks van to go back to LNV.

Ezekiel came over to me and climbed onto my lap as if he were but two years old. We hugged each other and cried like babies, both of us. I cried for Ezekiel and wondered what would happen to the one I should be able to protect, help and keep. He had to leave, and I had to let go.

Most everyone had gone and I couldn't stop the tears from running down my cheeks. Sure, missionary Kimberly Johnson, the Brazilian dentist, Marina, and those that worked at LNV tried to console my broken heart. Why would I, or how could I allow that? Who would be able to console and protect my son, my god-son? I did not want him to return to the dark, evil streets where Satan has such control over those in the streets in *Araras, Brazil.*

Monday came with no choice for me but a plane ride, to fly thousands of miles away. So off I went and at this writing it's been four years now since I've been back. Could I ever go back? I will be gone but God can help him, heal him, save him. I pray that my god-son will forgive me for all I could not do.

*Note: The last time Shirley was in Brazil, Ezekiel rode up to the church on his bike with his Bible in one hand. He asked if Deborah and Brad would be back someday. Who knows?

Joann Wood, Oklahoma

My husband, Lynn, and I have opened our home to many preachers and missionaries over the years. In fact, our friendship with the Combs began when we hosted them in our home in 1964 while they were intenerating.

Who's Clapping At Our Gate?

Who knew that 38 years later I would be taking a short-term mission trip to Brazil?

There were several members from Rejoice Free Will Baptist Church in Owasso, Oklahoma and the Central Free Will Baptist Church in Grandview, Missouri that wanted to be the hands and feet of Jesus by embarking on a trip to Brazil.

Each of us took a backpack full to give to one of the children at the orphanage. *José Carlos Batisteli* was to get mine and I made sure the backpack was stuffed as full as possible. I was humbled to watch these beautifully gracious children of God be blessed with the items we brought.

I learned this year that José Carlos is now married and is active with his family in church. He plays drums with the praise and worship team.

There was a lady that came to the orphanage twice a month to sew for the children, but the donations of material needed to be organized. I was able to help organize the sewing room while I was there. I helped make dresses for the little girls and left enough royal blue material for a girls' singing group to have skirts.

We prepared soup and bread to take to one of the poverty stricken areas close by. I became alarmed when we were told to be sure and get out of that area before dark. We handed out soup to everyone that brought a bowl. One girl of 13 or so had a child and it saddened me that she was so young and lived in those conditions. I still think of her often!

During this visit while folks were standing in line to get their soup, an old woman came out and wanted one of the men to dance with her. When he wouldn't, she started dancing with a broom. I can still remember the satanic feeling that overcame me. Shirley began singing "God is So Good" and the rest of us joined her as we gathered our things and left.

The congregation of both churches services we attended received our group warmly and our team participated in several ways.

We received a wooden flower in a wooden vase which had written, Deus *e' Tremendo* (God Is Tremendous). I still have it in my kitchen and it reminds me to pray for Brazil.

We've hosted in our home about thirty missionaries and preachers over the years. (Ex. Bessie Yealey, Molly Barker, Brenda Sanders family, Jim and Shirley Combs, Dr. Miley, Pat Tyson, Ella Rae Jones, Bill Jones, family of six from Hawaii, Marie Cousineau, the Hannas, Fred Hersey family(3), Lonnie, Anita, Noel Sparks, Doc Caton family (3), Lynn Midget, Trula Cronk, Auxiliary day in California).

Many of those told stories and testimonies to our four boys of their missions and call of God. Lynn and I offered our home to those needing a place to stay, but we know we've reaped the blessing since each of our boys has taken a short-term mission trip. Coincidence? I believe it was God ordained.

Who's Clapping At Our Gate?

Pastor Leonard Pirtle, Oklahoma

Pastor Leonard Pirtle

"Lenny, why don't you come down and visit us in Brazil?" Jim and Shirley Combs had invited me on several occasions but I really did not take it seriously, that would be a waste of a lot of money (or so I thought at the time)!

I sent three staff members ahead of me before Shirley convinced me to go down myself. I took Brad Bickerstaff with me because he had traveled a lot and I knew I could keep him in sight with his bright red hair in São Paulo airport. I soon learned that there is nothing like seeing a mission work in person to really get missions in your heart and mind.

My first impressions of Brazil centered on the sheer size of São Paulo and the unbelievable poverty that could be seen all along the highway. The city of Araras was another story. It was beautiful, especially as I entered the "*chacara*" of Jim and Shirley. The sights, smells, and sounds surrounding their compound were wonderful. I especially remember the truck that delivered natural gas to the homes. It played musical sounds that were haunting in my mind when I first heard it. I was shocked to see it come from a delivery truck.

The taste of food, fruit, and beverages were great to me. I remember on our first trip Brad and I tasted Brazilian coffee for the first time; strong and sweet and a boat load of caffeine! Brad drank at least five or six of them and was wired up the rest of the evening!

Getting to the meat of what made these trips so wonderful to me centered on the children's home, *Lar Nova Vida,* and the FWB Candida church. We watched both of these literally rise from the ground and soon touch the lives of the children in the home and the people who came to worship at the church. The lives of many of the people who made this journey south on mission trips will have lasting affects for all eternity.

Jim and Shirley Combs are more Brazilian now than American. Shirley's tireless energy and love for the children was amazing to see. Jim had a pastor's heart as he not only helped meet spiritual needs of the people but also helped build many of their personal lives. Helping them to help themselves and climb out of poverty.

On one occasion Jim, Brad, and I had gone fishing and on the way home, Jim took the fish we had caught by the home of a man that had had his feathers ruffled the night before. Jim took him the fish as a peace offering.

I don't want to leave you with the idea that those trips were just fun and pleasure: there is spiritual darkness, troubles with government authorities, bad decisions by the children in the home, conflict between parishioners in the church, and the constant battle for good leadership in Brazil.

The summary after all the trips, of all the dollars invested, labor projects completed and uncompleted, relationships established, and the victories (and losses) of both us who went and those we went to visit can be simply stated "worth it all".

Janita Hendricks, Oklahoma

John and Janita

John and I received such a blessing from our visit to Brazil. We went with the intention of giving, but received much more than we gave. The trip instilled in us a sense of compassion and humility that will never leave us. What the children at the *Lar Nova Vida* placed in our hearts was one of the greatest gifts we have ever been given. I just hope one day we can do more with this precious gift.

The atmosphere there seemed so pure. There

wasn't all the materialistic "stuff" that we deal with here. I am envious, in a good way, of the simple, childlike faith. I know that the children who are placed in the hands of the *Lar Nova Vida* are truly blessed by God, and I think they realize that.

On several occasions, someone would raise their hands to God and pray that He would rain down blessings on us. Tears still come to my eyes when I think of this. And it was in response to such a small act.

John loved playing with the kids, because he has never really grown up! He loved playing soccer and flying kites with the boys. The children loved their kites!

My favorite memory is piling in Tia Shirley's car to go buy shoes for the children. And I do mean piling! And from the back of the car comes a sweet little voice that said, "*Tia* Janita, *Dona* Shirley's car is just like her heart...always room for one more!" Just precious, and so true.

CHAPTER 9
Pastor Alan Led the Kansas/Missouri Teams

Pastor Alan Kinder, a retired military man and his wife Sharon, who works in human services, made many trips to minister in our city. Sometimes Pastor Alan, from Central Free Will Baptist Church in Grandview, Missouri, went as a group leader and sometimes he went only with his wife. Whether it was with a group or their two-member team, they got a lot done!

The kids loved them and ask each year if they will be returning. Besides helping in *Lar Nova Vida* on various projects, they spoke at our son Kemper's Language School. In their military career experiences, they traveled to different countries and had no problem conversing with the students from another background.

They helped a brother and sister set up housekeeping when they left LNV. They even bought used bicycles for them so they could travel to work and school. But their untiring sharing of hugs, prayers, and tears pass all language and culture barriers.

Pastor Alan Kinder, Missouri
I had recently completed my third short-term mission trip to Brazil, my second time as the team leader. Before we even left for this trip I had to wonder what in the world were we going to accomplish? There were only three of us going this time, and the work usually requires more willing hands than three can

provide. Of the three of us going this time, one was a teenager! Maybe it was time to put a stop to these short-term, cross-cultural mission trips that I seemed so bent on leading. After all, what can three of us accomplish that the money we raised could not do? I decided to examine this question, and see what possible reasons I could come up with for continuing these things.

First, I had to admit that there was no substitute for a ministry of presence. The Apostle Paul stated this very idea in many of his letters when he wrote of desiring to be present with those brothers and sisters in Christ who were far-removed from him.

Our financial support, prayers, cards, letters, and e-mails to our missionaries can only do so much. I'm saying we should keep doing those things (especially the prayers and financial support), but sometimes our physical presence is needed to provide the support that the missionaries on the field need. They sometimes need someone to lean on, a shoulder to cry on, in order to continue in their fight.

Second, I had to admit that even three sets of helping hands were better than none. The work is often tiring, thankless, and sometimes even a little hard to stomach, but it still needs to be done.

The children's home in *Araras*, *Lar Nova Vida* (New Life Home), always has children who need a lot of attention and affection. The *sem terras* (literally Portuguese people without land, or homeless people) also need to know the love of Jesus. While our ability to help is limited due to the length of time we can spend, it is still a big help. Our missionaries deserve whatever support and assistance we can provide, even if it is just three sets of willing hands.

Third, I had to admit that we could (and did) encourage our missionaries, the people in the local church where we ministered, and people in the community at large. Everywhere we went we were introduced to people as missionaries from America who had come into their city of 110,000 people to minister the love of Jesus to their children and homeless people.

Pastor Alan and Sharon with
Kansas and Missouri mission team

The people of *Araras* were encouraged that we would come so far to help them and their city. The missionaries were encouraged to know that they didn't bear the entire load alone, at least not for the few days we were able to spend with them. The people of the Second Free Will Baptist Church in the *Jardim* Candida neighborhood of *Araras* were encouraged by our ministry to the children and to the church as a whole. We did our best to lavish our missionary hosts with love and support for nine days. I only wish we could have done more!

Fourth, I had to admit that going on these trips is a tremendous way to confirm God's purposes. Seeing another church, from a different culture, struggling with the same issues we struggle with made me realize that the church is much bigger than I ever imagined. Believers in Brazil have God's ear in prayer for their cities just as much as people in the United States. Hearing some of our favorite hymns sung in Portuguese opened my mind to the reality that Jesus really did die for all people. God does intend for the whole world to hear the gospel, and that means it really is my responsibility to do my part. I can't ignore missions when I see it in action!

Pastor Alan and Sharon Kinder from Kansas City, Missouri

Finally, at the end of the trip, I had to admit that going on these trips could also be the means for the confirmation of God's calling on someone's life. Remember the teenager I mentioned? Her name is Mikayla Smith, she was seventeen years old, and she announced to our church on August 19, 2007 that she intended to follow God's calling on her life and enter missionary service upon graduation from college. I had asked her if being a part of these trips (Mikayla was a member of our team that went to Brazil in 2006, and has also made five trips to Mexico with her grandfather) had helped her make up her mind or not. She was adamant! These trips had cemented in her heart God's calling upon her life. What a blessing we would have missed if we had decided not to go.

Yes, short-term trips are expensive, but the intangible benefits to the missionaries on the field as well as the short-term missionaries are of inestimable value. We couldn't have done all that we did by just raising the money and staying at home. We wouldn't have experienced, once again, the life-altering time on the field that God provided through these types of trips. We might never have seen God's hand on a young missionary from Missouri who may one day, Lord willing, be a missionary on some foreign field.

I'm going back to Brazil if the Lord allows, and I have several more teenagers who want to go along. I'm praying that some more adults will come along, as well. It'll be costly, but the return is of eternal benefit. (From an article in the Missouri FWB magazine, GEM)

Experience Results in Sermon Illustrations

Many pastors have shared with me that they catch themselves using illustrations in their sermons from their experiences in Brazil. An illustration Pastor Alan Kinder recently used at his church was based on his visit to Brazil.

Pastor Alan Kinder, Missouri
What is it about the change that causes us to become upset? If it's simply because it's different and unfamiliar, then we probably need to adjust our attitude toward it. I learned a long time ago that different wasn't good or bad, it was just different. It may not be to my preference, but my preferences are most often of secondary importance, at best!

My first missionary trip to Brazil was all about learning to accept "different isn't bad" as a way of life. The food in Brazil is different, the language is different, the culture is different, the music in church is different, and I could go on and on about the differences.

If I had focused on those differences, I would have been miserable the entire time I was in Brazil. Instead, I tried to focus on the people! They were different culturally, and yet they were much like me. The children played different games, and yet they still loved to play and laugh. The adults enjoyed different pastimes, and yet they still loved to relax and spend time with friends. The people spoke a different language, and yet they still responded to the language of love when it was coupled with a sincere willingness to accept the differences. I was willing to accept the differences because I felt it was far more important to share the love of Christ with the people I came into contact with than it was to promote my preference. Let's accept those changes with a positive attitude that reminds us that different isn't good or bad, it's just different.

By the way, once I determined to accept the differences in Brazil, I started really enjoying much of what Brazil had to offer. The food was excellent, the people were loving and accepting, and the culture is fascinating! What I would have missed had I not accepted changes.

Pamela Wilson, Kansas/Missouri

"We're going to Brazil, so do you want to go along?" That was the question Pastor Alan and Sharon Kinder of Central Free Will Baptist Church inquired of me.

"Why are you going to Brazil?" was my response.

Pam
Wilson

A few years before this, I had been a flight attendant and had been to Brazil. I didn't really have any desire to return. But Pastor Alan told me of the children of *Lar Nova Vida* and I immediately responded with a "count me in!" I think he was really kidding when he proposed the question, but I was not when I answered him. Thankfully, he and Sharon were, and are, two very big hearted persons who allowed me to become part of a wonderful team leaving in just four months.

The trip from Kansas City to Brazil was quite long. After traveling for more than 21 hours, we were greeted in São Paulo by a truly lovely woman named

Shirley Combs. She accompanied us on the last three remaining hours of our journey to *Araras*.

That evening we met the children of *Lar Nova Vida* and my heart has never been the same. To look into each face and see the master piece that God had crafted and to realize God had given me the opportunity to share his love with these little ones, was priceless.

It was amazing to see each worker at *Lar Nova Vida* and watch how they interacted with the children to help mold them into the boys and girls they were intended to be. Many of the children had stories so horrific it could make a grown man shutter, and yet they all had smiles on their little faces. Most realize just what a blessing it was for them to be in a safe, comfortable, loving place which afforded them a new chance at a bright future. Others had no clue, but they knew they were getting real fruit and vegetables to eat each day and did not have to fend for themselves in dangerous situations.

Everyone on our trip had a wonderful time playing with and then worshipping with the children. The language difference was not an obstacle, as one might think. The children were very creative in expressing their thoughts and ideas.

During that first trip, I observed several times the difficulties of dealing with the government of Brazil, and their complex regulations. Here was a selfless group of Americans living in Brazil, only to be a blessing to the Brazilian people. Pastor Jim and Shirley were definitely examples of how "not to take offense". It was an eye opener for me to watch true life missionaries walk in love, regardless of the situation.

I saw the most undesirable people running into the arms of Shirley as we went into their poor neighborhoods to minister to them. We prayed over people and saw God answer prayer immediately.

I had a normal childhood for the most part. I was a curious child and got into more things than I probably should have, and got more spankings than all my siblings put together. We all still laugh about that. I say all that to say, my parents loved me and I knew it. I cannot for one minute imagine what it would be like to not have one person in my corner, pulling for me. Each time I would think of these little guys left to their own demise, it would break my heart.

Thank God someone loved them enough to get in their corner!

It was a blessing to have such a lovely place to stay each night. Jim and Shirley had a beautiful property on which they had built a Hospitality House for mission groups with four bed rooms and four baths. We all bunked in, ladies on one side and men on the other.

When the weather was cold, we would use rice bags you heat in the microwave to keep our feet warm, since there was not heat in the homes. And in the summer, we had ceiling fans that pulled the air through to keep it comfortable.

We would pick bananas right off the stalk and depending on what was in season, we could pick tangerines, guavas, mangos, persimmons, avocados, star fruit and others I don't know their English names for.

I returned to Brazil several more times over the next six years. Each trip I would think, "It just can't get any better", but each time it did. I was blessed more than I could ever have imagined.

Jesus told us to look after the children and the widows. He just never told us how fun and rewarding it would be. So, I will. It was truly amazing. So if you ever get the opportunity to go, GO. You will be glad you did.

*

On the day I was writing this article, Pam was flying to India to be with other orphans she helps there. Fortunate kids. This is a portion of the letter she sent me today.

"I spoke three different times and had activities with the children on several different days. I spoke to the congregation of God's Faithfulness. Then the following Monday I spoke to a group of Indian pastors. They came in from hours across the area.

The children were wonderful and very appreciative of all that was done for them. All the children now have bedrooms and bathrooms. There is no furniture in the rooms for the children, so they are still sleeping on the floors. But at least they have real floors. Something to be thankful for.

The children were so beautiful and loving. Of course I wanted to bring them all home with me. Instead, it is my desire to see what else I can do from this end to make their lives just a little better. It is my desire to show them how good a God we serve and how much He does love them."

CHAPTER 10
Tennessee Couple Strummin' and Preachin' and Lovin'

Pastor Vern and Delma Gunnels, Missouri/Tennessee

Vern and Delma Gunnels were pastoring in Adamsville, Tennessee, and accepted our invitation to come visit us in Araras. We had been friends for many, many years and ministry had led us both to many addresses far from each other. What a festive day when they arrived at our gate in Brazil.

I will let them both tell you in their own way. If they could share with you in person, you would probably soon be laughing and crying.

In case you have never been there, you will have an idea of missionary life as you follow Delma in her daily journal. If you have been there, you may nod your head and heart and think, yes, I have been there and have seen that.

From Delma Gunnels

Monday, June 6.

Vern and I left our home in Adamsville, Tennessee, around 12:15 p.m. A couple from our church drove us to the Memphis Airport. Our plane is scheduled to leave Memphis at 4:40 p.m. It was an easy, uneventful flight to Houston, Texas. We left Houston at 8:50 p.m. (about 45 minutes late) and the monitor says we're 4,917 miles from Sao Paulo! The flight will take approximately 10 hours.

Tuesday, June 7.

5:45 a.m. I think Vern and I got enough sleep on the plane where we can actually function today! We're supposed to be landing in two hours!

I'm so anxious to see as much of our mission works as we possibly can – especially *Lar Nova Vida* children. Jim and Shirley Combs have been my close friends since our days together at FWBBC in the early 1960's (now Welch College). They became Vern's friends after our marriage. We even spent a couple of nights with them in Moore, Oklahoma, as we were

Delma Gunnels

moving to Arkansas and they were on furlough and teaching at Hillsdale College in the early 1980's.

Our plane was only 25 minutes late. We had

to go through the long customs line, but all that smoothly. All of our luggage made it – we're here!

The airport facilities were just like the States. Jim and Shirley were there to greet us and let us know they live only two and a half hours away from São Paulo – Ouch! More traveling! But it really wasn't that bad since we were so happy to see each other.

We stopped at a restaurant to eat *churrasco* (meat on a stick). They prepare every imaginable meat on a shishkabab. The buffet table has every kind of salad you can think of. You get your salads at the buffet table; then waiters bring the meats to your table and cut a slice (you pull it off with tongs). At the table were also bowls of rice, beans, cheese balls, and cornbread-like crispy bread. After we were thoroughly stuffed (for about $5 each at that time), we continued our journey to *Araras!*

The Combs have a beautiful home in a country-like setting. They have a hospitality house that can accommodate 15 people with a small living/kitchen area; a swimming pool, and a game porch. There's also a small caretaker house for a family of five who help out.

We rested a while. Later the four of us went riding to try to find Messias, a 12 year old boy who ran away from LNV to try to find his brother Elias (who was messing with drugs). Their mother was in the hospital. Our concern was that the drug people were also looking for Elias and threatening to kill him.

We prayed that Messias will call or come back home as he's done two or three times before.

Wednesday, June 8.

Vern was up early and I awoke at 6:15 ready to go with Shirley to LNV! We have three Free Will

Baptist churches in *Araras* and were able to see all three of them. We also saw the shanties and poverty while searching for Messias.

Transportation in *Araras* means lots of motorcycles and bicycles, buses and, of course, cars. The stop signs in *Araras* are pretty much ignored – drivers just kind of "slide' through them – first come, first served!

Shirley and I spent all morning at LNV. She took care of business matters while I enjoyed those precious children! We had brought suitcases full of clothing and supplies. It was fun to watch the ladies and older girls sort through our gifts. EVERYONE wears flip flops! Next time I come I want to bring a whole suitcase full of them. I did have pockets of lollipops and gum which made me very popular with the children!

We ate lunch at LNV – rice and beans with a meat and tomato sauce; it was very tasty. After our meal, we were offered a glass of water or Kool-Aid.

Shirley and I went to tell the *Vila de Barro* children there would be no soup tonight because of a broken down stove. When the children saw our vehicle, they came running "*Sopa, sopa, sopa!*" (Soup, soup, soup!) We also met *Messias'* grandparents; still no word from him.

When we returned home, Pastor and Mrs. Martin were at the Combs' with their two daughters. He is the pastor of one of the FWB churches in town. We all had supper and enjoyed visiting.

Thursday, June 9.

Shirley and I ran errands and did a little shopping today. She had two meetings and I went with her.

We dropped by LNV and wished Marianna a happy seventeenth birthday.

Vern will be preaching tonight; Jim will interpret. I'm going to play the keyboard since Kemper has to work. Kemper teaches English and has a great working setup in *Araras*. Shirley and I went by to see his office and enjoyed his visit.

We had a good service tonight. Vern spoke from Matthew 6:33 and did a good job. We sang several songs. The children sang a few songs. We broke into prayer groups, and church was over.

Friday, June 10.

Vern, Jim and I enjoyed a leisurely breakfast and coffee while Shirley is working on a report due today for a grant (she just found out yesterday at the meeting). *Araras* and the Combs' home are beautiful with poinsettias and orchids growing here like daffodils do in Tennessee. They also have lots of banana trees, oleanders, orange trees, lemon and tangerine trees, avocado trees, cacti, and a papaya tree. The parrots and toucans fly around wild. Such a sight to behold!

The police called at midnight last night. Shirley went to the police station to pick up Messias and take him back to LNV. He and his brother were at a party. Their grandmother was at the hospital with their mother. She asked a policeman to help her find Messias. He took her to the party and there they both were!

Messias was ready to go back to LNV – cold and hungry. His brother can't because he's 14. Only children 12 and younger can go to LNV and then they can stay as long as they need to stay.

Who's Clapping At Our Gate?

At the time of our visit, LNV had 24 children plus house parents' children. In one house were 12 children with a couple as house parents, and they had children of their own. The second house had 12 children with a housemother and her five children.

We worked at LNV all afternoon making soup – scraping carrots and potatoes, and a squash-like vegetable that looks similar to a cucumber. We made two HUGE pots of soup and went together in the van to *Vila de Barro* (Mud Village).

Children and adults came out of their makeshift shanties with their own containers. We ladled the soup and handed out bread until it was all gone, which took 30-45 minutes. It was gut wrenching to run out of food! I felt guilty because I had already eaten – all these hungry children!

Messias had gone with us to help pass out bread and interpret for Vern. Afterwards Shirley and I took him to the hospital to see his mother. She had been released, so we went to his grandmother's (so he won't run away) and no one was there. We took him to LNV and promised tomorrow we will find his mother.

Saturday,June 11.

Jim, Vern and I went to LNV for art sculpting classes, only to find out they had been cancelled because of immunization scheduled for later today. Shirley had gone to a meeting with Marianna's teachers. Marianna is doing well in everything except English!

While waiting for Shirley at LNV, I tried to demonstrate to the children how to play kickball, a favorite with children in the States. Every time I stopped for a break, they'd go right back to soccer – THEIR favorite sport in Brazil!

Shirley and I took Marianna to town and tried in vain to find the shoes she needed for modeling school (spike heels and pointed toes). She is the tallest girl at the children's home, and we couldn't find shoes long enough for her.

Today the children are sharing pictures they've drawn which I will treasure!

After lunch at the Combs', Shirley and I went back to LNV to observe the volunteer art teacher giving lessons to six of the older children. The volunteer music teacher was also giving lessons.

Even more volunteers were there with their TV and VCR to cuddle with the children, watch a children's movie, and have treats.

Shirley and I went by Marcos' home. I got to meet him, his wife Claudiana, and his six year old daughter, Vitoria. Marcos was a street child before he lived with the Combs for nine years. He sings and preaches – a precious family. They also have a little son, Jessé, who was with friends that day.

Service was good tonight. The children's choir sang and two boys played instruments.

<u>Sunday,</u>June 12.

Shirley is letting me proofread her second book (now published!). It is as touching as her first book. This second one will be more meaningful to me because I have met some of these people, and they have become a part of my life!

We only have extended Sunday School on Sunday mornings (with an opening program and closing program); preaching is tonight. Sunday School was so much fun. I was sharing my testimony with the 9-12 year old class; then the younger teens asked to come and join us. The teacher said they were jealous and wanted to sit in, too. Shirley interpreted for me.

They learned the song "This is the Day" in English and sign language and sang it for the closing program. Sunday School lasted from 9:00-10:30 a.m. It felt funny not to have preaching but this is how it's done in Brazil.

After lunch, Shirley and I went to LNV; the children had invited us to play soccer! Vern and Jim stayed home to rest. Only the older boys were playing soccer, so Shirley and I cheered them on. The girls were busy with another project – witnessing to *Eliani*. *Eliani* and her three year old son were temporarily staying at LNV. She had been held captive by her husband and gypsies for over five years and was trying to escape to her family. She had made "a pact with the devil" to help her escape with her son.

The older girls from the home had rented "The Passion of the Christ" and were watching it with *Eliani*. They're showing her there's a better way!

Vern did an excellent job preaching tonight from I John 5:11-13 and *Eliani* was saved! The entire service was a blessing – even though we couldn't understand the words, you could feel the Holy Spirit's presence in the service.

Bruna (a 10-year-old girl) came to spend the night with us. Her mother is in jail; her father has remarried and his new wife doesn't like *Bruna* (because of her own children). So **Bruna** has been living with an aunt who "wants to turn her back in today." Shirley and

I stayed up late talking with Bruna and praying for guidance as we take her to the authorities.

They rarely place a child in LNV who has family capable of taking care of them; except right now it seems that no one wants *Bruna*, a beautiful 10-year-old girl.

Monday,June 13.

Bruna stayed with Shirley and me to run errands. Since *Bruna* made a decision at church last night, her Christian aunt persuaded the uncle to give her another chance so they decided to let her stay with them. The aunt has non-contagious leprosy and is on medication.

The weather has been perfect during our visit here. Shirley and I shopped in the afternoon while Vern and Jim relaxed.

We were all planning to relax tonight but Shirley got a call about a five-month pregnant woman with a one-year-old child who is in transient and has nowhere to stay. Shirley gets constant phone calls and is enormously busy!

Shirley found out later that the Tutorial Counsel had a mattress in a back room for the lady and her baby to spend the night.

So many needy people; so little time!

Tuesday,June 14

Vern and I went to buy and deliver groceries to LNV. Shirley and I drove an hour away and found the pottery mecca of the world! I bought several pieces to take home with me.

We met at LNV for lunch, then went by Carlos' home, the volunteer art teacher. I met him and his mother and bought some of his art work including a beautiful wood carving. We also went by another FWB church, and I got to meet that pastor.

That evening Shirley and I went to Adriana's for their weekly ladies meeting. We had about 30 women and girls, and I shared from Philippians 2:3-19. We had such sweet fellowship and refreshments. We drew names for prayer partners, and I drew *Flavia* and *Jessica.* These people are all so loving and precious!

Wednesday, June 15

Our last full day in *Araras*– I woke up crying. It has always been hard for me to leave people I'm attached to, especially children!

I helped Shirley prepare the hospitality house for the E-Team and Curt and Mary Holland who are arriving tonight. This group will be in charge of Thursday evening service; then they will sand and paint the playground at LNV. Then they're traveling on to Campinas.

This afternoon we helped again prepare the soup and served it one more time at *Vila do Barro.*

I have bought several pieces of art from the children and will treasure the memories we have made here! Shirley took me back by LNV to say goodbye to my friends. My life will never be the same.

I will be eternally grateful that we were able to make this journey.

Thursday, June 16

We're packing up and visiting briefly with the E-Team and the Hollands. I admire these young people who are so mission-minded and the adults who guide them into such an awesome ministry.

Who's Clapping At Our Gate?

Jim drove us to the airport in Sao Paulo. We made it through customs again with no problems and had an uneventful flight back to Houston and on to Memphis. All our flights were on schedule, the weather was perfect, and no luggage was lost.

While a student at FWBBC in Nashville, my minor was in missions. I've always had a special place in my heart for those serving on foreign soils. Vern and I are committed to continue this world wide mandate until the Lord sees fit to bring us all the way to our celestial Home.

P.S. I've relived this awesome trip just typing my journal notes. We love and pray for Jim and Shirley on a regular basis!

From Vern Gunnels

Pastor Vern Gunnels

In my forty-plus years as a Free Will Baptist pastor, I was never invited to a foreign mission work to see how my offerings were being spent until the Combs said, "Come and see us in Brazil!"

Man – what an experience: poverty, heartache, distress, hard work, compassion, gratitude, love and joy in every area.

Who's Clapping At Our Gate?

On one of our trips into *Araras*, Jim and I walked downtown to buy meat, bread, and vegetables to work that afternoon at *Lar Nova Vida* for the soup ministry at *Vila de Barro* (mud village). Never before had I seen so many native parrots flying free in the business district of *Araras*. We see pigeons, ducks, and geese; but never parrots!

The church services were teeming with love, joy and praise. Even though my Portuguese was very limited, it was refreshing. Preaching with an interpreter was an experience, but Jim and the Holy Spirit did a swell job with one lady trusting Christ as Savior.

CHAPTER 11
Student Internship Missionary Program

Years before the student internship missionary program was named in our colleges, we were hosting North American Christians in our home and reaping the blessings. The young student visitors were special blessings with their youth, energy, dedication and vision. Some of their stories are included with their own personal experiences and impressions.

Lori Gaw, Oklahoma

On May 23, 2001, I, Lori Gaw (from Hillsdale College, Oklahoma) and Jullie Biggs (from FWBBC (Welch) College, Tennessee) arrived extremely early in the morning in *Araras,* São Paulo, to stay for ten weeks. We returned to the states on July 31. The experiences we had there impacted our lives.

While there, we participated in various ministries of the Second FWB Church in *Araras*, one of the churches Jim and Shirley Combs started. Those ministries included the *Lar Nova Vida* children's home, the nursing home ministry, and the soup ministry as well as acting as conversation partners to English students at Kemper Combs' language school.

All of the ministries were effective in allowing us the opportunity to get a glimpse of the life of a missionary and the responsibilities involved. The people, the culture, and the experiences have made a lasting impact on our lives.

Who's Clapping At Our Gate?

Julie Biggs, Tennessee

Well, not enough can be said about the *Lar Nova Vida!* The kids are wonderful, and were the highlight of the trip for Lori and me. Every day was spent with the children. We participated in events ranging from cleaning the storage room to helping the cook in the kitchen. Many days were spent playing games such as soccer and "tickle." There were many kids at the home, ranging from eight months to 18 years old. Many great times were shared there that summer. It is going to be a long-lasting memory for both of us as summer missionaries and the children at the *Lar Nova Vida*.

We helped the Combs host other mission team groups who went that year to their home. We were blessed to have a group of people from South Carolina to come visit. The group consisted of over 20 people, led by a native Brazilian, *Rosana*, who now lives in the states. While visiting the states, David Aycock led her to the Lord in her own native Portuguese language. After she was saved, she learned of the *Lar Nova Vida* and felt a strong burden to come and experience. Her group brought gifts for the children, hardworking attitudes, and much love to the kids at LNV.

A couple from Oklahoma, Tim and Heather Adair, also came and stayed for about 10 days. They worked at LNV, and on July 16 - July 18 a day camp for the LNV kids began. It was a good time for all. Brother Tim Adair brought a devotion for each day, translated by Kemper.

The kids got a lot of exercise in. The older kids, including Julie, played a serious game of soccer for two of the days and the younger children flew kites.

The food was the best ever eaten by the Americans. *Churrasco* was made every day for us by the house parent, Max. Fellowship was enjoyed by all.

One of the main outreach ministries of the church that Jim Combs was pastoring at the time, is the soup ministry. Every Friday beginning at 3:00 pm, participants meet to begin preparing the all-homemade soup. About three hours are spent cutting vegetables and preparing the ingredients for this soup (all donated). The

Rita and Carmen study with Erin and Amy

soup gives the people at the "Villa" at least one good, hot, nutritious meal per week. Two huge commercial size pots of soup are prepared and taken there, which fill multiple bowls for waiting people week after week. That year represented the one-year anniversary of that ministry which has continued all these years since. It was a blessing to serve the community in this way!

(Copied from a prayer/news letter written by Lori and Julie of their ten weeks as student missionaries.)

Who's Clapping At Our Gate?

Erin Williams

On May 20, 2002, I embarked on several firsts in my life: first airplane ride, first trip from home for more than two months, first time overseas, and first mission trip. My destination was *Araras,* Sao Paulo, Brazil, through the overseas apprentice program.

My ministry focused on *Lar Nova Vida* (LNV), a children's home for street children, with missionaries Jim and Shirley Combs. Amy Lankford, a college classmate, was going with me.

I thought I would go to Brazil, have a wonderful time, do a lot of work, and learn a great deal. I was excited, but I had no idea I would grow to love the children's home so much. I had met missionary Shirley Combs two years before at the National Association and was anxious to see her again. The tearful goodbye stuff was not for me. I was ready to go. Most of all I looked forward to meeting the children.

We didn't meet the children until after we had a day to rest in *Araras.* The second night after our arrival, a special service was held at one of the churches and the children were present. That night we met several of the kids and a tradition was quickly established. In almost every church service during my stay, a child sat on my lap. Each time, the child was asleep before the end of the service.

Messias and Elias regularly fell asleep on my lap. These brothers were seven and nine years of age. They had come to the children's home shortly before we arrived. The boys had lived behind a gas station and made money for their family by shining shoes. When they came to *Lar Nova Vida*, they left their shoe shining kit at the service station.

These little guys hated school (they didn't do very well and fell behind) so they cut classes, ran away, and reappeared at the Home at night. After several times, we discovered they were going to the gas station to shine shoes and make money to take to their parents.

Shirley went to the gas station, retrieved their kit and brought it to the Home. Then she rounded up all the shoes she had and others and let them shine them. The boys asked if they could shine my shoes. I agreed and asked how much it would cost. They said, "For you, it's free."

Not long after that, we learned the boys had a Christian grandmother. She wanted to take care of them, so the boys went to live with her. The day they left, they asked us to visit them at their grandmother's house and indicated they would miss us. One boy said his heart was half happy and half sad.

Each child at the Home has personality, but two of the girls kept us laughing. Anna Paula and Ivani, the oldest girls at LNV, have been there since they were five and six years old. Now at 17 and 18, these sisters are the only two residing in the house for older girls with missionary Kimberly Johnson.

The first day we arrived at the Combs' house the phone rang. It was Anna Paula and she wanted to talk to one of the two American missionary girls. When Amy took the phone Anna said in her accented English, "Hi, my name is Chicken: I likey chicken." We really laughed and from that day on I called Anna Paula "Chicken." For some reason she called me "Giraffe." She would often say, "You is beautiful for me, *Girafa*."

Ivani was often my shadow. One Sunday after church she pulled me aside. Half teasingly and half seriously, she asked me to be her mother. I was honored and will never forget that.

Not long after going to *Araras* we met a 15-year-old named Lucas. He came to the children's home at the age of five and now lives with the older boys. Lucas loved to tease us. Whenever we saw him he would either be really friendly or really a pest.

On our first encounter, Lucas said in English, "It is beautiful, no?" as he pointed to himself. Sometimes he would flirt with us and kiss our hands. Other times he would walk away saying, "You Americans! You always come here and say you love it, and you never come back."

Leaving Brazil was very difficult. I hugged each child and told everyone goodbye as bravely as I could. That night at the airport I let the tears flow. Though the last goodbyes were tearful, I didn't care. I knew I was going to miss the children terribly.

It has taken me a long time to get reaccustomed to sitting through church without a child asleep in my lap. I know one day I will have to return to Brazil. My shoes need shining. I need to tell "Chicken" hello. I have to prove Lucas wrong.

(Taken from an article in HEARBEAT magazine, January/February 2003, page 8)

Mandi Springs and Kimberly Johnson
Hi, our names are Mandi Springs from South Carolina and Kimberly Johnson from Oklahoma. We had the pleasure of spending ten weeks helping the

Combs with their ministry in *Araras*. We were involved in teaching English classes, working with the children at *Lar Nova Vida*, helping with the soup preparation and distribution, hosting TEAM students, giving testimonies, and ministering through music and drama presentations.

Besides our involvement in the ministry, we were full time students of the culture and language of Brazil. After a month in Brazil, we had seen a graduation, a funeral, and had firsthand knowledge of the hospital. We have learned how to answer the telephone in Portuguese and how to make Brazilian desserts.

We have also learned many words. They include: *Oi* (hello), *tchau* (goodbye), *bom dia, boa tarde, and boa noite* (greetings), *comida* (food), *banheiro* (bathroom), *carro* (car), *pronto Socorro* (emergency room), *obrigado* (thanks), *de nada* (you're welcome).

Mandi Springs and Kimberly Johnson

At church we also learned: *Senhor* (Lord), *oracao* (prayer), *vamos orar* (let's pray), *Deus* (God), *cantamos* (let's sing), *versiculo* (verse), *capitulo* (chapter), *Igreja* (church), *Cristo* (Christ), and *Paz* (peace).

We would like to say *Obrigada* for your *oracoes.* We ask that you continue to remember the Combs and us in your prayers.

May the *paz de Deus* be with you.

(Copied from a prayer/news letter written by Mandi and Kimberly about their ten weeks in Brazil in 2000.)

Hollie Hubbard, New York

It was my missions studies at Welch College (Free Will Baptist Bible College) that took me to Brazil

Holly Hubbard on the keyboard accompanies
April and Moacir in worship service

as an overseas apprentice in the summer of 2003. We had the privilege of staying in Jim and Shirley Combs' home for our ten week assignment. We had no idea what adventures awaited us.

Who's Clapping At Our Gate?

Along with April Thomkins (Illinois) and Jessica Crider (Arkansas), a large amount of our time was spent getting to know the kids at *Lar Nova Vida*. I remember how loved I felt by all the kids there. Each day was filled with hugs and games, despite the language barrier. I still remember the excitement I felt when I was able to use my broken Spanish to have "conversations" with some of the kids! The night before we left, Mariana, one of the teen girls, wrote a message in my Bible that I still treasure and look at often.

I was impacted so much by the love Jim and Shirley had for the children and their willingness to serve and help them any way that they could! They took us in and made us a part of their family for that summer and I was able to see firsthand what it looks like to give your life to serving God overseas.

In reading over the journal I kept while in Brazil, I was reminded of so many instances of Mrs. Shirley's generosity and kindness. We were driving somewhere, and ran into a man who needed a ride to the bus station. Mrs. Shirley not only give him the ride he requested, but also helped him buy the ticket.

Another time I was able to go with her as she visited the home of a little boy. He had bad eyes and she told him she would take him to get his eyes fixed. We took him presents for his birthday and she helped the family send him to the children's home. Her love for the children was so apparent, and she was always encouraging them and doing all she could to help each of them and make sure they felt loved!

We attended a few of Kemper Combs' English classes and at the children's home I had my first experience trying to teach English. I say *trying* because I am not sure we taught them much of anything! But we loved spending that time with the kids. A few years later, I moved to Japan to teach English with the Free Will Baptist International Missions.

After returning from Japan in 2007, I was presented the opportunity to move to New York City for a summer ministry opportunity. Lorene Miley, FWB missionary to Ivory Coast, West Africa, had been living for a while in Hephzibah House, a guest house in downtown New York City. She invited me to join her there for a summer position. I jumped at this chance to spend valuable time with her and experience life in the big city.

I fell in love with New York City and the international flavor it has! One of my jobs at the guesthouse was working with internationals. What began as just a summer job has turned into a wonderful adventure of working with students from all over the world. In May of 2013, I celebrated five years in New York City.

While working at Hephzibah House, I began volunteering with International Student Inc. on the campus of Columbia University. ISI is a great ministry that reaches out to international students living in the United States. The majority of international students never have the opportunity of visiting an American home! What a great opportunity we have to befriend them and share the love of Jesus. We reach out to students through English conversation groups, Friday night fellowships and cultural events. Our vision is to share Christ with them and equip them to return home and take the gospel with them.

(You may find out more about this ministry by visiting www.isionline.org).

Hillsdale Athletes Play Soccer with Kids

Our colleges have a ministry of Student Internship/Overseas Apprentice that sends students who meet the qualifications to work on mission fields with invitations from missionaries. For many years we received students into our homes in the states of *São Paulo* and *Santa Catarina*. In May 2010 I had the opportunity of traveling with a group from Hillsdale FWB College in Moore, Oklahoma, to our gates in *Araras*.

The mission director at Hillsdale, Dr. Janice Banks, had signed up and oriented a fine group of

Hillsdale College athletes

students. A special group. The college girls (Lauren, Tara, Krishna, Darci, and Jessica) were all part of the softball team and the young man, Tadd, was on the men's baseball team. Another softball member Bailey was the chairman of the group, but early on she found out that there was a problem with her passport. The girls' coach told me to please get them all safely back home because the college athletic department was counting on them. There are no softball or baseball teams in Brazil, but these students were going to be introduced to Brazilian soccer.

Another member who went was my assistant, Janiria Kay Talley. She met me after a District WAC meeting where I had spoken and asked to go with us. She travels all the time and had been to several countries. She also is in the Softball Hall of Fame! A perfect match.

That year Hillsdale College sent groups of students to Haiti, Canada, and Brazil. Besides the orientation dynamics they had with their groups, they filled out forms for passports and visas. The other groups didn't need visas. At the time they were finishing their end-of-the-semester studies, our group to Brazil raised money for their trip and ministry.

Our group was to leave on a Monday, and on the Friday before, Tadd's papers had not arrived. Dr. Janice Banks and I told him to keep packing and believe. After all, he was our guitar player and we needed him.

Monday arrived and guess what? Tadd arrived with a great smile and a big envelope with his needed documents. They just experienced one more reward in their young journeys of faith.

We met in the college parking lot with the coach and Bailey, and after photos, prayer and hugs we were off to the airport.

When we arrived at the Will Rogers International Airport in Oklahoma City, we sat together to wait for our flight to Dallas to catch the night flight to Sao Paulo, Brazil. We waited. The first announcement came of a delay due to a mechanical problem, and the passengers around us groaned. Other announcements came as hours passed. The other passengers hurried to the counter to change to other airlines so as to not miss the night flight to Brazil.

We waited. Should we try to change? My opinion was to wait on the regular flight and pray. And wait upon the Lord.

I commented, "The Lord has called us and helped each one to arrive here in these seats in the Oklahoma City airport. He knows. Perhaps the night flight will be delayed. Perhaps the plane in Dallas will have mechanical problems. Who knows? God knows."

The group agreed to wait, and some scattered to find snacks!

We boarded our plane in Oklahoma City after the time the night flight was to leave from Dallas. Oh, well, off we went.

As soon as we arrived in Dallas, officials met us to hurry our group to a shuttle bus to take us to a plane. Have you guessed it? The night flight plane to Brazil had been delayed with electronic problems in the cockpit of our plane. Right. Again the student athletes received rewards on their young journey of faith.

For the other rewards of their mission trip, I will let them tell you in their own words.

Darci Scott Goldesberry, Oklahoma

I clapped at the gate of *Lar Nova Vida* in May of 2010, when I went to Araras with a group from

Hillsdale Free Will Baptist College. The process to even go was, for me, a learning experience. I was fighting the battle – maybe fueled by the devil – of whether or not to fill out the application, based solely on the assumption that I felt I was not in a very strong spiritual state. Not only that fear, but also the question of how I was going to get the huge sum of money required to go was delaying my decision.

I was completely taking for granted that my just being willing to go was a huge spiritual step, as well as the fact that all I had to do was ask God for His will to be done. If it was His will, the money would come as well. In the end, God answered my prayers and I found myself on a plane to Brazil. This in itself was a testament to the will of God in the lives of my group members. Delays in visa arrivals and delays in flights are just among the many examples of the possible tampering by the devil in our plans to serve.

My experience in Brazil showed me several things. It showed me what true giving looked like. Throughout my schooling, I have had several opportunities to volunteer my time; but throughout my schooling, my emphasis was placed on serving my time to get the requirements out of the way. The boys at *Lar Nova Vida* showed me that true giving is not selfish, not to fulfill a requirement. True giving comes from the heart. Even though they don't have much, the boys still give a lot.

Also, it showed me that God's love is indeed universal, as is His praise. While there we sang; we sang a lot. The greatness of God was revealed in the fact that, though two languages were being sung at the same time,

Portuguese and English, praising God still makes beautiful music!

I went to Brazil hoping to be a positive influence: but, in return, I came back a better, more spiritually sound person. I went hoping to change the life of a least one person, when in fact, I came back as the one who was changed.

Not a day goes by that I don't think of my experiences in Brazil. It is a time that I will carry with me always.

Kay Talley, Oklahoma
Praise the Lord there are always more and new ways to serve God, even after retiring from teaching and coaching!

It was a special Women Active for Christ meeting when I first met Shirley Combs. She spoke about our missionary work in Brazil and the needs there. In my mind's eye I could see those young boys learning about Jesus and immediately God led me to GO.

From our home church (Trinity FWB in Oklahoma City, Oklahoma) we could help with offerings and such, but God seemed to say, "You need to do more!!" Then He provided the way. Hillsdale students were going, many were softball/baseball players (I was a coach at the high school level), and I would be allowed to join them.

Coach Kay Talley

From the preparations before leaving to go to Brazil, to our final destination at the airport to depart for the USA, God blessed us with smiles, tears, joy, and sometimes sorrow.

When our church started collecting clothes, shoes, toys, games, and money to take to the boys, God was good to us. The fundraising activities, meetings with the team, all the excitement and eager anticipation, everything made us grow in God.

We finally clapped at the gate of the Children Home, *Lar Nova Vida* in *Araras*, Brazil. The thrill of meeting with the boys and staff at their home made my heart jump with joy. I got a warm and fuzzy feeling as we felt their love for God, the workers, and the "new" missionaries from Oklahoma.

We sang songs, prayed, ate, and played with them. Every evening was an opportunity to witness to them, even though they did not speak our language, nor we theirs.

Some things stand out about our visit to *Lar Nova Vida*:

Babysitting with the very young, playing on the floor with cars and balls, hugs, rocking, feeding, singing to them.

Nightly services – singing, praying, scriptures,

learning about Jesus.

Playground time – playing ball, swinging, chasing each other, jumping and romping. All was such great fun for them and for us.

Painting and cleaning rooms for the older boys, and they were allowed to help.

Sorting and passing out the clothes we brought with us. They were so excited about new hats, scarves, and jackets.

Hospital visits – rocking, comforting and playing with the little boys from LNV in the hospital.

Soup ministry – preparing and delivering food to the needy on the street.

Purchasing collection books and stamps for their favorite soccer players.

Visiting their schools, churches and neighborhoods.

Even crying when they had to be disciplined.

Besides the activities for the boys at the Children's Home, we enjoyed lunches with the staff, church services, and meals with pastors and church members. Watching the children's band music lessons, the singing services, and trips to stores as shopping was done for food and supplies.

The workers were eager to teach us about their culture, how work was done, and to show us their handiwork. In exchange, I taught some of the ladies how to make jewelry from russet potatoes.

The experience of bunking in the hospitality house with the Hillsdale college students, learning their new songs, sharing housekeeping and meals with younger Christians, and sharing church services and devotionals with another generation, what a blessing!

I had previously been on a mission trip to Mexico where we helped build a church. It was a great experience and it blessed us a great deal.

Thanks to God for workers such as Jim and Shirley who continue in the Lord's work in their retirement age. God blessed me so much with each smile and song.

I will never forget the young men and the staff at *Lar Nova Vida*. We are remembering them with prayers daily, with love and photos.

TO MY PEERS: Accept God's challenge. Step out on the waters. "We'll Work 'til Jesus Comes" is a good motto. We are never too old or too shy to stretch out our arms to reach across the world to take the hand of our fellowman and lead them to Jesus.

Tadd Wagner, Missouri

The trip hadn't even begun yet, and I was already seeing God at work. It was my first time to ever leave the country, or board a plane, for that matter. I guess I didn't fully understand the amount of time that obtaining a visa would take. I had already seen God at work throughout the fundraising process, but when my visa finally arrived just a couple of hours before we left for our flight, I couldn't deny God's hand in it all.

On the ten hour overnight flight from Dallas to Sao Paulo, Brazil, I remember interacting with a man probably in his early 20's who – simply put – needed some Jesus in his life. (Don't we all.) He had no joy. As I listened to him tell his stories, I could see that he had hurt and pain in his life that had caused him to be resentful and angered at the world. I cannot remember all I said to him, but I had the feeling that I had given him hope. While I do not know what became of this man, I do hope that he was able to see Christ in me that day.

When we finally reached Brazil, and caught up on sleep, we had the opportunity to become acquainted with the kids of *Lar Nova Vida* (the New Life Home). Many of these kids have literally been rescued from the streets of *Araras*, Brazil.

We were able to form amazing relationships with the awesome kids through soccer, music and the time that we spent in the home with them. One of my favorite memories is standing before them at a Sunday night service, being blessed by their hearts of worship as they cried out in a Portuguese song to the same God that we worship with our English tongue.

While I can't tell you every story or experience from our team's trip to Brazil, there is one that I would like to share. Our team was eating at a pizzeria with a group of people from one of the Free Will Baptist churches in *Araras*. The pastor of the church, running late, showed up with a brace around his neck. He had been in a car wreck and had minor injuries. He said something while looking at me, and *Dona* Shirley interpreted what he was trying to tell me. He said that it looked like I would have to preach for him the next night. I laughed. He didn't.

I went back to my room that night and began to prepare for my first overseas sermon. I remember presenting the gospel to the people, through *Dona* Shirley's interpretation, and offering a time of response at the end of the service. I was told later that a Brazilian college student had made a decision for Christ that night. Because of my great preaching ability? Ha, certainly not. But because I had allowed God to use my life as a tool to bring His kingdom glory, and because of the power of the Holy Spirit to move in the lives of weak and broken people.

I encourage you – as Christ did in Matthew 10:39 – to lose your life for His sake; to be a tool for His kingdom; clay in the Potter's hands. Then you will find life.

I'm so thankful for *Dona* Shirley's example for the work that she and her husband have done in Brazil throughout the years. I wish to one day see the faces of the many people – young and old – that I met while in Brazil. Such a great experience. I find it fitting to end this writing the same way that I ended my daily journals while I was in Brazil: God is good. *Deus e' bom.*

CHAPTER 12
Bobbie Lee Leads Georgia Team

Bobbie Jo Lee, Georgia

I had finally gotten back in church after having been away for many years. Little did I know the adventure I was about to embark upon. I suppose everyone can look back and determine a defining moment in their life. That fork in the road where, if you had gone the other way, your life would have been very different.

Bobbie Lee with Flavia

It was a Wednesday night at the Frist Free Will Baptist Church in Albany, Georgia. I had finished a class with a group of girls early that night so they could go to a choir rehearsal. I thought I would catch the end of Bible study/prayer meeting but when I looked through the window of the door before entering, I saw a gray haired man I did not know speaking and almost did not go in. If I had not followed the urging to go in and sit down, I would have missed Jim and Shirley Combs telling about their experiences with the children in Brazil.

But sitting there, the stories gripped my heart and I knew then and there, when Shirley offered an open invitation to go on down to Brazil and help out, that somehow I would be going. That was in 2004.

That first trip I went alone. Jim and Shirley picked me up in São Paulo and the whirlwind of activity didn't stop until they deposited me back at the airport in São Paulo about ten days later.

There are so many stories I could tell, but I guess the thing I remember most about that trip was spending time with the children. There were two houses at that time and the first night I was there, Shirley told me they were short a housemother at the smaller children's house and she had a meeting to go to so she was going to drop me at the house to sit with the kids and would be back in a couple of hours.

I was so excited about meeting the children. The only problem was I spoke no Portuguese and they spoke no English. I found out a smile communicates in any language and a digital camera is a great icebreaker. Just like kids in the US, they loved to have their picture taken. I took pictures of them…they took pictures…then we looked at all the pictures and laughed and laughed.

I helped the older girls prepare some food and hugged and played with the little ones. My heart was so full of love for these children. I felt like my heart would burst!

In an instant I realized it was God's love pouring through me for them and I was humbled and honored that I was fortunate to be able to participate in His work that was going on in this place. This work that Jim and Shirley had begun and sacrificed so much of themselves for. I understood then what a great joy it is to be His hands and His feet. They showed me what "walking by faith" really means.

Shirley had given me suggestions of items to take so I had shopped and stuffed suitcases with all kinds of "stuff" for the kids. Kites, kites, and more kites. The kids all love kites. Friends from church were very generous with donations. One year a generous benefactor donated money for playground equipment, the next year someone donated their "beanie baby" collection (a very large collection of about 300). We gave beanie babies to all the kids, ladies at women's meetings, and everywhere we went, actually!

The next year I found "salvation bracelets" – beautiful bracelets with beads and charms telling the story of salvation. After hearing the devotional using the charm bracelet, each woman, Christian and non-Christian, repeated the story of salvation and received a bracelet. Many of them still wear them when we return on our visits.

Every year (coincidentally or providentially) I would come across something, somewhere – marked down to rock bottom and lots of them. Always something great to hand out as a gift wherever we went.

One year it was American flag pins marked down to about seven cents. We have given away a couple hundred of those. Each year (we'll be making our ninth trip next time we go) I am amazed to see how God works as He brings everything together to make each trip more amazing than the one previous.

We have a very generous friend who met every donation given with an equal dollar amount. This generosity allowed us to buy shoes for all the children for the last two years, bicycles for the boys, and bedding and supplies for each house.

Since our first year, my dear friend, Marie Glover, has made the trip with me every year. My mother made the trip two years running and her friends Maurene and Christine Daniel accompanied us one year. These ladies have such a heart for these children and are so loving and kind.

One of the most amazing things to me remains the fact of how we are received in Brazil. Being a Christian makes you part of the family of God…and that is how we are treated…like family. The overwhelming outpouring of love from our Brazilian sisters and brothers in Christ is hard to describe.

I can never thank Jim and Shirley enough for allowing us to be a small part of something bigger than ourselves. While tagging along we were able to help out when they were doing their weekly "soup" ministry, to visit nursing homes where we would sing and visit with the residents. We visited local churches, visited people in their homes, prayed with and for the sick, prayed at a baby dedication in a home, gone to baby showers, attended a funeral, visited and helped kids who moved out on their own, and met and made friends with some wonderful people.

Of course, the greatest thing was being with the children and hopefully making a difference in their lives. We like to think we have helped and blessed them in some ways, but the blessing of having known these children and watching them grow and flourish far outweighs anything we have done. I will always cherish the memories of those sweet smiles and the hugs and kisses from children who just want to be loved and appreciated.

My husband, Jimmy, accompanied Marie and me for the last three years. He has enjoyed working with the boys and has been instrumental in starting a program of Jiu Jitsu training for them. Donations from his friends and Jiu Jitsu buddies allowed him to

Bobbie and Dr. Jim Lee With Soraia and baby

buy mats for the training and uniforms for all the boys.

I am so glad I listened to that still, small voice that urged me to go in to the meeting that Wednesday night. It was a defining moment that changed my life forever.

Dr. Jim Lee, Georgia

Bro. Billy Hanna, my pastor, regularly states, "I don't understand everything I know about this scripture or topic." I like that.

With this in mind...I don't understand (1) what made a fifty year old man (me) walk into a Brazilian Jiu Jitsu class, (2) what made this old man stay through the first bruising years of training, (3) and what made him decide to compete in tournaments (local, Atlanta, Los Angeles and Rio de Janeiro, Brazil).

About this time, my wife, Bobbie, attended a meeting with Jim and Shirley Combs at our church in Atlanta. Bobbie decides, if I'm going to Rio to fight, she'll go to Brazil to help out at the children's home.

Dr. Jim and his Jiu Jitsu warriors

She returned telling of all the blessings and also discipline problems, runaways, family crises, etc.

Over the years, I met more and more Jiu Jitsu practitioners. It became apparent to me that if you train Brazilian Jiu Jitsu...you are family. This family accepts you no matter from where you came (geographically, socially, or financially). I have befriended Jiu Jitsu guys that don't understand a word of English and have very little in common with me and as my family says, "didn't know me from Adam". I was still Jiu Jitsu family.

However, early in my training I suffered a miscommunication with a "black belt" who was giving me a private lesson. This miscommunication led to me being *choked* unconscious and left lying on the mat! You see, there is a mindset attained when a Brazilian man earns his Black Belt. He demands respect.

While sitting on the back pew totally absorbed in one of Bro. Billy sermons, it came to me…a Jiu Jitsu school in the children's home in Brazil. Perfect! The boys get to burn off some energy training. They would have a strict, disciplined, unwavering father figure, and a pathway to and through previously unattainable doors. Many belts (especially black belts) use Jiu Jitsu as a tool to get to other countries and opportunities.

Initially it was just a thought. Over time the idea would not go away. After a while I asked my wife about this…sounded good to her…she asked Shirley and she liked the idea.

So, how do you start a Jiu Jitsu school 5,000 miles away? Turns out, groundwork was already laid out. Marina, a volunteer dentist at the children's home had a black belt professor, Japao (pronounced Jap-a-own), who arranged for an instructor. I called Marcio Feitosa (my black belt instructor in California). Marcio sends seven crates of used *gis* (uniforms). Okay…I had *gis* and a black belt instructor…needed money. I approached my Jiu Jitsu family here in Georgia. Regular guys like Glenn, Rodney, Steve, George, and more, gave money. The money bought mats and continues to pay the black belt instructor Rangel (pronounced Han-gell). George keeps us in *gis*. To date, we have had several companies give us gear at no or greatly reduced costs. (Heroes like Suzzi Dahl of BJJ Mart and Howard Liu of Howard's Combat Kimonos).

Remember what I said earlier? The groundwork was already in place.

I pray the Jiu Jitsu School continues, for there are overwhelming positive results that can come of the discipline these kids learn from this project at *Lar Nova Vida* of Brazil.

A Letter from Dr. Jim (the last day he was with the boys)
Dear Renan and boys at Lar Nova Vida,

Now you are young. One morning you will wake up and you will be a man. You will be this man who is the result of what you have experienced.

Let me explain – If you are a bad boy and only know other bad boys and bad things, you will become a bad man.

You are very fortunate to be exposed to many good things and people. You know that God loves you and will look-out for you. You are surrounded by people who love you (Mrs. Shirley, Pastor Jim, Kimberly, Vicente, Marina, and many others.) And yes, me! (Very much.) It is important for you to know this. You are a young boy now, but you will know this better when you are a man.

One year ago, I did not know I would ever come to Araras. But God said to me (I don't know how) "Jimmy, go and take Jiu Jitsu to those boys in

Who's Clapping At Our Gate?

Araras...5,000 miles away"
    God provided kimonos, mats, many helpers, and your teachers. No one knew God would put Rickson Gracie, Bobbie Joe, and me in Paulinia last Saturday morning. Rickson has never seen you boys. When Rickson Gracie woke up that morning, he did not know God would have him make a video for you, Renan, and the other boys.
    I do not know why God chose Jiu Jitsu to get me to Araras. There are too many things to try to know. You and I must have faith that God knows what He is doing.
    If I had not obeyed God...I never would have met you. I discovered right away that you are a very special and kind boy. I learned over these few days, that you are also a very smart boy.
    I wish my heart was as pure as yours.
    Bobbie and I love you and will miss you very much till we meet again.
    I am sure God has a special purpose for you. Make God proud of you every day and one day you will discover that purpose.
    Renan, if I were your father or your big brother, I would tell you, "always ask yourself – Would God have me do this?" Trust God to do the right things. You will probably not understand this until you are a man. But that man will be the end product of God's will! (And you will probably be a very good Jiu Jitsu warrior, too!)
    We hope to return. You work on your Jiu Jitsu and always help the smaller boy and all girls and ladies.
    Love, Jimmy Lee

P.S. Renan, it is important for you now to let God be your father. I will always be your big brother.

The following is a loose translation from Portuguese to English of a letter young Renan wrote to Dr. Jim Lee.

Dear Dad Jim,

Thanks for all that you did for LNV. You became my Big Dad because when you came to LNV, I felt a big emotion because you came to our home to help try Jiu-Jitsu for us. You are making part of my family and of Dona Shirley's.

I'm going to give the best of myself to be a great warrior. I always will pray for you that all will go right in your service and also for our family. I, Mom Bobbie, and you Dad Jim, and my brothers Alex and Dalvan.

Dad Jim, continue following the path of God. He always will show the path certain and also don't stop going to church. Since the day that you left, I have been missing you because that you went away.

I and you and Mom Bobbie Lee will always be a family united. Nothing can us separate. We always will be firm in the promises of the Lord Jesus. In the bathroom I cried because you were not by my side.

Dad Jim, I thee love for what you did for me and for everyone.

I thank Aunt Shirley for caring for me. She always will be in our hearts. You, Bobbie Lee and Aunt Shirley.

I love you, Dad and Mom, Kisses and Hugs. Send me a letter for me to know how you are.

I love you and God, too, Renan

Bobbie Jean Deese, Florida

My daughter, Bobbie Jo, invited me to go to Brazil on a mission trip with her and a friend, Marie Glover. They had gone the year before and had a great time.

Shirley Combs, a missionary from Brazil, had come to the States on a states-side assignment and told about their ministry and an orphanage that the missionary

Christine Daniel, Marie Glover and
Bobbie Jean Deese

and her husband, Jim, had started. They visited the Free Will Baptist Church in Albany, Georgia, and presented a program about their work there and all the homeless children in the town.

After the program, Shirley Combs invited people to come up and talk to them. My daughter and her friend, Marie Glover, fell in love with the pictures of all the children and the needs there. They decided they would love to go on a mission trip to Brazil. So they started planning to go in 2005. They loved it and invited me to go in 2006.

Shirley Combs and her husband met us at the airport in Sao Paulo. The drive to *Araras* was beautiful.

We stayed busy all the time – we helped cook, clean, paint, go to lady's meeting, and church. The most memorable thing we did was every week the ladies cooked two large pots of vegetable soup and loaded them on the back of their van and went to a very poor area. People actually lived in huts covered in plastic and card board. People came from every direction with a pot, bowl or whatever would hold soup. They had wonderful bread there and each person received a small loaf of bread with their soup.

The trip was a great experience and I am happy and blessed that I went twice.

From the journal of:

Christine Daniel, Georgia

<u>Wednesday</u>, August 15

There were four us who left Albany, Georgia, in 2006 to go to Brazil. We met at Dr. Jim and Bobbie Lee's clinic and spent about an hour waiting for Bobbie Lee to "wrap up" her work there. She had been there since two or three o'clock am trying to finish her work so she could leave.

Doc Jimmy helped us load all of our luggage. And we did have a lot of luggage! Two of Bobbie's bags looked like "body bags". (She took lots of things for the children at the Children's Home, *Lar Nova Vida.*) We wanted to help but Doc Jimmy said to "stand back and put our hands in our pockets".

We drove to Atlanta and got on a shuttle bus to take us to the airport.

Three of us went through security fine. Bobbie's mom was pulled aside to be checked more thoroughly. They found a small knife in the pocket of one of her carry-on bags. She had no idea she had that knife. We all had a good laugh about that.

We left Atlanta at 4:40 pm and arrived in Miami at 6:40 pm. We flew out of Miami at 8:30 pm in a HUGE plane – a Boeing 767.

We were served supper around 9:30 pm and then tried to sleep some. We were served breakfast around 3:00 am. We were half asleep when we were told they were serving breakfast and I said rather loudly, "YOU HAVE GOT TO BE KIDDING!"

We got to São Paulo airport around 5:30 am, Friday morning. We had to wait in a long line to go through customs. When we got to the baggage claim, Jim Combs was waiting for us. Jim had rented a van and a driver to take us to Araras where he and Shirley live. Shirley's leg was in a cast so she waited for us at their home.

Jim and Shirley have a nice country home. It has a stucco-type exterior with a red slate roof – even the dog house had this type roof. They had lots and lots of tile floors – even the front porch was tiled. It was interesting to note that they had no carpet, no air conditioner, no heat, and no closets. They have beautiful pieces of furniture, which reminded me of chifferobes.

All of the interior doors were arched. Their windows and doors are left open most of the time.

Their property reminded us of a compound – with a tall concrete fence/wall around it. It had a tall iron gate that operated with a remote.

We stayed in their hospitality house at the back of the property. Jim renovated an open building specifically to accommodate large groups. Each one of us had our own bedroom and bath. Three of the bedrooms had two sets of bunk bed in them and one had a double bed. They could easily sleep 14 or 15 people. In the middle was the sitting area, the dining area, and a fully equipped kitchen.

We were immediately introduced to the warm hospitality of the Brazilians, because placed on the counter was a beautiful potted mum, a bowl of candy, and some fresh tropical fruit.

We unpacked, freshened up, and after about an hour, we walked down to the Comb's house for lunch. Lunch is the big meal of the day in Brazil. For our first Brazilian meal, we had some boneless fried chicken, beans on rice, slaw, and a delicious chocolate pudding/cake that Shirley had cooked in the microwave. Jim showed us how to add strawberries and cream to it to make it even more delicious. The meal was scrumptious.

Jim and Shirley had an 18 year old girl who was in the Children's Home, but now lived with them. She had no family to go to so she helps Shirley in the day time and goes to school at night. Her name is Mariana and is very pretty. She usually sits at the table and eats with Jim and Shirley but, for some reason, chose not to do that when they had visitors.

Thursday, August 17 –

After lunch we rested and then got ready to go to church. They have their mid-week services on Thursday nights instead of Wednesday nights. We went to II *Igreja Batista Livre* (Second Free Will Baptist Church in JD. Candida) for our first exposure/impression of the Brazilian people.

They are so friendly, loveable, and seemingly happy. They greet you with hugs and kisses on the cheek - men, women, and children. This is the church the children from the Home attend. They are transported there on a large bus with the Children's Home name on it, *Lar Nova Vida.*

The children came up to us and hugged us and wanted to sit beside us. They behaved well and really enjoyed participating in the singing. A teen-age boy from the Home played the guitar. And, they were so glad to see Bobbie Jo Lee. This was her third trip there. She had also been listening to a CD teaching how to speak Portuguese and she impressed us and them with her ability to communicate with them.

In the services, they sing a lot of praise hymns and hymns (none we knew). They pray really long prayers, both men and women. The pastor spoke. The pastor's wife seems to be the Song Leader and the Children's Director. They also have a Praise Team.

They put a lot of feeling in worshipping and all of the children participate. They have a keyboard – no piano nor organ. They have two or three banners in the Sanctuary. The Sunday School rooms are up-stairs.

Their "offering plate" was a wood pedestal that was small at the top and big at the bottom – probably three or four feet tall. It has an opening/slit where you drop your money and was located at the front of the church. (All ages marched to the front and reverently placed their offering while music played).

The services must have lasted one and a half hours. Time doesn't mean much to them. They just enjoy worshipping the Lord. Jim and Shirley have started churches and founded the Children's Home since they went to Brazil in the 1960's.

Friday, Aug. 18 –

After breakfast at the Combs' house, Shirley went over our agenda and answered any questions we had. There were two interesting things Jim and Shirley told us about. One was to use "thumbs up" for the okay or good sign – do not make a circle with your pointer finger and thumb. That evidently meant something vulgar. The other was to always say "hotel" instead of motel. They associate motels with prostitution.

After breakfast, we went to the Children's Home which was about 15 minutes away. Bobbie Lee drove because, the week before, Shirley had fallen and fractured her ankle. She was wearing a big shoe and was on crutches.

The children ran out to meet us and to hug us and to kiss us and to help us if we had anything that needed carrying in. The workers are so friendly and sweet and treated us like royalty.

We entered the Home after clapping at the tall iron gate. We ate lunch with the children who were not in class. They have three sessions of school – morning, afternoon, and at night (for those who may have jobs, like Mariana). The house parents feed their children breakfast and dinner in their individual houses to keep the small group atmosphere. Lunch is the only meal everyone eats together in the dining hall.

After lunch, we proceeded to see what we could do to help get ready for the big celebration to be held the following day to celebrate the Home's fifteenth anniversary. It opened in 1991. We raked, used the blower, picked up the trash, hung photos on the walls, but the majority of the time we washed the white plastic chair that were to be used the next day. Everyone was helping – the workers, as well as some of the children.

The large room where the celebration was to take place reminded me of our gymnasium. It has beautiful tiled floors. Some of the workers came in with soapy water and water hose and cleaned the floor. It didn't look that dirty but it was shining when they finished.

Shirley showed us where the tables and chairs could be set up. There were tables with pretty lace tablecloths on them for framed pictures of the children and for the refreshments.

We went back to our place rather tired. But we went back that night to *Lar Nova Vida* for an evening praise service. There were other adults and young people there, in addition to the LNV children.

There was lots of singing, special and praise songs. There was a boys' quartet which sounded great. One of the boys was in a wheelchair. Shirley introduced us and had us to say a few words, with a Brazilian lady interpreter, of course. The same lady told a Bible story with another girl using a puppet.

Saturday, Aug. 19 –

THE BIG DAY. At breakfast, Shirley showed us the local paper and was reading an article and pictures about *Lar Nova Vida's* fifteenth anniversary. They had sent a reporter out the day before to interview Shirley and to get some pictures.

The program was to start around 2:30 pm. There was a sign-in table for all of the attendees which was estimated to 300 to 350. There were beautiful potted mums everywhere and ficus type trees. The floor was shining like new money, the clean white chairs in place, and the children's pictures and photos were proudly displayed around the room. Everything looked beautiful!

The cooks made three or four huge rectangular cakes with white icing and strawberries on top. Sandwiches were made with some kind of meat spread inside that reminded me of a small hot dog bun. Their drink was something like ginger ale which they poured straight from the bottle into glasses without ice. They also served everyone instead of your going up to the table and serving yourself.

There were several speakers (local preachers from different denominations, local merchants, city dignitaries.) Shirley spoke and thanked the visitors from the community who had helped during the years. The children sang and some played musical instruments. The program lasted about two hours. Time just isn't important to them – they just enjoy themselves.

Everyone was talking to Shirley and we were the last ones to leave. We also took a couple home. They wanted to show us their place – especially Marie and Bobbie. They acted like it was an improvement from where they lived last year. It was so sad – just a hole in the wall, literally. Shirley said he got a small disability check each month – hardly enough to live on.

We came home to get ready for ten or eleven girls to come and spend some time with us. Bobbie's mom brought some crafts for them to do – jewelry making, etc.

The girls got to our place around nine or nine thirty that night. They had a ball making necklaces, playing games, etc. It was about eleven fifteen pm when they left. They all spent the night at Shirley and Jim's house with Mariana.

Sunday, August 20 –

We went to Sunday School. They do not have preaching services until Sunday night, but with opening exercises, the lesson, and closing exercises, Sunday School lasts one and a half hours.

We went back to Shirley and Jim's for lunch and while we were eating, their son, Kemper, and his Brazilian wife, Simone, came in with two desserts. Everyone moved over and made room for them.

That afternoon the boys from the Home came over. They swam. There is a pool near where we stayed. I think I heard that Jim used it for a baptistery. The children played at a pool table that was on our porch. They flew kites that Bobbie had brought them. They played soccer some. You could tell they had been to Shirley and Jim's house many times before because they were right at home there.

The night services at the churches in Brazil are the main services. The Children's Home bus brings all the children and workers to all of the church services. When we arrive, we get more hugs and kisses and the children want to sit by us. The little boy sitting next to me turned right to the Scripture reading in Nehemiah. Shirley said most of them know the books of the Bible.

Monday, August 21 –

We went downtown to have hot dogs at a street vendor, Christian friends of the Combs. We sat on stools right there on the sidewalk a few feet from the vendors while they cooked them. Very different! The hot dog consists of a huge bun with a long wiener, a fried egg, corn, lettuce, potatoes, and the dressing. It was very good. For that and a canned soda, we paid the equivalent of three dollars, I believe.

We took a walk around the square and afterwards, we stopped by Kemper's house. He teaches English classes and was teaching two girls who looked to be in their early twenties. He left them to talk to us. They told us a little about themselves and we did the same. We then went to the piano to sing a song for them. I just randomly chose "The Family of God". I couldn't believe it when we got to the second verse. It goes like this:

"From the door of an orphanage, to the house of the King.

No longer an outcast, a new song I sing;

From rags unto riches, from the weak to the strong;

I'm not worthy to be here, but praise God, I belong.

I had sung that song many times but never had the words had such meaning as they did right then.

Tuesday, August 22 –

Jim took Shirley back to the doctor to get the cast off her foot. She had a seven am appointment. When they got back, they told us the

Home called and wanted us to go have lunch there, which we did.

We befriended a lady in the grocery store a few days before who sought us out when she heard us speaking English She told me she spoke five languages – Portuguese, English, Spanish, Italian, and French. She is an artist. She visited the Home that afternoon and hopefully we made a friend for the Home as a volunteer to give the children art lessons. Shirley loves to have volunteers come and give the children special lessons and attention.

Wednesday, August 23 –

In the last few days, several of our group had felt puny but I really pushed myself all day because I wanted to go with everyone to serve soup in a really, really low income area of town. Some of the people are relatives of the children in the Home. The Home does this every Wednesday evening. They cook two huge (and I mean HUGE) pots of soup with donated ingredients. Then all the volunteer workers eat some for dinner, load it up, along with donated bread roll, and take it to the area and park at the end of a street.

People start coming from every direction, adults and children, with bowls in their hands to get some soup. It is really a humbling experience. They come out of houses that are nothing more than shanties. They are the epitome of the poor.

Thursday, August 24 –

We had a wonderful last meal with Jim and Shirley. They are such a sweet couple. She is from Oklahoma and he is from West Virginia. They met at Free Will Baptist Bible College (Welch College) in

Nashville, Tennessee. All three of their children (Kemper, Cindy, and Tânia) graduated from Hillsdale Free Will Baptist College in Moore, Oklahoma. Shirley told us we could go back to the Children's Home one last time before leaving.

We went to *Lar Nova Vida* for our very special send off. Everyone, workers and children, came outside on the veranda for us to stand in a circle holding hands. Each one of the adults said some of the sweetest things to us (through Shirley's interpreting) and we were able to say something to them. Then Pastor Oscar prayed the sweetest prayer. There were lots of hugs and kisses and tears as we said goodbye.

That night we arrived at the São Paulo airport. Bobbie Jo Lee was flying on to Rio de Janeiro to meet her husband, Jimmy. Now we were without our fearless leader. Jim went with Bobbie Jo to help her get her luggage checked and Shirley stayed with us while we got ours checked.

While we were in line a young woman with a small baby approached Shirley and asked her for some help. She told her she couldn't give her any money, but she would be glad to buy her something to eat and buy the baby some diapers, if she needed some. Shirley did both and talked to her about the need for the Lord in her life. The girl said her husband was backslidden. Shirley told her she needed to be an example to him and it might bring him around.

Jim said it seemed they were always like magnets to people like that no matter where they went.

It will be a long trip home to Georgia and we will arrive tired, but with a lifetime of memories.

CHAPTER 13
David led the North Carolina Group

Youth minister, David Mizelle and wife, Christy, took a good group of young people from their Free Will Baptist church in western North Carolina to help us with ministry. They were there in Araras on July 4, (which is not a holiday in Brazil, of course, and it is winter time). Our son Kemper took his students from his language school to our hospitality house to visit with the American visitors.

David and Christy

At first, his students were a little shy to use their English as a second language skill, but the Americans' friendliness broke the ice.

The Brazilians commented that they didn't know what to expect. But as the mission group sang, played the guitar, laughed, preached and shared, their hearts were *warmed*. I remember Brother David preached about Independence Day, then challenged the group with how they could have true independence and freedom in Jesus Christ.

Kemper and some of his students finally

arranged some fire crackers and sparklers (difficult, since it wasn't a holiday there) which were shot before the group left. Our home is outside the city limits, and the sky was clear and full of fantastic stars.

Each Brazilian student took home a small American flag. Perhaps on their Brazilian Independence Day on September 7 they have thought about that message of liberty in Christ a *gringo* and his group shared with them through English as a second language.

The following is from Pastor David Mizelle.

David Mizelle, North Carolina/Virginia

One of the greatest privileges of serving as a student minister was the opportunity to involve the group in missions. Short term missions served several purposes in local church ministries.

These purposes at times were not planned, but the results were welcomed. First, they gave the opportunity for students to see other people and cultures and values, to see them as God values them. It is easy to stay in the south and see that the south, with all of its people and traditions, will be the only region that God sees as valuable. Second, it gave students the opportunity to prepare themselves spiritually. That gives God a wonderful opportunity to speak truth to the students and call them into His work

I thank God for these opportunities.

The Road to Brazil

While serving as Student Pastor at Rocky Pass Free Will Baptist Church in Marion, North Carolina. I began praying for an opportunity to take a group into a different area of the world on a short term trip.

We had served at a number of home mission churches in the States. We served two summers in Puerto Rico with the Bevins and Fannis. Our group had grown spiritually, and my desire was for them to experience God's work in a different area. I began looking at our works in South America and praying for each of the missionaries.

I reached out to the Combs who were more than willing to host a group. We began making preparations to go to Brazil. After many yard sales, car washes, and spaghetti dinners, our funds were raised and we were off.

Hodge Podge of Memories

After landing in Brazil, we all loaded into a small bus that would take us a few hours from the airport to where we would be staying. There are so many memories that I still have that bless me when I think about them.

North Carolina youth

Who's Clapping At Our Gate?

We had many services that we attended in the ten days. I remember a quote from Mr. Combs that I still laugh about. Mrs. Combs had us planned to attend a service almost every night. Mr. Combs spoke up and said, "I'm going to take the boys fishing. I'm not that spiritual." I don't know if that will make it into this book

Our boys loved spending time fishing, preparing stools for the children's home, playing soccer with the children, or sharing and singing in various services. We drove from place to place in a 60's VW bus. I often thought that bus would make a great bus for our youth group at home. We were in the middle of Brazil's winter. They suffered with 60-80 degree weather. While their youth were wearing sweat shirts and coats, we were in shorts and t-shirts.

There was a young girl that worked for the Combs. She came out to see what was going on. Our group had jumped in the pool and the boys were messing around. She was too close and one of the boys grabbed her and jumped in the pool with her. She thought she would freeze.

One of the events that we organized was a Fourth of July celebration, USA style. Since our trip was over the holiday, we invited the English students that Kemper taught to come to be a part of this celebration. We tried to get as many typical "cook out" types of food and prepared a meal and a message to share.

I spoke about freedom. Freedom that is synonymous with the Fourth of July and freedom that we can have in Jesus Christ.

Mr. Combs knew a guy...so, the boys loaded up and went to the "guy" that made fireworks. They were bombs! They were bigger, louder, and more powerful than anything I every bought in the states, and they were cheap. Needless to say, we had a lot.

While the girls made lime slushies with the fruit from the trees on the property, the boys were anticipating darkness so they could light their fireworks. With little warning, we set off one of the best individual fireworks displays and one of the loudest I had been a part of.

I learned some things through this. Brazilians must not like loud noises. They all ended up in the house wondering why we like everything loud. All of the students ended up in the house.

The other event that impacted our group the most was the time of serving soup and bread in the *villa*. I suspect that no one in our group had experienced lines of people waiting to be served soup out of the back of a pickup truck. There were children as small as two to three years old standing with their containers waiting for the only hot, nourishing meal they would get for a week. We all went away feeling so blessed and yet so spoiled to live in the abundance that is available in North America.

Worship

I love to worship with God's people. I am often convicted when I have the privilege to worship in other countries. My experience with worship in other cultures has always been an area of conviction. I love the freedom and the excitement that is there in other countries, especially those in Latin America. It feels so encouraging to be in their services and I would always go away feeling encouraged.

Conclusion

Our trip to Brazil was one of the most memorable. For me it was a time that God was speaking to me and changing direction in my life. For our group, he was shaping them and calling them into a life of ministry.

It was good to meet other believers that all we had in common was Jesus. For me, that was enough. That is a lesson that I have tried to remember all throughout my years in ministry.

I thank our missionaries for their examples and lives of service to peoples that, most of us, will only meet outside of this life time. To all of our missionaries who give opportunities to disrupt their lives for a week, thank you. The results of our short time with you all changed us and blessed us. May God continue to bless each of you.

(At the time of this report, David was pastor of First FWB Church of Bristol, Virginia church. They have four children since their Brazil trip.)

CHAPTER 14
North, South, East and West Clapped at Our Gate

From Sugar Land Came Sweet Autumn
Autumn, a young lady from the Sugar Land FWB mission (now Eagle Heights FWB Church) was sent by her church, and was she a "wow" success. While she was in *Araras*, she wanted to be baptized with a church group at our *chacara* pool. We advised her to call Randy Puckett, her pastor in Texas, and he gave his blessing. That really impressed the Brazilians present at the baptism.

Autumn played the guitar and helped in the worship music and soup ministry and was especially loved by our youth. I'll let her tell her own story.

Autumn Downing, Texas
Brazil...how do I start? It's been since I was 18 and I'm 28...so over ten years ago. It was right after I graduated from High School, and it's still a vivid memory in my mind. When you go on a mission trip, big or small, it makes an impact. Most go to make an impact on people, but I believe it makes an even bigger impact on the ones doing the work.

When I look back on that trip, sometimes I'm like, "How did I do that?" That is when I'm reminded that it was definitely what God wanted me to do. I think about how I went to another country, all alone, not knowing the language, not knowing the culture, or a single person there. So it was definitely inspired by God. It had to have been, because of all the things that lined up so perfectly before, during, and after the trip. From moment one, you could tell that it was something that God wanted me to do. Now I know why, because two of the biggest life lessons for me were learned on that trip to Brazil.

Like any mission trip, you have to find a way to raise money, and if you know me, you know I'm not someone that was really a door to door knocker. I never really did those fundraisers in school either, and I didn't really feel comfortable asking people for money. Not even my family. So when I knew I had to raise money I was a little worried.

Even though I knew God would help me, if this was what he wanted me to do, this trip gave it deeper meaning of how true that really is to me. For me, going to Brazil taught me a deeper faith in that if God wants

Autumn at the baptism

you to do something, it's going to happen whether you are open to it or not at the beginning. Yes, I can get caught up in worrying about things or get emotional and dramatic about life issues, but once I ground myself it has been easy to have faith that God will provide, because of when God sent me to Brazil.

When I arrived in Brazil, I really had no idea what I was going to do and how I was going to do it other than I was to work with orphans. I was just there to help in any way that I could or in any way that I was needed.

I just needed God to be in control and not push myself to meet my goals and agenda. Just to be a servant, just exist, just be. I felt so taken care of in Brazil. I had no wants or needs, and it was beautiful. Mr. and Mrs. Combs were wonderful people to work with and for, and they were and still are amazing examples of God's love.

It was very interesting to me how relaxed I was and how not being able to speak the language never really got to me. If you know me, you know I can talk and that it's a huge part of me. But in Brazil God took care of me, because I didn't know any Portuguese. I was unable to verbally communicate every day for about five to seven hours a day for six whole weeks, unless the Combs or some of the Brazilian college students who spoke English were around. So God gave the people I met and me peace and it made things easier.

You really had to focus on the person, not just what they were saying, but also how they were saying it and the context. There's something so very valuable about nonverbal communication, and we take it for granted: a simple smile, a nod, a gesture, a hug, a tear, a laugh, a stare, a grunt – they're universal. It just makes us closer to the person we're trying to communicate with.

Every day was something different. I had a location and a job given to me most every day, but it was having only a general direction that enabled me to be open for whatever I was meant to do or learn, or help with, or give, or receive. Whatever God wanted.

Like for instance, every Wednesday I would make soup with the church and take it to the nearby villages, where people would come running with their buckets ready, and I would wonder why they weren't in tears because of their lives. Some hardly had any clothing. These people had nothing, or so I thought, but when I met the people, they had more joy in their hearts than most people I know who have a lot of "stuff". They focused on what they had, and not on what they didn't have.

It gave true meaning to the scripture in Matthew 6:25-34. "Therefore I tell you, do not worry about your life, what you will eat or drink; or about your body what you will wear…but seek first his kingdom and his righteousness, and these thing will be given to you as well".

I remember a lot of people telling me before I left Texas, "Don't eat the fruit, don't drink the water, don't eat the vegetables, be careful what you touch", and it can really make someone not want to go. What Brazil taught me is that when it gets to a point and someone is in need, your worries about A, B and C are pointless. You need to recognize that God is not going to let anything happen to you that you can't handle. You can sit here all day and say do, don't do, even with good reasons, but if you have a calling, go into it knowing it is what God wants you to do, and do not hesitate. James 4:17, "So whoever knows the right thing to do and fails to do it, for him it is sin."

Will you meet every need out there? No. But you will meet every need that God allows you to, if you respond to it in faith. I guarantee it. But you have to be open to it, and you have to not let your fears get in the way.

Luckily, God taught me that early on in my trip. Later in my time there, three new children came to the orphanage, and I was asked to help bathe them. They were covered with sores, smelled like they hadn't bathed in a very long time, and they had been living in the streets. Every disease known to man could have been on them, and could have been transmitted to me. How selfish of me if my thoughts would have been on that? Those children needed me, and fine, if I got a disease. But I am a firm believer that nothing happens without a reason and God allowing it.

In Brazil my life was changed. I felt a call on that trip to do something that really only had full meaning to me. I wanted to be baptized again. I had gone through confirmation already, and for those of you that don't practice or know of infant baptism, confirmation is the moment you decide to take on your faith as your own, and you accept Christ.

I wasn't converting and it wasn't that I didn't believe in God before and accept him as my Lord and Savior. It was that at that point I finally realized what I had been looking for. I wanted a purpose. I thought it was to be a missionary, to be a music minister, and to work with children...but it had nothing to do with that. Yes, those are things I feel strongly about and still do.

In Brazil, I was given a vision by God for me to fulfill a life calling and I accepted it. My vision was something I didn't really share because I didn't want to sound crazy, but the experiences and moments of humility had opened my eyes to receive my calling. So I took part in the most significant non-verbal expression possible in front of the very people that had helped me realize what my vision meant. My baptism was not the beginning of my faith, but the beginning of my ministry and accepting my calling.

Ever since Brazil, I've encouraged people to understand that work is all over the world, even in your own back yard. You just need to be open to the places God sends you to every day or the people God puts in your life, especially the difficult people.

Don't forget that things like a simple smile, a nod, a gesture, a hug, a tear, a laugh, a stare, a grunt, can go a long way. It is the condition of your heart, a daily attitude. You will have your ups and down, just like me. Satan is always trying to knock you down. We have to fall on our faces sometimes in order to see God's will for us, but I welcome God putting me there because certainly it is easy to get off track and to get in a bad attitude.

No matter where you are in your faith, missions can be a life changing event for you, and God can use you no matter what. Psalms 11:25, "Whoever brings blessings will be enriched, and one who waters will himself be watered."

Who's Clapping At Our Gate?

June Brunkhorst, California

I was sitting in my living room when I got a phone call from Jim and Shirley Combs, missionaries to Brazil. We had met Shirley's mom and dad, Marie and Tom Roberts, who were pastoring in Oklahoma in the 1950's. Marie led George to the Lord in 1959. They were a great people and over the years our families have kept in contact.

My husband, George, wasn't home at the time Jim called. Jim said, "I have a proposition for George. I want him to come to Brazil and paint the new orphanage here in *Araras*. I can't pay him but we can feed you and give you a place to stay." I said I would have George call him when he came home.

As soon as George found out Jim called, he was on the phone calling Jim before we even had a chance to talk about the situation. He told Jim that he would be glad to do it. George had a passion for children living in this situation since he had lived in one from the ages of three to five.

When he hung up the phone I asked him, "How can we go to Brazil with no money?? He said simply, "God will provide."

Two days later we got a settlement check from a fall that happened to George on his job as a painter. A scaffold had not been attached to the building properly and had collapsed. It fell on top of George and injured his ankle.

Fortunately, we already had our passports from a previous trip so George told me to look for tickets. Since this was now the middle of August and we needed to be there by September first, I contacted a travel agency. I found two round trip tickets for $1,400, well within our budget.

When we arrived in Sao Paulo, Jim met us in a borrowed car. In the capital city of São Paulo there is so much traffic people can only drive their cars on certain days of the week (according to the last number on their car license plate). Unfortunately this was the day he couldn't drive his own car the 100 miles between the two cities.

When we arrived in *Araras*, we drove by the orphanage to see what we would need. Jim didn't know the surprise that was waiting us. While Jim was at the airport to get us, someone had sent to the home a donation of paint and painting equipment. However, they didn't have any paint sprayers that would normally be used for such a big job. So Jim, George, and a helper from the orphanage brushed and rolled it all!

We were there 30 days, with George painting by day and preaching at night. I played the piano (in Portuguese!), and George and I sang in English.

They treated us well. Jim and Shirley were living in a country home in front of the estate of a famous soccer player. We slept in their guest house and took our meals in the main house with Jim and Shirley.

There were around forty or more kids in the orphanage and they really took to us. The children certainly loved to go and participate in the church. On the day before we left to return to the states, we baptized 15 people.

The Lord answered our prayers. George went to be with the Lord two years ago. He was a great soul winner. One of his dreams was to go to Brazil and thanks to the Combs and their hospitality and trust, he was able to do that. We love them both very much.

E-Team, CMP, and Hanna Project Youth Clap at Our Gate

Tania with the E-Team

E-Team Members from the USA

E-Team is a Free Will Baptist ministry of high school groups from many states that visit mission fields. The College Missions Program (CMP) is a group put together by the International Missions of FWB. When these groups go to Brazil, their main base may be in *Campinas* or *Ribeirão Preto,* but the different groups spend at least one day at *Lar Nova Vida* Children's Home and the *Araras* churches. They ministered through music, pantomime, and testimonies in the churches. In the children's home, they painted playground equipment, or furniture, or walls, and played with the children. The adult leaders were Missionaries Ken and Marvis Eagleton, Dr. Kenneth Eagleton or Curt and Mary Holland.

The Hollands, who were my students at Hillsdale FWB College, continue to influence and impact young people who have participated in these groups and they continue to influence and train others. Mary has had a great ministry and influence working with international families that are right at our doorsteps. Curt shares with us his vision for students' impact through these groups.

Curt Holland, Oklahoma/Missouri

At the ages of six, two and a half, and one, our daughters, Amber, Brooklyn and Kelsey, arrived in Araras, Brazil for the first time. They arrived at their new home because mom and dad were new missionaries. During their next ten years, they grew to love and adopt Brazil as their home.

What they also learned was that not all children in Brazil were as blessed as they were. The *Lar*

Nova Vida was also new in Araras and our family began to visit the home and meet many of the children who were being cared for. We painted, installed ceiling fans and a variety of other things during our time in Brazil. However, those things didn't compare to the love and attraction we had for the children at the *Lar Nova Vida.*

One of our most memorable Christmas times spent in Brazil was the one in which we were able to have little David and his sister Sue Ellen from LNV in our home for a week. Our daughters still have fond memories of our visits, the children's smiles and even friendships that developed through the years.

THE HANNA PROJECT

Some 20 years after our one-year-old lived in Brazil, she had the chance to return to Brazil with The Hanna Project, the NGO arm of FWB International Missions. She along with a number of our adults worked non-stop painting and giving the *Lar Nova Vida* a "new"

Curt Holland and Hannah Project Team

look. Endless hours were spent during the day preparing and then painting the walls, the gates and windows of the residence for the children.

Throughout the day and evenings, giggles, smiles, and meals were shared with the children being cared for at the LNV. Some of the workers were on their first visit to Brazil, and one young lady was from France, while others were returning to Brazil to *matar saudades.*

Curt Holland,

Hard work, fun times and lasting memories were made along with lots and lots of pictures.

E-TEAMS

Having served in Brazil as a missionary because of the impact a short-term experience in Brazil had on my life, I want to continue to provide the same for today's students. Leading two groups in 2003 and 2005, E-TEAM members from the USA had the opportunity to visit the *Lar Nova Vida* in Araras.

Small work projects were always a great way for the students to be useful. These projects also served as a means to help expose many "overly" blessed students from America to the challenges of street children in Brazil.

Each year, during our debriefing time and discussions about their experiences while in Brazil, the students always referred to the impact the LNV had on their lives and realities. Many students found that little pieces of their hearts were left with the children at the LNV and many of them determined that the Lord wanted them to be involved in rescuing children and sharing the Good News of Christ with them, no matter where in the world God placed them in the future.

Brooklyn Holland, RN

WORLDVIEWS

As the Campus Pastor at Hillsdale and the Director of Missions/Ministry Programs, there are so many ways in which I get to rub shoulders with and impact students' worldviews. Along with the challenges given in chapel by a variety of speakers to reach our world and community, our students are challenged in the classroom on a daily basis.

Because of the daily contact I enjoy and the countless "chat" times I get to have around the breakfast, lunch and dinner table, the Lord provides many open hearts and attentive listeners.

In the classroom we have a chance to share our views and insights as well as summer and short-term mission experiences with each other. However, the friendships, the stretching experiences and impact of cross-cultural events that I get to lead each semester are a highlight of my work at Hillsdale. Our students have a chance to make a difference in places where they serve on short-term trips. Plus, outside of the comfort zones, they learn to trust in the Lord, hear His voice and see His hand around the world and the USA.

One of our first E-TEAM students wrote Jim and me, in 1996, after she left Brazil and went back to Arkansas. Then, she wrote me 17 years later.

Bridget L. Bowman Riley, Arkansas/Tennessee
Dear Ms. Shirley,

I hope you haven't already forgotten us! I know I will never forget you and Bro. Jim. I am writing to share some things with you that God showed while I was in Brazil, and to ask you to pray for me.

The last day we were in Brazil, Bro. Jim took several of us girls to the neighborhood that a lot of the children had come from. Seeing that neighborhood changed me. God gave me more compassion than I ever thought I could have for people and their circumstances, especially children.

As I looked around the neighborhood, many of the stories in your book finally became real life to me. Your book was very touching, but it was honestly more than I could imagine. Not until I actually saw the neighborhood did I see the need.

While Bro. Jim drove us around the neighborhood and I looked on what those precious children had come out of, I felt this overwhelming desire to rescue them all. I felt like I could not go back to the United States without bringing some of the children that were yet to be rescued. I brought them in my prayers. That was all I could do. I saw that no one but Jesus could be their Savior. He is the only one that can rescue them.

We must be willing vessels, as you have been. God showed me many things while I was in Brazil, and I tried to be still and listen to Him.

Many things about Brazil were completely new to me, as I am sure you can imagine. One of them was Spiritism. One night as I sought God to give me understanding about this, He gave me Ephesians 6:12, "For our struggle is not against flesh and blood, but against the rulers, against the authorities, against the powers of this dark world and against the spiritual forces of evil in the heavenly realms." I used to read the armor of God verses daily, but this verse had never meant to me what it does now.

Since I have returned to America, I am still trying to seek God's voice about everything. It is so much harder (for me) to do that here. The world has many distractions. Please pray for me. Pray that God's guidance would be continually upon me.

Your work truly helped change my life and viewpoint of many things. You will never be forgotten. I will pray without ceasing for the Children's Home, the church, and especially the lost and dying of the community.

They you so much ...for everything.

Love always in Jesus, Bridget L. Bowman Riley, Ark., 1996

Bridget Lavinia Bowman Riley, Tennessee
(17 years later)

As a teenager, most people have various experiences that *seem* monumental at the time but turn out not to have much significance. Nothing could be further from the truth with regard to the three weeks I spent in Brazil when I was sixteen-years-old. Apart from the amazing cross-cultural experience, I was also able to see poverty and riches co-existing in the lives of Brazilians. It was in Brazil that I first truly realized a person can be rich, blessed, and joyful despite living in immense material poverty.

As young and underexposed Americans, our team walked the streets of Brazil and saw everything from shelters constructed of mounds of garbage to children pan-handling in the street to help support their families or to carve out their existence. They are images that have stayed with me and that have shaped how I view people born into difficult circumstances, as well as how I view personal riches that exist quite independently of material wealth.

Who's Clapping At Our Gate?

I will forever be grateful for my opportunity to meet the amazing children who "clapped at the gate" of *Lar Nova Vida*.

Bridget L. Riley

P.S. Our team consisted of: Christy Zimmerman, Joy Taylor, Jason Harbeck, Tim Ferguson, Roberto Morgan, Jennifer Dycus, Amy Scott, Kari Ferguson, Kimberlee Scott, Bridget Bowman (me), and Missionaries Ken and Marvis Eagleton.

Miranda Grimes, Oklahoma

I was in Brazil, May of 2013. I was given the opportunity to apply for the College Missions Program in February. I was so excited when I found out I would be going to Brazil. I have very good friends that are always talking about Brazil, and I just knew I had to go one day.

The program CMP is a group put together by the International FWB Missions for college age students. The whole group was put together by Hanna Mott, who did an amazing job getting all the visas, money, and the flying stuff. She even was there to help train us for the trip. So we definitely had to bring her back some *guarana'* (national soft drink).

Our team leader was Pastor Jeff Caudill from Nashville, Tennessee. Toward the middle of the trip we started to notice his Michigan accent! But we were all a much accented group of people! I certainly made lifetime friendships with my teammates. Lauren and Dustin are from Alabama, Sarah from Mississippi, Erin from Tennessee, and I from Oklahoma. We all seemed to struggle with the Portuguese language, all except Mrs. Erin. She picked it up quickly.

Who's Clapping At Our Gate?

My experience in Araras, Brazil, was wonderful. The people were so nice and caring. I wanted to put every one of them in my suitcase to bring home with me. José (Zé) and Walter were our national hosts. They drove us everywhere and if we asked for one thing, they would get it to us with no doubt. They both showed their dedication to the church and I could see how gladly they want the church to succeed. And their hearts for evangelism shone through their every action.

Miranda and CMP team

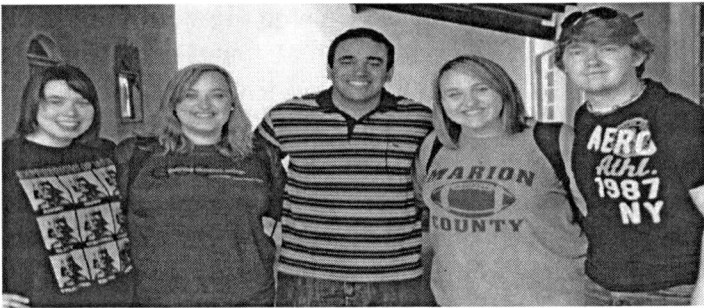

Our first dinner was at Ze's house. He spoke little English so it was difficult to communicate, until he brought out the guitar and the piano. Using Portuguese and English we all praised the one thing we had in common, our Savior, The Lord Jesus Christ.

I'm so happy to have met my brothers and sisters in Brazil. We were also blessed with the chance to hand out *folhetos* (pamphlets). The nationals taught us three phrases to use to hand out tracts to the neighborhood. Luckily they stayed with us, because most that came to the gate didn't understand my

Who's Clapping At Our Gate?

Oklahoma Portuguese. I wonder why?

That night as our team debriefed, we talked about how many rejections we received while handing out the pamphlets. We realized there were **no** rejections! Each person received the pamphlet without harsh tones and most with a smile and questions about the church. I hardly got that when I handed out pamphlets in St. Louis.

We discussed how thankful we were and how surprised they were so kind. A lady even invited us in to have *café*. And she brought out her guitar and we worshipped, in yet another stranger's, at that time, house. She fed us and prayed for us before we left her house. That was a true blessing.

We participated in the Berean Free Will Baptist Mission in the Maraba' neighborhood, the First Free Will Baptist Church downtown, the Second Free Will Baptist Church in Jardim Candida. We were given the opportunity to sing just about everywhere we went.

We sang *Amazing Grace* while Ze' played the guitar. It was very special to us and Ze'. When we had down time at the church, we always seemed to be in the sanctuary singing and playing hymns. Sarah played the guitar, Erin, Lauren and Dustin played the piano while Lauren, Dustin, and I sang. Our favorite was *It is Well*. Which just happened to be Pastor Jeff's favorite. He always joined in to sing with us. The sanctuary had amazing acoustics that would just echo, so it sounded really neat when we all sang.

That definitely had to be our most vulnerable bonding moments. We all really began to get very comfortable with each other and the jokes began. Really, mostly about Sarah and her possum. But she was a good sport.

The memories we made on that trip will forever stay close to my heart. I believe God gave me this trip to show me how so many different people can come together and speak one language which is the Gospel.

My heart is forever changed and I realize that I must fulfill His plan for my life and be willing to go wherever He leads me. I may have to learn a new language, maybe sleep on the ground, and get a few shots, but His plan is ultimate. And He definitely planned for me to go with CMP to Brazil.

International Fellowship at Our Gate

The International Fellowship of Free Will Baptist meets with representatives from many countries. It was organized to unite Free Will Baptist churches from around the world for the purpose of identification, communion, mutual edification, and encouragement in order to better fulfill the Great Commission and the establishment of churches among all people.

The Executive Secretary Melvin Worthington approached Foreign Missions to consider an international organization of Free Will Baptist. In 1992 Foreign Missions Director Eugene Waddell and Overseas Secretary Jimmy Aldridge met with representative from seven countries in Panama. They formed a statement of intent to move forward with the organization.

Their first meeting to officially organize the International Fellowship was in *Jaboticabal, Sao Paulo*, Brazil in 1995. The members decided upon a triennial general assembly hosted by various member countries.

International women's tea

The presidents elected from the past meeting were: 1995 – John Poole, Brazil; 1998 – Daniel Dorati, Panama; 2004 – José Manoel Parron, Spain; 2007- Gerardo Acevedo, Uruguay; and in 2010 – Luis Felipe Tigerina, Mexico.

When it met in Brazil, we had the opportunity of receiving members of FWB international communities clapping at our gate in *Araras* to visit in our home and our churches. After the meeting, we hosted national Christians from different countries and one special missionary couple, June and Fred Hersey in our home.

June is the widow of Sam Wilkinson, and they were pioneer missionaries in Brazil for many years. Their children and ours grew up together as missionary kids (MKs). Fred is the widower of Evelyn and they were pioneer missionaries in Japan. How special it was to have our friend June back in Brazil and to hear how she and her new husband had been back to his beloved field of Japan.

Brethren gathered around our table from Africa and Uruguay, Japan and Cuba. What a thrill to sit with a combination of experiences, cultures and languages enjoying food and fellowship in Christ. And best of all they could visit in our churches and share stories with our Brazilian Christians of souls being saved around the world. You can read about great stories, but it is so thrilling when the messengers arrive personally at your gate.

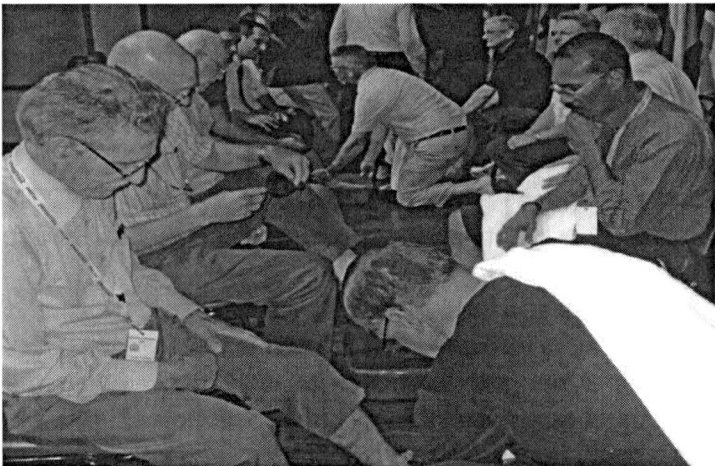

International men's feet washing

The next International Fellowship met in Uruguay in 1998. In 2001, because of the 9/11 crisis, it was decided to postpone the next meeting until 2002. Delegates met that year in Tennessee. In 2004 it met in Panama, and in 2007 France hosted the meeting. In 2010 it met in Oklahoma City at Hillsdale FWB College where we were privileged to attend and to host friends. One of the highlights for me was to experience the Lord's Supper and feet washing with fellow believers from all over the world. The president elected was Luis Felipe Tigerina from Mexico, the Vice President was Keiichi Kimura from Japan, and the Secretary was Dr. Thomas L. Marberry from Oklahoma. The next International Fellowship was scheduled to be in Brazil.

Guess who stayed in our home after the International Fellowship in Oklahoma? After 15 years, Fred and June Hersey once again came to our home. We were in Oklahoma where they rang the doorbell instead of clapping at our gate, but the hospitality fellowship was the same.

We have discussed the importance of hospitality evangelism together and I have asked them to share some things with you now.

Fred Hersey and June Wilkinson Hersey, Alabama

Having lived in two countries other than the United States of America and visited others, international hospitality evangelism has been a part of my experience. I have observed it as a result of many different efforts, methods and activities.

Inviting someone to experience life in one's environment for the purpose of showing why or how to live a Christian life or visit him/her in their environment for the same purpose is necessary for in implementation of hospitality of any kind.

I'll endeavor to give some examples of efforts, methods, and activities in the two countries with which I am most familiar, Brazil and Japan. In order for these to be effective one must become familiar with the culture so as not to become offensive in trying to evangelize. A very important factor is one must win the confidence and respect of the potential convert.

I heard someone say recently that Jesus had an "eating" ministry and I agree and believe that He set a good example for us in this regard. He ate with government officials, fishermen, friends, foreigners, family, and even enemies as he went through Samaria.

In both countries much is done around the dining table. In some instances there was no living room in Brazil so one was entertained at the dining table. In Japan in the morning the sleeping mats are stored in a special closet and there will be a low table placed in the middle of the "living" room where the meals are served, homework is done, crafts are done, games are played. The same is for the table in the "living" room in Brazil.

I learned some interesting things about serving guests early in my life in Brazil. Something to eat or drink is not served until the visit is over. I made the mistake of offering some pecan pie to a guest and she refused, which I thought was strange. Not until later did I learn that the host must offer three times and the guest must refuse three times before accepting what is being offered. My guest later told me she learned quickly that when offered something by an American, one must accept or there will not be another chance!

In Japan it is the opposite. Something is served

at the beginning of the visit. Nothing is served in "fours" as the same word is another way of saying death and no one wants to talk about death. Things are served in three's and five's.

In Brazil, as is eluded to by the title of the book, one claps at the front gate or enters the yard (if there is not a dog) and retreats to outside the gate and waits for someone to answer. Fred said that years ago in Japan one would enter the front door of the house where the shoes are taken off and stored and would announce, "I'm here." Someone from inside would then come, offer slippers or "inside" shoes and invite the guest into the house proper.

Find out what people's interests are and participate with them if it isn't against Godly principles. Once when entertaining some college students around our dining table, the question was posed regarding something being discussed. The question was, "Is this American tradition or scriptural? If it is an American tradition, we are not Americans (meaning North American), but Brazilians. It if is scriptural, we can accept it." Nationalism is very strong in most countries and one must be careful to honor it.

Some methods or activities used in other countries but can be used in the USA with internationals are: English classes usually concluded with a Bible lesson; cooking, sewing and craft classes Bible studies for children and adults; retreats, youth camps, Daily Vacation Bible School; Child Evangelism clubs; E-Teams and College Missionary Teams; family outings; games and entertaining in the homes; birthday celebrations and other special events; a card of encouragement or a small gift.

In Japan, however, if a gift is given, then the recipient feels obligated to give one in return. Times of crisis or transitions in someone's life are always opportunities for hospitality evangelism. Missionary children are a vital part of the family international hospitality evangelism.

One such opportunity that Fred related happened several years ago for him and his family in Japan. They became acquainted with a family who had lived abroad and they wanted their first grade boy to retain his knowledge of English. Paul, Fred's youngest son, agreed to teach him on Saturdays.

The child became ill and the doctor couldn't determine the cause and the next morning he died. The father called and asked Fred if he would perform a Christian funeral because he preferred that to a Buddhist one. The grandparents were shocked because Fred didn't charge for his services. The Buddhist priests are very expensive. Fred had the service and was able to share the gospel with many family members and friends.

Paul also taught English to a neighbor's grandchildren in Japan and as a result the father, mother, daughter, and son became Christians.

One of the leaders of the Japanese church is a result of Paul's willingness to teach English to a neighbor boy who became one of his best friends. He liked going to the Hersey's house because Evenlyn always had some cookies or other goodies.

The boy's mother would not allow him to go to church, but one summer when Paul was home in Japan for the summer, he told the boy that he was old enough to make his own decision about church. He began attending the services and after Paul returned to the states, he continued to attend, became a Christian, and was baptized. He says he is Fred's fifth son. He is married and has a lovely Christian wife.

The Wilkinson family lived several years on the mission property in Brazil and were responsible for youth camps, retreats, and field council meetings. The property also served as a vacation spot for missionary families as personal funds were most times in short supply for other places.

Youth camps were held during summer and winter vacations from school activities. These played a very important part in the evangelism ministry. Many can point back to those times as the time in their life when salvation decision or a Christian service commitment was made.

On Sunday afternoon sometime people from the local church or acquaintances from the city would come out for fellowship to enjoy the good fruit offered by the orchard trees. Many weekends I would look in my daughter's room to see how many girls were sleeping in there or Sam would look in the boy's rooms to see for how many I needed to prepare breakfast.

Gatherings on the front veranda for singing and playing of instruments were a common occurrence. On several occasions Sam allowed the local soccer team to stay overnight in the camp dorms and practice on the soccer field.

Today one does not have to leave one's country to be a participant of international hospitality evangelism. People are on the move all over the world.

Do not be afraid of someone who looks different, speaks a different language, has a different belief system, or eats some strange things.

The human needs are the same, the main one being a personal relationship with the true and living God, love and acceptance by other human beings, sustenance for the physical and spiritual life. Look for opportunities. There are many and each of us can do something to fulfill our part in the international hospitality evangelism part of the Great Commission.

Dr. Mark Brashier covered with kids

Hero Makers
Hero Makers (**H**elping **O**thers **R**emember **O**rphans) enables and inspires ordinary people to do

extraordinary things through first-hand field experience aiding children at risk. It provides an opportunity for people to share with others the experience of being a HERO through short-term missions; thereby each HERO becomes a "Hero Maker" as well.

The scripture they use on their web-site is: "Pure religion and undefiled before God is this, to visit the fatherless and widows in their affliction, and to keep himself unspotted from the world." James 1:27

Before one of the Kansas City FWB group trips, Dr. Mark Brashier met representatives of that group that builds homes for children in foreign lands. They were commenting about the hot temperature in the months they were building in Mexico at that time. Dr. Mark told them that May in Brazil was not summer, and that the weather was much milder. He also told them about our *Lar Nova Vida Free* Will Baptist Children's Home there.

Two of the members of this Hero Makers group visited us with Dr. Mark and a mission team group. When they offered to help, we explained that, even though we needed the house, with our strained budget to cover monthly expenses we could not build one. They said if we own the land and can put down the foundation, they could take workers and money to buy materials to build a third house in *Araras*.

Our plans were for a one-story house someday, but upon their suggestion, we had an engineer draw up a blueprint for a two- story house. LNV traded a donated plot of ground for a lot next to the LNV playground, and Rejoice FWB church in Oklahoma helped us put down the foundation.

Hero Makers took a good group to *Araras,* and they worked hard. Whole families went. They impressed the entire community. In other countries they had worked on wood frame buildings but learned to work with mortar and bricks in the entire construction.

They worked together with a Brazilian brick layer, Eduardo, and his son, Eduardinho, (who spoke a little English), but still didn't get as far as they planned. It was so different from the building system they were used to. They raised the brick walls up to the second level, and their time ran out. As of today, they have not returned to continue building, and we still do not have the funds to finish it.

Maybe one day it can be finished, but the wonderful example they gave as generous, hardworking Christians still lingers in the hearts of our children and workers. The t-shirts and jackets they left behind with the Hero Makers logo can be seen proudly worn by people all over town.

CHAPTER 15
Okies via Bolivia to Brazil at Our Gate

We were in the *Escola de Portugues e Orientacao* in Campinas, São Paulo, Brazil, in 1965 to study Portuguese. Bud and Ruth Bivens, fellow Okies and Free Will Baptists, appeared at our gate during that year. They were in the Peace Corps in Bolivia and were on a short break that had not originally included clapping at our gate. How wonderful to share time with friends at the same time we were adjusting to the culture and language of our new country.

They shared their interesting experiences and opportunities to live the Gospel in a new land, Bolivia. It encouraged us since we dreamed of God giving us the experience of witnessing for Him in a new language one day. At that time we were only able to get by with "baby talk" in Portuguese. During the following years the Lord gave the Bivens a variety of ministries which led them to dedicate many years of their lives to teaching Spanish speaking peoples.

I asked Ruth to tell how they left family in Oklahoma, went to primitive Bolivia, and then "accidently" spent a month in Brazil. Here is her first-hand account of those amazing adventures.

Bud and Ruth Bivens, Oklahoma/Mexico

Bud and I met at Central Avenue Free Will Baptist Church in Oklahoma City in the spring of 1963. He attended Central State College in Edmond, Oklahoma at the time. I was studying at Saint Anthony's Hospital

School of Nursing in OKC. After we dated a while and I proposed to him, he mentioned that he had applied to enter the Peace Corps. Living in the student Nurses' Dorm, studying and working in my spare time was almost like living underground. I heard no news from the outside world and, had not even heard the term "Peace Corps."

He explained a bit about it and, since he was scheduled to leave for West Pakistan right after his graduation in 1963, he contacted the Peace Corps officials in Washington and asked about my joining him. The official he spoke with gladly granted him a delay so that I could apply. He announced they much preferred volunteers who were married couples because they seemed to do better in the remote areas of the world where the Peace Corps served. So, August eighteenth, 1963, the week after I graduated from my Nursing School, we were married.

While we were awaiting our assignment, I went to work at Saint Anthony's Hospital and Bud found a job teaching business classes at Bishop McGuiness High School (Catholic High) in the northern part of the city. He also agreed to teach night classes at the Oklahoma Bible College (which later became known as Hillsdale Free Will Baptist College). At that time classes were being held at the Capitol Hill Free Will Baptist Church in the southern part of Oklahoma City. So, I worked part time at the hospital in order to maintain a day time work schedule. That way I was able to attend Bible classes at OBC while Bud taught in the business department to pastors at night.

Bud finished an entire school year before we received our assignment. We were to fly to Seattle, WA where we would enroll at the University of Washington

Missionaries Bud and Ruth Bivens

and receive our Peace Corps training. This would prepare us with language and knowledge of the country for our volunteer service to the South American country of Bolivia.

In mid-September, 1964, after two months in Seattle and six weeks in Puerto Rico, we landed in La Paz, Bolivia. Our group of volunteers was in the process of receiving our initial orientation to the country when a revolutionary war broke out. We were confined to our hotel while truckloads of indigenous men road up and down the streets of La Paz pointing their ancient looking shot guns and rifles skyward. The air force's two planes flew over the city firing on the rebels. As the war progressed there were even guns fired from the street up toward the hotel's upper floors. One night bullets came through the window of our room and lodged in the ceiling.

After the Peace Corps officials determined that the revolution was confined to the city of La Paz, they started taking us out to our village assignments, one or two at a time. Bud and I were delivered to the village of Coroico Nor Yungas on a Saturday. The assistant Peace Corps director loaded our suitcases into a jeep and took us north out of La Paz, over the most hair-raising roads we had ever seen.

It was a six hour trip down and up and down and up again over a one lane mountain road down from the 13,000 feet altitude of the city of La Paz to the more moderate 6,000 feet altitude of the Nor Yungas. Much of the trip we were hugging the mountain side while the valley floor lay hundreds of feet below us. We left the frigid, high desert and entered a lush, green, semi-tropical community nestled on the only level spot on the side of a huge mountain. Our driver deposited us in a room at a boarding house a block off the plaza and left us there.

The very next morning, as I was reading my Bible, we heard someone singing hymns. As soon as it was quiet below us, we went down stairs and met Agustin Luna, a young pastor. His Aymara congregation rented a room for their worship services exactly underneath our room.

He had lost his parents in an accident when the truck they were traveling in went over one of the many cliffs on the road out from La Paz. His only brother was studying in a city hundreds of miles away. So, we three clung to each other like long lost kin.

As Peace Corps Volunteers we had been forbidden to attend any Evangelical church lest that cut us off from 99% of the local people. But, we ignored that instruction and attended Agustin's church regularly. He would preach a while in Aymara, then change to Spanish just for our benefit.

We got acquainted with folks in the town and began to figure out what we could do to help them. I went to work at a clinic with a nun from Bogata, Columbia; delivered two babies; taught health classes in the elementary schools; and Bud and I both taught English. Bud worked with the men from a rural community getting a road built out to their area; worked with men in town trying to get safe water piped into town; helped one community finish the construction of their school house-which was named for him; and played basketball with the local young men.

Once a month we rode into La Paz, on top of a load of produce on the back of a big truck, with all of the other travelers. They were going to the city to sell their bales of coca leaves (the source of cocaine), sell chickens, or coffee. We climbed up on top of the load, hunkered down, and prayed hard for safety on the whole trip. We quickly understood how Agustin's parents had been killed.

Our excuse for going in to La Paz was to buy supplies and pick up our mail. We did those things. But, we always scheduled our trip when another couple from Texas who had trained with us could be in the city as well. They worked in the high Altiplano, above the altitude of the city of La Paz. As much as we enjoyed spending some time with another American couple, the truth was that the trip served to get us out from under the constant scrutiny of the locals. It seemed we were everyone's main source of entertainment and curiosity.

We lived in four rooms on the second floor of a normal Bolivian house, right on the main cobblestone "street" that came into town from the mountain. The purpose in renting four rooms, which all opened to a narrow balcony, was to have a bit of privacy. Normally four families would have lived in those rooms. We had no electricity, and no running water. However, there was water in a bathroom about half a flight down. A shower head placed in the center of the ceiling provided cold showers, and the drain in the middle of the floor kept the rest of the room from being flooded. The commode flushed, but, had no seat. When Bud bought a mahogany toilet seat, the owner of the house would not use it. They were not accustomed to a toilet seat. Most of my baths were taken with a pan of water heated on our three burner kerosene stove.

We were carefully instructed NOT to drink the water, nor use anything that had a drop of water on it. Just a drop of the terrible contaminated water could carry severe illness, hepatitis, or any number of parasites. Every day I boiled a pan of water for 20 minutes. I covered it with a tight lid, and when it was cool, I poured it into our drinking water tank. This unit looked like a tall, tan crock. It was a glazed, clay container with its own tight lid, and a white, unglazed, clay stem about three inches in diameter in the center. The stem, that could be replaced when it got too dirty, filtered the dirt out of the now sterilized water into another glazed, crock tank below. Using a small spigot on the bottom part of the tank we could pour ourselves a glass of safe drinking water. The only time I used water from the bathroom faucet for cooking was if I knew that what I cooked would be boiling for 20 minutes minimum.

After a short time, Agustin introduced us to Maria, an Aymara girl, who walked in to town to go to school. I hired her to help me with house work. She would come from school at noon and eat lunch with us. Before she went back to school, she would wash up the dishes and sweep or mop as needed. It did not take me long to find a neighbor who would do all of our laundry, too. She washed everything by hand, dried and folded it and returned it for 80 cents U.S. a week – and she was glad to get it.

I quickly discovered that I could spend all day just getting meals on the table. Everything had to be made from scratch. Vegetables and fruits that would be eaten raw had to be washed and then soaked in an iodine bath for 20 minutes. Since we had no refrigeration, if we were going to have meat, I had to walk down to the market first thing in the morning to buy it. I soon decided that we would only have meat every other day. And, shortly we agreed that we would eat supper each evening at a large hotel down below the village. It was cheap and gave me a break from so much cooking.

When we completed a year of service as Peace Corps Volunteers, we were granted a month's vacation. With our friends from the Altiplano we plotted and planned our vacation. We were scheduled to be in the eastern city of Cochabamba for a few days of additional training so, we agreed to make that our jumping off place. We traveled from La Paz to the training site by bus, hours and hours, down more mountains, but, just in another direction.

Toward the end of our training session, my friend Sandy and I took a taxi out to the airport and bought tickets for our flight to Rio de Janeiro. Our plan was to take a short tour of that area, visit the statute of Christ that is so popular, then continue on. We outlined a complete tour around the southern coast of South America, returning via Peru to La Paz in a month. It sounded like a good plan. However, as often happens, our plans hit a snag. Due to bad weather, our plane set down in the Brazilian city of Campinas.

While we were waiting for the storm to pass, I mentioned to Bud that I knew we had Oklahoma Free Will Baptist missionaries who were living and working in Campinas. He just walked over, picked up a phone directory, found Earnie Deeds' name and phone number and called him. Earnie told us to stay right where we were. It was not long before he walked into the airport. He invited us to get our luggage off the plane and come visit them for a while. We talked it over for a minute or two and agreed. Earnie spoke to someone who retrieved our luggage. We said "Good-bye" to the Johnsons, and in no time at all we were traveling in a car down a beautiful highway in the lovely city of Campinas.

You cannot imagine our surprise when we saw the American style home where the Deeds lived. They had running water, electricity, a refrigerator, even a television! We attended services at their mission with them, met the warmest people, rejoiced in the familiar songs, and even understood a good part of what was said since Portuguese is so similar to Spanish.

Earnie and Jean treated us like long lost family and, we loved it. They drove us from one place to another and introduced us to other missionaries there. We tried all kinds of Brazilian food and the tiny cups of coffee so strong it could have walked out of the cup.

Jim and Shirley Combs were in language study there in Campinas at the time. We visited them in their little rented house and felt like we had known them forever.

Little by little we worked our way from one mission site to another, getting acquainted with the rest of our missionaries who were working in Brazil. We spent a few days with Dave and Pat Franks and enjoyed playing with their little boy Dave Junior.

Bud has never forgotten the hard, corn shuck mattress we slept on at their house. I remember the lady who did their laundry spreading the clean, just laundered clothes on the grass in their back yard to dry. With my background, thinking about all of the bacteria that would be on the grass, I wanted to run grab it up. They explained that the chlorophyll in the green grass made the white clothing look whiter.

We attended church services with them too, and again, were made to feel so welcome by all of the Christian brothers and sisters. Then they took us out to the camp ground where Ken and Marvis Eagelton served. They took us on a tour of the facility where youth camps, retreats, and associational meetings are held. We enjoyed visiting and playing with their five little boys. I remember eating supper with them and suddenly someone noticed that the smallest boy was missing from the table. They looked for him and found him lying on the floor. He had fallen asleep as we were all eating and slid down from his chair to the floor under the table.

We felt like we had run into long lost family at every stop. And, life in Brazil seemed so modern and up to date, so far removed from our primitive life style in Bolivia. We drove modern highways, stayed in homes that looked like 'home'. We attended Free Will Baptist missions and churches with each family we visited. Everyone was so gracious and loving toward us.

I visited some of the ladies' groups, and was delighted that we could visit and for the most part understand one another. For the first time in our experience of being so far from home, we realized how much we had missed those familiar things. We both dreaded the thought of heading back to the hard life of the Nor Yungas.

When we learned that the missionaries' children attended an English Speaking Christian School, we discussed the possibility of just coming to Brazil when we finished our second year in the Peace Corps. Bud could probably get a job teaching there. And, with a little language study, I could probably go to work in nursing in a hospital. We agree that it was certainly something we should pray about and seek the Lord's direction.

Too soon our month of vacation came to an end. Brother Earnie took us back to the airport and we returned to La Paz. I wrapped my winter coat around me and walked, with heavy step, through the market place, buying a few items that were not available at the market in Coroico. Then, early the next morning, with sweet memories of our trip fresh in our minds, we lifted our luggage up on top of a load of produce headed out to the tropics on the back of a truck. As soon as we arrived, we were once again busily involved in all of our jobs back in Coroico.

It was not the Lord's plan for us to go back to Brazil to work. We came back to the states after our Peace Corps service ended, and plunged into life here. Thirty years passed before we felt the Lord leading us to sell out and go to the mission field, and although it was south of Tulsa, Mexico is much closer to Oklahoma than Campinas. But, we still treasure the friendships we were blessed to make during that one sweet month we spent in Brazil in 1965.

Who's Clapping At Our Gate?

PART FOUR

CHAPTER 16
World, Here We Come!

It has been our privilege to *entertain angels unawares* in our home and reap the benefits. We have received mission teams into our home in Brazil and worked alongside them to see God do wonderful things.

But we found ourselves *clapping at gates* in other fields.

Opportunities opened up for us to be part of mission teams going to other countries. On these trips others opened their gates and homes in their own countries for us and our groups, and we participated in the wonderful things God did in those fields, too.

In these past years our own adult children have participated in trips to Haiti, Mexico, Dominican Republic, and Europe. Their bi-cultural experiences helped them to evaluate other countries' poverty and starvation, as well as the ultra-modern sights that more fortunate places in the world have to offer in material goods and gadgets. We have nieces who have gone as missionaries to Africa and Egypt.

The first family story is taken from my own journals.

Shirley and Brazilians Go to Ireland and England

"It will be great to go to Ireland with you and the students. Thanks for asking!" I hung up the phone very surprised and happy.

Missionaries Bobby and Geni Poole, Brazilian Pastor Jeancarlo Ache, and Renata Poole were planning a mission trip for the Brazilian Bible College students from our school in Ribeirão Preto. Some had been my students and they had studied missions. Now they wanted a *hands on experience*. What made the trip even more personal is that the missionary family in Ireland was from our *Igreja Batista Livre* (FWB Church) in Jaboticabal, São Paulo. Also, Brazil was playing in the World Cup Soccer Tournament and would be playing the last games while we were there in Ireland!

We got our passports and tickets, packed our bags with lots of green and yellow flags and *props* for the World Cup games, and the ten of us left São Paulo airport for our first stop in Frankfurt, Germany. We stayed there for five hours and found out that if we *left out* the gate and came right back in, they would stamp our passports as having entered Germany. Some of us did just that.

Mission team to Ireland

Who's Clapping At Our Gate?

Over the airport's giant screens, hundreds of us watched the US soccer team play the German team. Our Brazilians were surprised at how reserved the Germans were when they scored. Quiet. Calm. Not at all like we would have been. Well, Germany won the game and beat the US team. As we passed through the gate, we congratulated the German officials on their win. They said in accented English, "Oh, it was luck. The US deserved to win." It was a surprise, but helped us take the loss a little better.

Then to Ireland. The Emerald Island. Lovely, lovely green Ireland. A pastor from southern Ireland met us at the Dublin airport and had a mini bus waiting for us. We had a long drive to Carlow where we were to stay in the home of a pastor, Pastor Seamus (pronounced Shamus). He and his family left for a week's retreat and gave us the use of their whole house for our time there. They didn't leave us a car so we walked and walked. Their house was not close to town, the churches or any places we visited. But it is a thriving town pleasantly situated on the River Barrow and we enjoyed walking its streets.

Visiting and encouraging our Brazilian missionary family from *Jaboticabal* was the purpose of our trip. We wanted to encourage them and help their ministries in some way to bring Glory to God. They are Raul and Rosane Goes and their children, Aline, Ludimila and Ariel. They live and work there in order to help in the music of two churches. They all sing and play instruments. They are examples of modern *tent maker* missionaries since their teen children worked at Burger King and the parents worked in a packaging company.

The Protestant churches in southern Ireland are VERY small. But as in most places, the best thing about the country is the people. So, so, so friendly. We walked a lot, and strangers would wave to us from car windows and even from their living room picture windows. We took long walks to and from the bus stations, subways, and train stations, and folks were friendly everywhere. All the females seemed to have bright blue eyes and pink cheeks and easy smiles. The Christian people were very hospitable, always serving us hot tea with milk. Not bad.

One big thrill was to watch two World Cup soccer games with the Goes family. We were pleasantly surprised to see the city shops had decorated their windows with draped Brazilian flags and posters of Brazilian soccer players. Shoppers in the streets were wearing Brazilian soccer shirts. When they found out we were from Brazil, they engaged in friendly conversation wishing us luck in the next games. If Brazil won, it would be the *penta*, their fifth World Cup title.

We filled up their apartment living room on the second floor for the big game. We wore green and yellow head bands and shirts and were really worked up for the game. Theirs was probably the noisiest house on the street with each goal we made. We did it. Brazil was the world champion. We won the PENTA!

Another big thrill was to participate in the church services. Oh, yes, they speak English and Irish in Ireland. We were speaking to foreigners but in English. For most of the Brazilians it was a challenge to speak English, but Bobby, Geni, Jeancarlo, and I felt real liberty. Pastor Jeancarlo and his family had lived in

Carlow as missionaries before the Goes family moved there. He was lovingly received and preached several times in English in the churches. Bobby also preached and Geni gave a dramatic presentation.

I was able to teach classes, give my testimony, sing, and give information on the street children ministry in Brazil. After services I counseled and prayed with women. We met a young woman named Verna from *Goias*, Brazil, who works with street children there. The Brazilians gave their testimonies through interpreters, and sang. After services we visited and drank…guess what? Hot tea with milk.

The congregation in *Carlo* met in a rented senior citizen's building, but it was the last Sunday in that building. The second Sunday we were there they met in the Seven Oaks Hotel. They are led by Pastor *Seamus* with the help of the Raul Goes family. Refugees from Nigeria meet with them. Our women took photos with them in their colorful long dresses and turbans. Women of faith standing together and crossing barriers. We plan to see them in heaven!

The congregation in *Hacketstown* met in the Christian Centre, and is led by Sister Elizabeth Byrne and a core group. They were a small group but dedicated to "taking Jesus to people so that people can come to Jesus." They are about transformation and not just information. The Raul Goes family helped them on Thursday nights.

We visited the little town of *Wicklow* for a Christian leader's retreat. The bus left us on the main road so we had to climb up a steep road to the camp carrying our bags.

There are so few Christian leaders in southern Ireland. At the retreat there were participants from Northern Ireland, Scotland, England and South Africa. All spoke English with different accents. There seemed to be more blonds and blue eyes there than in Oklahoma!

The Church of Ireland in *Wicklow* was built in the 1500's. The cities are modern, but you take narrow, winding country roads and drive on the opposite side of the road. Rush hour is a flock of sheep crossing the road. After the meeting, we went to the beach. Only one car was taking us and was only able to take two passengers at a time. Since it was so cold, ten minutes was plenty of time to stand on the beach, so we made it fine.

We went to the city of *Kilkenny* by train and saw the famous *Kilkenny* Castle from the thirteenth century. It stands on high ground behind the River Nore. It remains today the property of the *Marquis of Ormonde*. It was magnificent. They said the county is excellent sporting country, with good opportunities for hunting, angling, shooting and golfing, but nobody had time for those things.

When we went to Dublin, the capital of the country, of course we saw the famous River *Liffey* and the sights around it. Everything was so ancient in contrast with modern parts. They call it the city of the Wizards with Words – Sean O'Casey, James Joyce, George Bernard Shaw, Sheridan, Swift, and a host of others writers are claimed as their sons. It was so friendly and gracious.

One of the high points there for me was the Trinity College. One thing I will remember is the fabulous library which contains the *Book of Kells*, one of the world's most beautifully illuminated manuscripts. A hand written copy of the Four Gospels was fascinating. Every margin and all spaces were filled in with hand painted designs. I bought my husband, Jim, and son, Kemper, ties with the same designs on them.

Soon it was time to leave the green emerald island and our dear missionary friends Raul and family and to travel across to England. Ireland is known for its writers and its traditional Irish music and instruments. Violins, accordions, bongos and pipes. But they are blessed to have Christians from another country dedicated to playing music with them for the glory of God.

The Irish have a saying, *"Is deacair ceann crionna a chur ar cholainn oig."* (It is difficult to put a wise head on young shoulders.) Well, mine was 60 years old at the time and I was thankful to travel and learn new things. Especially to sing the Lord's song in a new land for me. It was good to see ourselves multiplied by our Brazilian Christians being sent to the country of Ireland from our church in Brazil.

The last days of our trip were spent in a hotel in London, England. A young woman named *Manoela* from our church in *Araras*, São Paulo, lived there. She and her husband from Portugal and baby boy visited with us.

We took the regular tourist tour – St. Paul's Cathedral, Houses of Parliament, Big Ben, and other churches. We took a boat trip and saw other fantastic sights including the Wheel, the Tower of London, and the Tower Bridge.

Who's Clapping At Our Gate?

The day was the Fourth of July. Of course it was not a holiday there in England nor in Brazil, but I was very emotional thinking that we were in our mother country on that special day. Over the past generations our two countries have become allies, and we honor one another.

We visited the Buckingham Palace and saw the changing of the Royal Guard. All over London we saw posters of Her Majesty the Queen and Her Majesty the Queen Mother. All week we had been joking about the Queen coming out and waving at us. Guess what? She did! She left in a car and passed right by and waved.

We left that day – The Fourth of July – and flew back to Brazil to the São Paulo airport, and on to *Ribeirão Preto* airport on the fifth of July. Many church people were there to meet us.

The Irish have another saying, "*Nil aon tintean mar do thintean fein.*" (There is no fireside like your own fireside.) It was good to be back home to the beloved Brazil which had been our 'fireside' since 1964. We could share with our family and friends photos and experiences of that trip and give a good report of our dear Brazilian missionaries serving God far from their family and homeland. I am blessed.

At the time of this writing, Brazil has sent missionaries to Africa, China, Uruguay, the Amazon jungle, and Ireland.

They have been taught to "observe all things" that the Word teaches about reaching the world for Christ. And they obey.

Kemper Goes to Mexico and the Dominican Republic

Kemper Jonathan Combs, Oklahoma

In July 1993, I went with a group of 14 people from my church, which at the time was known as Norman First Free Will Baptist Church (Crosspointe FWB Church, now). The fourteen of us went by van to the town of Mission, TX where we stayed at a campground facility. All total, 180 Americans plus 40 from Holland were involved in the project. The organization that sponsored the trip was World Servants.

On Monday morning we crossed over the border into the town of Reynosa, Mexico. There are many neighborhoods in that town called *colonias* that are

Kemper in Dominican Republic

still undeveloped. Our group split up into two building crews and erected two houses. The lady my group built a house for had six children, and her oldest daughter was expecting a baby. They lived in a very small, run-down house. The house we built had two rooms, a living room and a kitchen. It has been twenty years, but I believe the house had a bathroom as well.

We worked on the house on Monday and Tuesday. At the same time we were building houses, another group was having Vacation Bible School for the kids at a local school. We worked on the houses from 7am to 2pm every day except for Wednesday. That day we took a much-deserved break at Padre Island.

By Friday we finished building the two houses. We visited the houses that the group had built the year before and the families were still enjoying living in their homes. We got back Sunday evening just in time to get a quick shower and head on over to church in Norman, Oklahoma, to give an account of our trip. That was my last Sunday in the U.S. I moved back to Brazil the following Friday, July twenty-third.

The highlight of my trip was getting to talk to the people of the neighborhood. I was one of the interpreters, so I had the opportunity to speak directly to the people. The lady next door to where we were building said that they lived in constant fear for their lives. At night the drug lords and their underlings would drive around the neighborhood and have target practice. Anyone outside their homes after 8pm was fair game. It was heart-breaking to hear the stories. We were able to present the Prince of Peace to some of these hearts that lived in constant fear.

Who's Clapping At Our Gate?

There was a horse that had been around the neighborhood near the watering hole. It was very skinny and didn't look like he would survive very long. On the last day we were there, he just fell over on his side and died. It was a reminder to us of how pervasive the poverty in that area really is. We went to help make a difference.

In December 2007 I decided to visit the Lighthouse Foursquare Church. On the first day I was greeted with hugs by member and the pastor. Coming from Brazil it seemed natural, yet at the same time out of character for some Americans.

When I sat down, a lady introduced herself as Sharon and asked me what I did as far as work. I told her I was teaching French and Spanish at Harrah High School. She started laughing and said she had been praying all week for God to send someone that spoke Spanish to go with them on their missions' trip to Mexico in May, 2008. She said they would be having their first meeting that day with the group that was going, and wanted to know if I would be willing to stay afterwards to participate in the meeting. I assured her I would.

In preparation for the trip, they asked me to help teach them basic Spanish on Saturday mornings, and to give them some idea of what to expect.

The big day finally arrived. Pastor Richard Thomas, Dale Keeton, Sharon Davis, Joan Richardson, and I traveled in the rented van all the way from Oklahoma City to Laredo, TX. (Two people from our team could not go; Pastor Lauryce, and Susan Keeton who had to go to Oregon for her father's funeral.) It took us close to 12 hours to drive that distance.

When we arrived in Laredo, we ate before attempting to cross over into New Laredo, Mexico. As always, there was a lot of red tape, missed turns, U-turns, and by the time we got into Monterrey, Mexico, it was already after midnight.

We had a reservation at the Best Western in town, but because we got in so late, they had given our reservation to someone else. We ended up having to stay in a low-end hotel. Pastor Richard and Dale were amazed at the size of the cockroaches. It was like being back in Brazil for me. In the hotel's bathroom, there was not a toilet seat lid, so you had to sit directly on the ceramic toilet. Again, it was like being back in Brazil for me, but it was all new and strange to them.

The next morning the American missionary, Jeff, came to greet us at the hotel and apologized for the confusion the night before. He went with us in the van and guided us to the church, right after we had a Mexican-style breakfast at Appleby's, near the church. We were ready for it, too.

The original plan was for us to build a prayer room as part of the sanctuary. When we got there, Jeff had changed all of the plans. We were now going to build a new platform-stage area. I went with Jeff's son to Home Depot (yes, the real one) to buy the materials we would need. It was my first experience driving in Mexico.

That afternoon, Pastor Richard and Sharon both got sick, mostly from the heat. There was no air conditioner in the building, only very powerful fans, and it was 100+ degrees outside. Dale started getting worried about not having a real helper in the construction part of ministry. Soon Pastor and Sharon both recovered and we were back in business.

That night, Friday, Dale and I stayed with some of the church family in their home. The other three stayed with two different families. Saturday morning was Mother's Day in Mexico (the day before Mother's Day in the US). Judy Kinder arrived by plane at the airport and we picked her up before going to the church to work It was nice to see all of the people going to buy flowers for their mothers, and all the hustle and bustle involved.

Saturday night we had our first service. It was an experience. The next morning we were at the church from nine in the morning until one in the afternoon. It was hot, but the people were enjoying it. Pastor Richard preached a short sermon with a lot of meaning. Jeff interpreted.

We finished building the platform on Tuesday evening, right on schedule per our timeline. To us it was nothing more than a platform, but they were not calling it that. They were saying: "The Americans built us a beautiful *altar*. Upon this altar people will be giving their lives over to Christ and answering the call to ministry." The dedication to the altar was similar to Solomon's dedication of the temple in Jerusalem. It was an unforgettable experience.

Our last day was a 'day off' for us. We took a tour of the city by boat. According to our guide, there are only three cities that have this city boat tour: Oklahoma City, San Antonio, and Monterrey, Mexico.

The way home took almost twenty hours, and

that was an adventure in itself. A lot of funny things happened on the trip and we still tease about them to this day, five years later. All of us felt like God had changed our lives. Everyone who participated was impacted in a very strong way.

Dominican Republic

In March 2011 my friend, Dr. David Duty, from the First Presbyterian Church in Norman, Oklahoma, invited me to go with a group from his church to the Dominican Republic. I checked my vacation schedule and found time available except for one day, and I felt like it was important enough to go ahead and go and just take points for the day missed. We would leave the weekend before Memorial Day weekend and return on Memorial Day, May thirtieth.

We met every two weeks on Saturday morning, between March and May to plan the activities, make crafts, practice songs, and pack the material the church had given to take with us. We left the Oklahoma City airport on Saturday, May 22, around 6:30 am. We arrived in Atlanta around 9:30 and left again for Santo Domingo, Dominican Republic. We landed in Santo Domingo around 2:00 pm and proceeded to pay entry fees, go through customs, and head on to the rental office to pick up our van. The church people were there waiting on us in another van so that they could take some of us and the luggage.

We were taken first to the home of Olga and Sr. Matos. (Mr. Matos is a judge, and Mrs. Matos has a degree in biology.) That was kind of the meeting place for everyone, and the home where Dr. David, Beverly and I stayed. After dropping everyone off at their respective homes, we returned with the van to the Matos' residence to shower and rest for a little bit.

After resting, we all went out to do some shopping and sight-seeing. Many of us had never been there, and some had been there three or more times. I guess the very first thing I noticed upon arriving was that, as bad as the traffic is in Brazil, it is nothing in comparison with traffic in the Dominican. There is no rhyme or reason to their traffic patterns. There are generally no lanes to speak of, and it reminded me more of a bumper car ride than anything else, where you go whichever direction you feel like going and hope you don't bump into anyone. You see beat up cars everywhere.

There were two designated drivers for the van – Dustin Camp and myself. Dr. David asked me it if would bother me to drive in the Dominican Republic, and I said I wouldn't mind. I did okay, but I preferred it when Dustin drove, because he acted like he was in his element. It was like he was taking out all of his frustrations from having to follow the rules in the US that now he was free to drive like he's always wanted to drive but couldn't.

A lot of the people we met there are descendants of American slaves who ran away and went to the Dominican Republic. So their last names are Smith and Jones and Miller, and some of them can communicate in English. There are also a lot of Haitian refugees who had left Haiti after the earthquake and gone to the Dominican Republic. After all, Haiti and the Dominican Republic both occupy the same island of

Who's Clapping At Our Gate?

Hispaniola.

On Sunday, we went to the morning service at the church that sponsors the trip and takes care of a lot of the logistics of where to house us and feed us. In the Dominican Republic, you never know when you'll have electricity. It may be on one minute and off the next, and you don't know when it will come back on, or what day. Because of that, the wealthier people in town have their own generators. The Matos residence has two generators – one for upstairs and one for downstairs.

We were blessed at church to be able to sit near the fan that was working that day. We were very grateful, because on the island besides being very hot, it's also very humid, and we were wearing our Sunday best clothes.

Most meals in the Dominican Republic will have plantains, a lot like bananas, so I expected them to be sweet. Plantains there are served as a salty side dish and are not sweet at all. Because of the heat, we were careful not to eat something that had been sitting out for too long waiting on us to get there, especially the sea food. The food was very good, and most people did not have any problems eating it.

In the mornings, Dona Olga would serve us her version of oatmeal, scrambled eggs, bread with all the fixings, a lot of fruit, fruit juice, milk, and coffee. After eating there, we would go to the church, where they had also prepared us breakfast. Believe it or not, in one week I lost more than ten pounds, even eating well! I think I sweated it out more than anything.

During the week we were at three different locations. On Monday and Tuesday, we were in the town of *Hainamosa*. There is a school for children there, run by a very sweet lady who knows how to keep those kids disciplined, and yet shows them a lot of love. The people of the community meet at the school to be attended by two or three doctors, who do exams and prescribe medicine, the medicine that we took from here, donated by generous American organizations. Some of us were helping to keep things organized, others were handing out medicine, separating the medicine into the containers, much like at a pharmacy.

There was also a dentist who went with us and he did all manner of dental work on the people in the community. We were there from ten in the morning to seven that evening.

On Wednesday we did the same things, but at the church in Santo Domingo, the host church. They also have their own school.

The last two days were spent in the poorest community of all. Funny enough, though, the place we were using to distribute the medicine was right next door to a Lan House, where we could pay a few cents to go online and send messages to our loved ones in the State.

The people in general were very grateful for all that we did for them, and were very respectful. We all agreed that the poorest community was the place we enjoyed the most, because they were the most grateful and really the neediest.

On Friday night all of the host families met with us for a big going-away party. Gifts were exchanged, there was lots of good food, photographs taken, and just a great time of fellowship.

Saturday morning we drove two hours to

Samana, where we had the opportunity to play at the beach. We were at Samana two days and then left on Monday morning in time to catch our plane ride back to the States.

We arrived here on Memorial Day around 8:30 pm or so. I was very exhausted, but losing those ten pounds was well worth it. I still keep in touch with some of the people I met there, through Facebook. The best part about it, though, is that I know where they will be when all this is over, and we'll meet again.

Cindy Goes to Haiti
Cindy Weinette Combs, Oklahoma

It was mid-December of 2011 and I felt in my heart I needed to do something more for God, but I was not quite sure what. I prayed about it and remembered I had had a desire for a long time to go to Haiti. It seemed like the right thing to do because at the time I was unemployed, but then how would I pay for my trip?

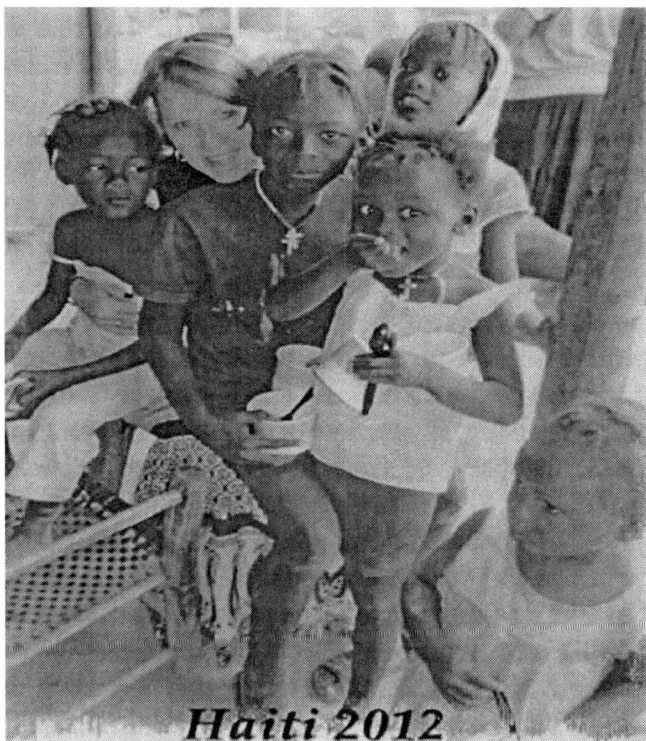

Haiti 2012
Cindy with children in Haiti

I made some tie blankets, 110 to be exact, sent out an email, and was able to raise the money in about two weeks.

I wasn't sure where I was going or staying so I googled trips to Haiti and only had one email response and it was from Mission of Hope. I called the person responsible and found out what dates they had available. I ended up going on January 12, 2012, which was the two year anniversary of the earthquake.

When I arrived at the airport, a member from

Mission of Hope picked me up in a van. The ride was very bumpy and hot. I had been in a third world country before, Brazil, but had never seen such poverty. Slums all over the place, people half dressed...I knew my time there would be very interesting. THANK YOU, LORD, FOR PAVED ROADS. THANK YOU FOR CLOTHING.

On the way to *Titanyen* where Mission of Hope is, I saw several people gathering to worship and remember the second year anniversary of the earthquake. The trip took about 45 minutes and it was very dusty and bumpy. Arriving at Mission of Hope, there were over 100 other people there from so many different churches in the USA.

They had a dorm where I put my things. Hot, hot, hot...and to think it was in the middle of winter! We had to take drinking water to the room to brush our teeth, and baths were limited to one a day for three minutes. You would not want to take a longer one because it was ice cold. Yes, no hot water. THANK YOU, LORD, FOR HOT WATER.

Meals were served in the cafeteria and were cooked by the Haitian women. They were very kind and we just smiled at each other because communication was very difficult.

There were several groups there from all over the US. They split us up each day into groups. Our group went to the villages the first day and took food (spiritual and food food) to the orphanages there. One orphanage where we arrived had several children in the hospital because they were sick with Malaria and other issues. It was sad, but we still ministered to the ones there.

First, we fed them real food. It was interesting watching the young kids feed the even younger ones oatmeal as if it were a candy bar. They were starving, as most of the Haitian people are much of the time. They normally have one meal a day. THANK YOU, LORD, FOR FOOD IN ABUNDANCE. Then, we put on a skit and one of the natives translated to the kids. It was amazing watching them laugh and pay attention. It was a great experience.

We headed over to another orphanage in the middle of a slum. When we arrived, some of the children had never seen white people. They were afraid and hid from us.

Most of the children were not dressed from the waist down, and if they were, they were wet and dirty. But they were all so loving and wanted to be all over us. I had a lap full of little girls in just a few seconds, then soon after, I also had pee all over me! But that's part of it. They were also so very hungry. We fed crackers to them and I had brought some candy. They were all excited.

I met a young 16 year old girl with a little baby. Her baby was deathly ill. She asked us if we could take her baby and take care of it. Sad, sad situation.

Every day we visited another village and a new orphanage. Orphans all over the place, poverty all over the place...the earthquake had left a nation full of misery and disaster.

We also went into the villages and painted and cleaned some houses that Mission of Hope was giving to the people. Many had been living in tents, or under tarps for two years. You can imagine how hot it was.

While walking around in that village, there were kids from all over. There was a cute little girl who was about four who jumped in my arms and never let go. She was with me the entire day we were there. Her parents never came looking for her.

The Haitians see their children as a burden. Either they are selling them as sex slaves or they are just ignoring them and wishing they would just disappear somehow. Yes, sex slaves starting at around the age of five all the way through whatever age until they can run away from it all.

One of the orphanages we visit, Oscar's orphanage, known as Victorious Kids Orphanage, had several children who had been rescued from being sex slaves. The kids were smiling, but you could see that look in their eyes. A look of someone who had suffered a lot.

At night we would participate in church gatherings. They would sing their praise and worship songs in English and in Creole. The preaching was in Creole but I was able to understand it a little.

I had an amazing week there in Haiti and met a lot of wonderful Americans and Haitians. There is a huge need there. Not only to feed the people, but just to love on them and touch them. They enjoy touch. Something they don't get very often. My hope is to go back some day. If you can't go, pray. Pray for the Haitians and pray for the people who are there every day ministering to them.

Help one at a time. That's all we can do.

Who's Clapping At Our Gate?

Tânia , Our International Hostess
Tânia Marita Combs Ferreira, Oklahoma
Tânia, our youngest Brazilian-born child, has traveled to (Europe) with business friends and to Italy

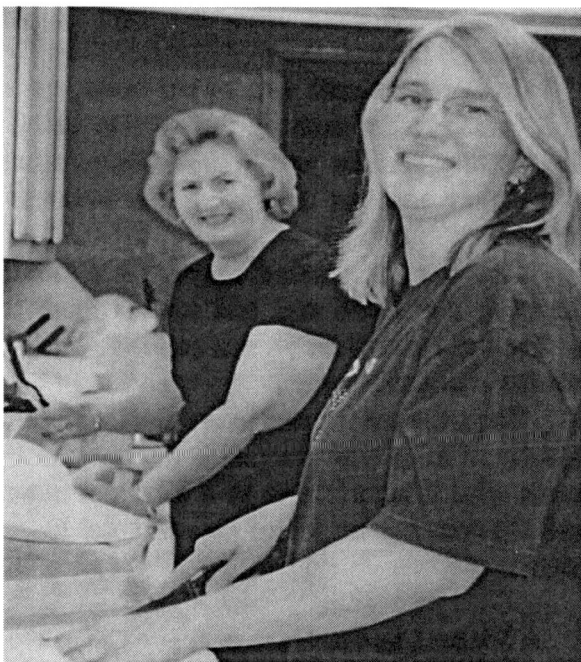

Tania in kitchen with Aunt Judy

with her husband for a friend's wedding. They have crossed our US borders on different occasions, but internationals seem to gravitate to their home. She is a good hostess and enjoys taking them on local tours to show some of our Okie beauty and culture. Being a good cook, she mixes American dishes with Brazilian cuisine along with recipes others pass on to her.

Her children, Daniel, Bianca, and Isabela, take home international friends they have met and her husband, Rodrigo, has contact with different nationalities through his business, Wood Creations. Most get invited to their home. Since her house is the largest right now, family reunions meet there often and there are usually several languages represented.

On one state-side visit to her home, we met a room full of foreigners meeting for a Bible study. The Brazilian pastor, Porfirio and wife, Liliane, moved to Boston and they host her now when her business trips take her there.

One week she asked prayer for a family she had hosted in her home and had invited them to her church. They did visit their church and their home. That is *hospitality evangelism.*

She has been the one in our family who visited the countries of folks who clapped at our gates in Brazil. She knows what it feels like to be a foreigner in another land, and she does a great job of *international hospitality* in her own home.

A Niece, Lancia, Goes to Ivory Coast
Lancia Puckett Berglan, Oklahoma
"Some trust in chariots and some in horses, but we trust in the name of the Lord, our God." Psalms 20:7 (NIV)

In February 2008, there were many *chariots* and *horses* I had come to rely on. Good health. Personal freedoms that, when combined with a determined, independent spirit and supported by a stable government and infrastructure, made nearly all of my goals within reach. I took for granted that these things were part and parcel of the fortunate lot that had befallen me.

I was in for a rude awakening when I visited Africa that spring.

I had sensed God leading me to participate in a medical mission trip to Cote 'd'Ivoire. As an R.N., I was excited about the thought of using my experience to serve God and help others. In retrospect, I suspect the trip was more about teaching me than any benefit my meager skills could offer.

At home, there was no reason to think about or be thankful for the supernatural hands that held everything around me together. When I ordered something by mail, I expected it would be delivered in a timely and correct manner. My trust was in the USPS.

Our shipping container containing all our medical supplies and food for our team of over forty members was held up by a corrupt government. After much prayer and appeals, it was finally released, not a day too soon.

When I paid for a utilities service, such as electric or water, I trusted that the infrastructure was there to provide it and the service companies would make it happen.

In Africa, we spent much time in prayer for our electricity to hold out long enough to complete a surgery. One time, after several hours with an outage, I began to pray aloud with a group, knowing our surgeons and nurses were desperately trying to finish the last surgery of the day with headlamps and flashlights. As I spoke, the lights flickered back on. God was showing me who was truly in control.

In my country, I take for granted the freedom to hop in my car and drive from state to state – point to point. Doing so in a country torn by civil war – where the measure of power is weighed by the number of automatic weapons or the amount of time each group can detain a busload of Americans

Lancia Puckett Berglan, RN

at gunpoint – you are not likely to arrive at your destination still alive and free without at least a breath of thanksgiving to the One who holds us all.

Probably the most dramatic showing of Who was in control came one Sunday in Africa. Our little clinic closed for rest and worship, and a group of doctors and nurses loaded into two vehicles with the intent of traveling two hours across a dry, dusty, crater filled African dirt road to a village to hold a service and minister medical care. But God had other plans for us.

About 45 minutes into our drive, one of our vehicles broke down on a dusty road right in front of a small village of huts. As we were assessing the vehicle situation, men, women and children from the village began to curiously approach. (The men were carrying machetes which was disconcerting at first, but we were assured there was no harm intended.)

Who's Clapping At Our Gate?

After it became apparent we would go no further that day, we happily began to offer food, medical care and supplies, and the Gospel – the reason we came. The African national pastor who was accompanying us shared the story of Christ's love and his relentless pursuit of His creation. Many accepted His love that day, and gave up their idols and fetishes.

After he spoke, the pastor was surrounded by a small group from the village. Later he would tell us this amazing story the group relayed to him.

"About one year ago, a group just like this one came. They offered medical help and told us of some God – the one true God. Many of us believed at that time – turned from our idols and gave up our fetishes. The men who spoke told us there would be people coming to follow them to teach us more. We had waited, and were beginning to question if this story was true. We prayed and asked this: if he was the true God, then send someone to us again, with the same story of this God. And you came!"

God is always moving, always controlling, always keeping. My trust should be in Him alone. I'm learning that more and more.

Another Niece, Jessica, Goes to Cairo, Egypt
Jessica Combs Martin

One of Jim's brothers Mark Combs died in 1988 when his two children were very young. A few years later his wife Lisa remarried, moved to North Carolina, and had another child. Ironically, also she died when the children were still young and living at home,

Jessica Combs Martin (lower left)
enjoys time with friends in Egypt

and they went to live with their grandparents in West Virginia.

For their oldest child Jessica, the desire to serve others was strong, leading her to volunteer with the Red Cross while still in high school. After studying at Concord University and West Virginia University, Jessica accepted a teaching position with the Free Will Baptist Christian School on Saint Croix, US Virgin Islands. The years spent there in a foreign culture gave her a taste of missionary work which she embraced fully.

In 2008, Jessica accepted a position as a medical assistant to a doctor in Cairo, Egypt, with whom she served one year. During that year of service, she fell in love with the people of Egypt, and determined to stay in spite of the turmoil the country was experiencing due to the Arab Spring revolution.

During the revolution in Cairo's Tahrir Square in January 2011, Jessica was urged by her family, and even the US Government, to return home temporarily. She considered her options and declined because she felt that God wanted her to stay and not abandon her Egyptian friends who could not leave. She volunteered at a makeshift clinic during these dark days, helping treat the injured as they came in. The people asked, "Aren't you American? Why didn't you leave?" This gave her an open door or opportunity to share her faith with many people during a time of upheaval.

From the beginning, Jessica eagerly adapted to the culture, learned Arabic, and ministered to the people around her. She loves to cook, especially to bake, and often opened her small flat to her international friends and neighbors, sharing her meal and her heart. She is a great example of friendship evangelism.

After the first year in Egypt, Jessica accepted a teaching position at the Modern Education School of Cairo, where she continues to teach children and minister to Egyptians.

CHAPTER 17
Stay-At-Home Missionaries

Since we were foreigners in a strange land, I was impressed at how many times the Bible mentions that we should show hospitality to foreigners. Foreigners who live right around us. Why?

Over and over the scriptures describe Jewish feasts and festivities and command them to call together men, women, children and the **foreigners** within their gates that they may *hear* and *learn* and *fear* the Lord God and *observe* the words of the law. They were to remember that they were foreigners in Egypt. (Deuteronomy 16 and 31)

Recently we were in the home of dear friends from McCurtain, Oklahoma, Gary and Rita Wilson, who first offered us hospitality in their home in Georgia while we were on deputation many years ago. Gary was teaching the course THE POWER FOR TRUE SUCCESS, from the Institute in Basic Life Principles.

In the chapter on Hospitality vs. Unfriendliness, it says, "True hospitality is bringing guests to a home in which the character of Christ is being demonstrated on a daily basis." It says that one of the two Greek words translated *hospitality* is *philoxenos. Philos* means "friend" and *xenos* means "stranger; guest or host."

The scope of hospitality reaches out with the love and light of God and it does not choose its recipients. It even reaches to the enemy (in Matthew) as well as to a brother or sister in a destitute situation. (In James.)

I hadn't really put the list together, but there are guidelines to hospitality. We are not to eat a meal with another believer who *persists* in immoral behavior. (I Corinthians), or one that promotes false doctrine (II John). It even covers an angry person (Proverbs) and a deceitful person or a liar! (Psalm)

But there are so many rewards of hospitality to strangers or foreigners because we are doing it unto Christ. Doing this we take on the work of Jesus Christ

LNV kids load up and head to the Combs' chacara

and can become a channel of His love to foreigners who really need and appreciate it.

What about the foreigners in Oklahoma and Ohio? In Tennessee and Texas? In Missouri or Mississippi? California and Colorado? Georgia and Florida?

Who's Clapping At Our Gate?

The instruction used in the Old Testament was: to make contact through hospitality. The mission field has come to our gates.

While teaching missions at Hillsdale Free Will Baptist College in Oklahoma, I spent a few hours a week teaching ESL (English as a Second Language) classes to international students at Oklahoma City University. Arabs, Latinos, Orientals, Europeans. That meant Muslims, Buddhists, Spiritists, and atheists. They were scientists, pilots, government workers, and members of royal families. They were right at my doorstep. I needed no passport. No visa. No plane ticket. It seemed so right.

A lot of times evangelism is fulfilling someone's needs before you can get their attention. What were their needs? Far from home, they needed friendship and help with a language. The students represented several languages and couldn't understand one another. We had great fun trying to communicate.

Because I met those needs, they were open to my invitations. I invited them to our home for meals and took them on tours of our Free Will Baptist churches in Oklahoma City. It opened up questions about food preparations, family cultures, church baptisteries, and even hymn book racks.

They were only in the university course for a few months, but our friendship was intense. My prayers were intense, also. Some told me that my friendship changed their opinions about American citizens. I saw no signs of spiritual change, but I planted seeds through hospitality. Telling them goodbye proved difficult.

You can do the same thing.
Please do the same things.

Internationals live in almost every neighborhood of our U.S. cities. Check with local colleges and universities, and public schools for foreign students enrolled there. You can survey your local government about international residents and high school exchange students. Contact international churches in your area.

Contact with internationals here in our state is becoming more and more common.

Recently after speaking in the Dibble District WAC meeting, I was listening to two beautiful, dedicated Christian sisters, Ginger and Linda True. They were excited about their "international evangelism" experience.

Their cousin had cancer and his body seemed to tolerate only Chinese food. That took them into the Chickasha, OK Chinese Grill many times. The owners were parents to two delightful children who eventually had contact with Ginger and Linda. In their natural, loving ways the sisters invited the children to an Easter Egg Hunt and then to Sunday School, with their parents' consent.

They didn't know how much the children were understanding from their experiences, but one day they heard one sing (from the back seat of their car, I believe) the song "Victory in Jesus". They didn't need a passport to China and didn't need to spend money for tickets, but they were missionaries and helped plant the seed of victory and love.

Who's Clapping At Our Gate?

One young lady that has a great ministry with international students at The University of Oklahoma happens to be our *niece* (former M.K. from Brazil). Who of us can say we have invited into our home foreigners from eight different countries? I was talking to her recently and she sent me this:

Ladonna Deeds Wolfes, Oklahoma
Even though I have been a Christian since I was a teenager, I spent many years of my adult life focused on things that don't have any eternal value – building a career and achieving what I considered to be "success". Until God, in His goodness, pursued me and began to change my heart. He opened my eyes and heart to care about the things He cares about.

I began to pray each day for an opportunity to do something that will have eternal impact. My goal became to live my life in alignment with Jesus' words in Matthew 25:35: "For I was hungry, and you fed me. I was thirsty, and you gave me a drink. I was a stranger (foreigner), and you invited me into your home. I was naked, and you gave me clothing. I was sick, and you cared for me. I was in prison, and you visited me."

I discovered that God is eager to answer our prayer when we ask Him to use us! He has given me amazing opportunities to touch many lives in big or small ways. One way is through friendships with international students attending The University of Oklahoma.

Each year, thousands of the brightest and most talented students from all over the world leave their families and everything familiar to them so they can study in America. Oklahoma University alone welcomes over 2,000 of these amazing young people from over 100 different countries each year!

While this opportunity is often a dream come true for these young people, it can also be a challenging time as they are suddenly immersed in a culture and environment very different from their own. Most are eager to form new friendships, learn about the American way of life, and share their own culture. But sadly, very few are ever invited in to an American home.

When I learned about Oklahoma University's Friends of International Students program, I knew it was a God given opportunity to show His love to young people from around the world, right in my own home town!

We have been so blessed to become friends with wonderful students from China, India, Colombia, Afghanistan, Korea, France, Cameroon, and Mexico. Many of them have never known a Christian personally until they met us.

By welcoming them into our home for meals, holidays, and simply being their *American family,* we have been blessed to form wonderful friendships that continue after they return to their own countries.

We know by "welcoming the stranger" into our lives and home, we are living in alignment with what Jesus wants from His followers. Our prayer is that God will bring a great harvest from the seeds that we are blessed to plant.

Who's Clapping At Our Gate?

Welcoming, Heavenly Gates

Be a 'stay-at-home' missionary through hospitality to foreigners. The Bible stresses the importance of hospitality, and we can testify to its benefits to our family and hopefully to all who entered our gates.

Gates? Gates. We are looking forward to arriving at the heavenly gates one day.

Just think about our being greeted by many who have come to our home and clapped at our gate. Those who have chosen the narrow gate to salvation so they can enjoy eternal heavenly **hospitality.**

Our niece, Deborah, visited us in Brazil years ago with her family. She recently wrote a poem after her mother's (Dean Hale, my sister) sudden passing from this life to life inside the gates of pearl. It gives a glimpse of what it may be like behind those gates for those who follow the Lord's footsteps.

Footsteps to the Gates of Pearl
Deborah Hale, Oklahoma

In the early morning dew I walked
Barefoot to look at a flowering bush...
When I stepped upon my porch it revealed an imprint
As I watched it fade away this thought came to mind...

Who will remember our footsteps...
To know where we have gone...
What they have done...

Who's Clapping At Our Gate?

What is our mark on this earth...
Maybe no one will remember our stay...
Or even know we were here at all...
Our lives are but a fleeting ember...

God knows it all: past, present and future...
If at the end of this life we know that God
Directed our path and we live to serve Him...
And He says "Welcome home thy good and
Faithful servant, welcome home"...
Then no matter whether the world remembers,
Our Lord remembers...

Our footsteps are ordered by the Lord...
Follow closely to His call...walk the
Straight and narrow...sometimes lonely...
Sometimes friendless...but always directed...

Leading us to the One who made us...saved us...
Gave us His grace...and opened wide His arms of love

With Him...never lonely...never friendless...
Never misdirected...

Guiding us ever so close to Him...
*And soon we will be walking through **those gates** of pearl*
Where we will know as we are known...
In a place where the only footsteps that
Really mattered were our Lord's...
And if followed, will lead us to His throne...
Where we will worship at His feet...
His precious feet.

How thrilling to think about being greeted by our **Host Jesus Christ** who will welcome us.
*"Enter into **His gates** with thanksgiving,*
And into his courts with praise:
Be thankful unto him, and bless his name.
For the Lord is good; his mercy is everlasting;
and his truth endures to all generations!" -Psalms 100

Another book by Shirley Combs
Available from her for $13/99

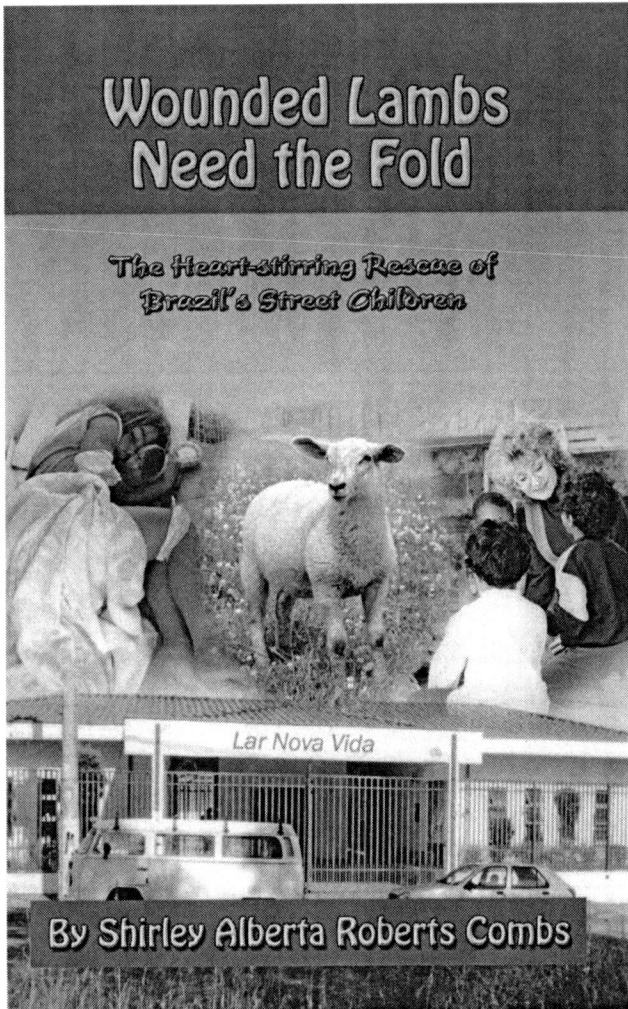

Wounded Lambs Need the Fold

The Heart-stirring Rescue of Brazil's Street Children

Lar Nova Vida

By Shirley Alberta Roberts Combs

CPSIA information can be obtained
at www.ICGtesting.com
Printed in the USA
FFOW05n0019311213

9 781940 609027